The Spirit Dimension in African Christianity

Published by the
Christian Literature Association in Malawi (CLAIM),
P.O. Box 503, Blantyre, Malawi
ISBN 99908-16-14-X

ISSN -1025-0964 (Kachere Monograph)

Layout and Editorial Assistance: Celeste M. Geddes and Fran Rout
Graphic Design: Patrick M. Lichakala
Cover Design: Deborah Kerr
Published with the assistance of a grant from *Feed the Minds*, Guildford, UK

Printed in Malawi by Assemblies of God Press, P.O. Box 5749, Limbe

The Spirit Dimension in African Christianity

A Pastoral Study among the Tumbuka People of Northern Malawi

Silas S. Ncozana

Kachere Monograph no. 10

CLAIM

Christian Literature Association in Malawi

Blantyre

2002

Kachere Series,
P.O. Box 1037, Zomba, Malawi
email: kachere@sdnp.org.mw
www.sdnp.org.mw/kachereseries/

This book is part of the Kachere Series, a range of books on religion, culture and society in Malawi. Kachere Monographs published so far are:

Andrew C. Ross, *Blantyre Mission and the Making of Modern Malawi.*

Harry Langworthy, *"Africa for the African": The Life of Joseph Booth.*

Kenneth R. Ross, *God, People and Power in Malawi.*

Isabel Apawo Phiri, *Women, Presbyterianism and Patriarchy: Religious Experience of Chewa Women in Central Malawi.*

Matthew Schoffeleers, *Religion and the Dramatization of Life: Spirit Beliefs and Rituals in Southern Malawi.*

Ernst Wendland, *Buku Loyera: an Introduction to the New Chichewa Bible Translation.*

J.C. Chakanza, *Voices of Preachers in Protest: The Ministry of two Malawian Prophets: Elliot Kamwana and Wilfred Gudu.*

John McCracken, *Politics and Christianity in Malawi 1745-1940.*

Klaus Fiedler, *Christianity and African Culture: Conservative German Protestant Missionaries in Tanzania 1900-1940.*

Ernst R. Wendland, *Preaching that Grabs the Heart.*

Martin Ott, *African Theology in Images.*

George Shepperson and Thomas Price, *Independent African.*

J.W.M. Van Breugel, *Chewa Traditional Religion.*

The Kachere Series is the publications arm of the Department of Theology and Religious Studies of the University of Malawi.

Series Editors: J.C. Chakanza, F.L. Chingota, Klaus Fiedler, P.A. Kalilombe, Fulata L. Moyo, Martin Ott, Shareef Mahomed

Contents

Series Editors' Preface

The Kachere Series is the publishing arm of the Department of Theology and Religious Studies at the University of Malawi. It aims to promote the development of a body of literature which enables students and others to engage critically with religion in Malawi, its social impact and the theological questions which it raises. An important starting point lies with the publication of essays and theses that until now have been inaccessible to all but the most dedicated specialist. It is also hoped, however, that the development of theological scholarship in Malawi will continue to stimulate the writing of many new books. General works with popular appeal are published as *Kachere Books*. Documents and essays, which are of value as sources for the study of religion in Malawi, are published as *Kachere Texts*. Full-length treatises, the fruit of sound primary research that meet rigorous academic standards, are published as *Kachere Monographs*. The Editors intend the Series to contribute substantially to the growth of a body of knowledge in the area of theology and religious studies in Malawi. As important resources for study related to this field, we are confident that they will come to be prized not only within Malawi but also in every academic centre concerned with religion and society in Africa.

When the appropriate time came, it took Africa only a few generations to transform itself into a Christian continent. Though this deeply changed her religion, the spirits of the old religion have not necessarily disappeared. Spirit possession or, using perhaps a more up to date term, spirit affliction cults, are still common, even in societies predominantly Christian. Dr Ncozana seeks to give answers to the role of such spirit cults, and to the role the Holy Spirit plays among the Tumbuka, and how the two relate to each other. As editors we welcome Dr Ncozana's contribution to both the study of pastoral care and of the history of the church.

We gratefully acknowledge the grant given by Feed the Minds, Guildford, UK.

Kachere Series Editors

Zomba, 2002

Acknowledgements

This book is the final result of my own work, much of whose material I took from the PhD thesis I did at Aberdeen University in 1985. With the current Pentecostal tendencies blowing over Malawi and many parts of the world, this book raises relevant pastoral issues. I could not have completed this book without the support of many friends.

Firstly, I owe much of whatever coherence and effectiveness this book has to my venerable supervisor, Professor Andrew F. Walls, then Head of the Religious Department at the University of Aberdeen. His patience in going through various drafts of this work, combined with his acute criticisms, comments and thoroughness, was rewarding.

Secondly, I would like to thank Professor Kenneth R. Ross and Dr. Klaus Fiedler, both from the Department of Theology and Religious Studies at the University of Malawi, who encouraged me to publish this book. Their interest in seeing the contents of this book go to print left no room for me to delay the work.

Thirdly, I am sincerely grateful to Ms. Celeste Geddes for meticulously editing the material for this book. I do not forget the many times she sat with me ensuring that I had correctly set the statistics and bibliography. The result of her untiring effort is evidenced by the attractive layout of the material.

Without the presence of my family, it would not have been possible for me to do this work. I thank my wife, Margaret, and our children for their moral support. They accepted me taking many hours out of our family time together in order to write this book.

I would also like to thank all those who helped me during the time I was working on my original thesis in Aberdeen, both financially and academically; too many to mention by name.

Finally, I would like to thank the staff in various libraries and archives for their assistance. These include the staff in Aberdeen University Libraries, National Library of Scotland, Edinburgh University Library, University of Malawi Library and the National Archives of Malawi.

Silas S. Ncozana

Illustrations

Abbreviations

ALC   African Lakes Company
CCAP   Church of Central African Presbyterian
CMS   Church Missionary Society
FMCCS   Foreign Mission Committee of the Church of Scotland
IRM   *International Review of Mission*
JAH   *Journal of African History*
JRA   Journal of Religion in Africa
LMC   Livingstonia Mission Council
LWCSBCA   *Life and Work of the Church of Scotland in British Central
           Africa*
MNA   Malawi National Archives
NLS   National Library of Scotland
UFCS   United Free Church of Scotland

Introduction

This monograph sets out to explore the implications of spirit possession among the Tumbuka when they converted to Christianity. It is not a study of possession as such. Where direct study of the phenomenon in Tumbuka tradition has been made, it is meant to aid our understanding of Tumbuka response to Christianity, a religion they have embraced since its inception in the area in 1881. Further, the study does not examine how spirit possession in Tumbuka tradition has assimilated Christian ideas thereby reordering its practices. Our concern in this study is with how Tumbuka Christians have moved away from possession in the traditional sense, to possession with the Spirit in the Christian sense, the power involved in this transformation and the pastoral task brought about by the shift.

Possession is a term which established churches hesitate to use in the religious experience of their converts. This is because, in the West, the term had generally been associated with demons and schizophrenic personalities. Possession in Tumbuka tradition was institutionalized in their religion. It often appeared among *basofi*, priests, *nganga* and *nchimi*, doctors. These people were highly regarded by their community. There was nothing unusual or frightful when possession occurred, as it was controlled. The appearance of possession signified the presence of a divinity or an ancestral spirit, warning the people of coming danger or endowing the possessed person with healing and prophetic power. However, when possession occurred in an individual for the first time, it caused anxiety to the family of the possessed person. This is because the novice did not know how to deal with the possessing spirit. To solve the problem, the novice had to be taken to a *nchimi* to be healed. Further appearances of possession in the same person were not dreaded by the family and community. These appearances were regarded by the community as a call to priesthood, mediumship etc.

The history of Christianity teaches us that wherever this religion has gone, it has been built into those cultures with which it has come into contact. This has caused certain modifications of the Christian message. For example, the Apostle Paul's message to the Greeks was appropriate to them:

> Men of Athens! I see that in every way you are very religious. For as I walked around and looked carefully at your objects of worship, I even found an altar with this inscription: "To an unknown God". Now what you worship as something unknown I am going to proclaim to you.[1]

---

[1] Acts 17:22-23 (NIV).

While Paul's message was viable in the Greek context, it would have had to be modified to be viable in a different context. Certainly there are risks involved in this process, like watering down or distorting the central message. But this process must be made if Christianity is to take root and be viable in the cultures in which it finds itself. Tumbuka culture is one such culture where Christianity has been embraced by many people. This study is a reflection of Tumbuka Christianity in relation to possession, a central belief in Tumbuka tradition.

This book examines pastoral issues which have arisen as a result of the Tumbuka becoming Christians since 1881. The Tumbuka tendency to possession colours their understanding of Christian teaching, especially about the work of the Spirit. For example, many Christians claim to be possessed with the Holy Spirit; dreams and visions occur to many Christians and are regarded by the Tumbuka as channels for communication and as gifts from God. Many people are possessed by evil spirits and look for healing in the church. When they do not find it there, they look for help in traditional religion. The drum-beat, song and the dance which accompanied possession ceremonies in the traditional setting were a doorway to the religion of the Tumbuka. Through possession, dreams, visions, drum-beat, song and dance the Tumbuka found effective means for communicating with deities. If the Christian faith is to be viable to the Tumbuka and their culture, the church ought to deal with the pastoral issues raised here with a sense of urgency, and it is my hope that this study may be a contribution towards addressing that pastoral problem.

This book concentrates on the Livingstonia Mission in Northern Malawi. Livingstonia, the oldest of the five Synods of the Church of Central Africa Presbyterian (CCAP),[2] began its work at Cape Maclear in the southern region in 1875. The mission moved its headquarters to Bandawe in the northern region in 1881. A large population inhabiting the highlands attracted the mission to move its headquarters once more. It was established at Livingstonia, Khondowe, from 1895 to 1978, when it moved to Mzuzu. Today Livingstonia Synod has about 90,000 communicants.[3] The influence of Livingstonia mission has been felt throughout Malawi and outside it. Many people who were trained

---

[2] The CCAP was formed in 1924. Then it was made up of Livingstonia Mission and Blantyre Mission. Nkhoma Mission joined the union in 1926. See minutes of the Livingstonia Mission Council 1926. The Synod of Salisbury was formed in 1964. See minutes of the General Synod 1969. The other two Synods are the Synods of Zimbabwe and Zambia.

[3] This figure is an estimate given by Rev. Dr. O. Mazunda, General Secretary of the Livingstonia Synod. The Synod of Livingstonia statistics are kept by congregations and no longer come to the central office. This has been the case since 1964. Personal interview with Rev. Dr O. Mazunda, 15 June 1998.

at Livingstonia have found work within the mission, in government and in the private sector. Many have achieved leading positions in these spheres.

The period of this study is 1881 to 1950. 1875 is the date when Livingstonia Mission was established in Malawi; coming into effective contact with the Tumbuka in 1881. 1950 saw considerable reduction in missionary personnel and leadership within the CCAP.[4] Local leadership became evident in mission stations. For example, Rev. P.C. Mzembe was in charge of Ekwendeni station while Y. Kaunda was responsible for a large area including Chasefu in Zambia.[5] Formerly these posts were occupied by missionaries. It may be said that 1950 forms a natural dividing line between the past and the present era. It allows us to study with a certain amount of detachment the notion of possession among the first three generations of converts and how the Livingstonia Mission dealt with the issue. In the light of the past, the Livingstonia Synod ought to consider how best it can provide pastoral guidance and adopt the possession method to assist converts who are perplexed by the activity of the Spirit in their lives. This study is a contribution towards providing such a pastoral strategy. It is our hope that others will improve and carry on what is begun here.

The method of approach to this study is historical. The study begins from 1875 when the missionary work of Livingstonia began. However, in order to provide a background to Tumbuka traditional religion, it is necessary to begin the study in 1780. This time is when the Tumbuka enjoyed peaceful socio-politico and religious changes under Mlowoka.[6] As already noted, the study ends in 1950 when missionary influence continued, but at a lesser degree than before.

---

[4] W.H. Watson, a missionary who joined Livingstonia Mission in 1933, informed this writer that the third generation of missionaries assumed a secondary role in the work of the mission in Malawi. He said that they were prepared to support and work under local leadership. The Livingstonia Mission Council whose membership was restricted to missionaries, was dissolved in 1935. The Presbytery of Livingstonia, then the only Presbytery, i.e. really equal to a Synod, was led by Malawians: the Senior Clerk was Patrick R. Mwamulima and the Junior Clerk was Rev. Y.M. Chibambo. The Rev. J.B.M. Mhone succeeded these men. Then arrangement of a Synod of Livingstonia was made with several Presbyteries; of it, the senior Clerk was Rev. P.C. Mzembe and the Junior (Clerk was Rev. W.H. Watson. The new Synod combined the function of both the Livingstonia Mission Council and the Presbytery of Livingstonia. [Personal] interview Rev. Dr W. Watson, Aberdeen. 12 December 1984). Dr Watson's comments in other areas of my work have been helpful. I regret not having met him in the early stages of this study.

[5] Livingstonia Presbytery Minutes 1950.

[6] T. Cullen Young, *Notes on the History of Tumbuka-Nkhamanga Peoples in the Northern Province of Nyasaland*, (Reprint) London: Frank Cass, 1970 [1931], pp. 7-8.

For our sources, we rely heavily on minute books, church reports and papers of the Livingstonia Mission found in the Malawi National Archives. These materials provide useful evidence showing how the Livingstonia Mission dealt with possession when it occurred among converts. Chapter Five, which deals with possession cases, makes full use of this material, showing the attitude of the missionaries to the phenomenon from 1881 to 1935.

While there are no books directly dealing with possession among the Tumbuka, most books written by Livingstonia missionaries at the turn of this century make reference to the phenomenon, pointing out its existence and some of its practices. In some books, the reference to the phenomenon is made in a few sentences. In others, the phenomenon is described in a paragraph or so. However, these have been useful in our attempt to reconstruct and interpret the religious history of the Tumbuka with reference to possession. Fieldwork carried out in four presbyteries, Livingstonia, Ekwendeni, Bandawe and Loudon provided useful information on Christianity as lived by the people. Many Christians who were interviewed admitted having visions, dreams and possession experiences, indicating that the Christian message has undergone some modification. Fieldwork provided us with useful information on how possession is practised outside the Church today.

The Tumbuka, who are our main interest in this study, are the largest ethnic group in the Northern Region of Malawi. They form ten percent of Malawi's population today. Dwangwa River north of Kasungu divides the Tumbuka from the Chewa in the south.

Another river, Songwe in the north, separates the Tumbuka from the Nkhonde. Within Tumbukaland, the Ngoni had their strongest hold in the 1845-1904 period. This resulted in a mixture between the two ethnic groups. It is for this reason that the Ngoni will continue to be mentioned alongside the Tumbuka in this study.

Malawi: People & Places
based on *Politics and Christianity in Malawi 1875-1940*
By J. McCracken

Brackets represent more modern names

The Livingstonia Mission: Sphere of Influence
based on *Politics and Christianity in Malawi 1875-1940*
By J. McCracken

Chapter 1

Spirit Possession as an African Phenomenon

The spirit world in African religions

Writers on African religions agree that most African peoples are sharply aware of a spirit world closely connected with the physical world. The two are one. This is what John Taylor calls "the unbroken circle".[1] A similar view is put forward by Duff MacDonald when he writes about the Yao view of the spirit world. He says that as the order of things is in this physical world, so it is in the spirit world.[2] K. Opoku alludes to the same point when he says, "the spirit world forms an integral part of the whole of human existence".[3] There appears to be agreement that the reality of the spirit world in African experience is linked to the everyday life.

However, writers differ in their description of the spirit world, especially about its nature. Understandably, this is because each writer was looking at specific peoples in a particular context and at a certain time in their history. For example, Evans-Pritchard observed that in the Nuer spirit world, God is regarded as the all-spirit; under him are the spirits of *the above* and then the spirits of *the below*[4] According to Evans-Pritchard, the spirits of the air or of *the above*, which are secondary only to God, derive from God himself. The lesser spirits of *the below* are historical, but nevertheless are dependent on God. As such, the spirit world is a replica of the physical and the Nuer view themselves and the cosmos as dependent on, and as a reflection of, God.

Another order of the spirit world is given by John Mbiti. From his general observation of African peoples' spirit world, Mbiti presents two categories: spiritual beings which were never humans, and those which once were.[5] The spirit world as presented by Mbiti is a two tier system: heaven and earth. The coherence of this spirit world, according to Mbiti, is in God.

---

[1]   J.V. Taylor, *The Primal Vision: Christian Presence amid African Religion*, London: SCM, 1963, p. 59.
[2]   Duff MacDonald, *Africana: The Heart of Heathen Africa*, Vol. 1, London: Dawsons of Pall Mall (Reprint), 1969 [1882], p. 69.
[3]   K. Opoku, "When the Spirit of Truth Comes", in S.J. Samartha (ed.), *Faith in the Midst of Faiths: Reflections on Dialogue in Community*, Geneva: WCC, 1977, p. 129.
[4]   E.E. Evans-Pritchard, *Nuer Religion*, Oxford: Clarendon, 1956, pp. 1-2.
[5]   John Mbiti, *African Religions and Philosophy*, Nairobi: Heinemann, 1969, p. 75.

E.W. Smith presents yet another order in the African spirit world. He writes,

> Above all forces is God, who gives existence and increase to all others. After him come the first fathers, founders of the various clans, who form links in the chain binding God and man. Next to them come the so called "dead" of the tribe who are other links in the chain or, say, channels through which the vital force influences the living generation. The "living" in their turn form a hierarchy according to their vital power. The eldest of a group or clan is the link between the ancestors and their descendants. The chief, duly appointed and installed according to traditional rules, reinforces the life of his people and all inferior forces, animal, vegetable and organic.[6]

Smith's description of the African spirit world is important in that it shows the homogeneity between the spirit world and the physical, a point agreed by other writers, as already noted.

From the examples given, it is clear that no one description satisfies the concept of the spirit world as held by different peoples in Africa. However, the linking factor is always the presence of spirits. Most people recognize the existence of spirits, and regard them as having great influence on the living.

The reality of the spirit world

Again, Mbiti emphasizes the reality of the spirit world when he says,

> Whatever science may do to prove the existence or non-existence of the spirits, one thing is undeniable, namely that for African peoples the spirits are a reality, and a reality which must be reckoned with, whether it is clear, blurred or confused reality.[7]

This reality of the spirit world is expressed in the importance attached to rites, sacred places and rituals. According to Mbiti, disease, death and other misfortunes are regarded by some people as an attack by spirits. Therefore, in worship, the spirits must be propitiated.[8] Sacred places are regarded with awe because the spirits, both malevolent and benevolent, are believed to be present.

A similar view of the reality of the spirit world is given by John Beattie. He explains that among the Bunyoro, illness and other misfortunes are regarded as the work of spirits. Beattie stresses the belief held about the existence of spirits as the driving force behind the Nyoro people. He says that their entire life is lived and passed within the vibrancy of spirits. At birth, initiation, healing, rain,

---

6   E.W. Smith (ed.), *African Ideas of God*, (2nd ed.), London: Edinburgh House Press, 1961, p. 18.
7   Mbiti, *African Religions and Philosophy*, p. 91
8   *Ibid.*, pp. 93f.

burial, harvest and planting, the potency of the spirit world is sought and felt.[9] This view of life is not an escape from realities, but the spirit world is a "vital force" of life by which the physical world is lived and governed. Tempels points to this fact when he says, "they [the spirits], serve to acquire vigour or vital force, to live forcibly, to reinforce life, or to assure its continuity in the descendants".[10] This reality of the spirit world, common in primal religions, also applies to the Tumbuka people of northern Malawi, as we shall see later.

God and spirits

In discussing the nature and the reality of the spirit world in primal religions, it has become apparent that components which make up that spirit world vary from one culture to the other. However, these components fall into three categories, God as the ultimate spirit, the fathers or territorial spirits and the spirits of the household. It is apparent that the spirit world has to be understood in its relation to the physical world.

First, God Spirit: Southall says that among the Alur, a Nilotic people, *Jok*, God, chooses mediums through possessing them. Usually this experience is preceded by illness or some suffering.[11] When the novice goes through the initial stage of possession, he learns the nature of the *Jok* he is becoming a medium of, as there are many *Jok* spirits.

According to Southall, no Alur man or woman consciously wishes to become a medium. Selection by *Jok* is resisted, but unavoidable. Because mediums are already initiated and cured, they do not easily get carried away at possession ceremonies. Instead they are the organizers and healers. Southall remarks, "I never saw the mediums in charge of these seances go into trances, or prophesy or even dance. They were occupied in drumming, singing, treating the patient and unobtrusively organizing the proceedings".[12] As such, mediums visited by God play a mediatory role. Because they have been elected and are able to communicate with *Jok*, they assist individuals and society to come to terms with cosmic forces.

Tanner offers a similar interpretation among the Sukuma people south of Lake Victoria. God, regarded by the Sukuma as having supreme power, is

---

[9] John Beattie, "Spirit Mediumship in Bunyoro", in John Beattie and John Middleton (eds.), *Spirit Mediumship and Society in Africa*, London: Routledge and Kegan Paul, 1969, p. 160.

[10] Placide Tempels, *Bantu Philosophy*, Paris: Presence Africaine, 1959, p. 30.

[11] A. Southall, "Spirit Possession Among the Alur", in Beattie and Middleton eds., *Spirit Mediumship and Society*, pp. 243-244.

[12] Ibid.

viewed as a stabilizing force. He is closely associated with the ancestors who are regarded as supporters of society. However, for the most part, the Sukuma would rather be left alone without God or the ancestors interfering. But when a medium is visited by God, the Sukuma believe that it is for the good of society. Through his power, the medium is able to diagnose and heal disease and to find causes for misfortune. [13]

Among the Sukuma, mediums come from the privileged class of society and enjoy a certain amount of respect. Their behaviour is characterized by gentleness and self-control. As Tanner points out, "There is no relationship to mental abnormality [in the mediums] or epilepsy, nor do mediums appear to be social deviants." [14]

God, among the Dinka of Western Sudan, according to Lienhardt, is viewed as being a Power above humanity. [15] *Nhialic*, that Power, is "a multiplicity of beings, the clan divinities and free divinities" [16] which manifests itself in humans through visions and through possession. [17]

Lienhardt points out that an individual who gets possessed by one of the Dinka divinities is highly regarded by his community as he joins a special class of people, "the great Dinka men of divinity". [18] These men are regarded as prophets and representatives of God on earth. Their effectiveness is demonstrated in their ability to heal various illnesses or to curse culprits. For instance, Lienhardt cites Bol Tol, a man who claimed to have been possessed by God towards the end of the First World War. "If he looked at a man, or even thought of him, and silently broke a blade of grass, that man would surely die, while if he thought of a man who was sick, that man would be well." [19] Thus, according to Lienhardt, the Dinka think that God possesses certain individuals, giving them a power which ordinary people do not have. However, Lienhardt notes that the Dinka also recognize that not all individuals are possessed by reliable spiritual powers. Some who claim possession by a divinity may only pretend to be possessed and therefore do not make an impact on society. [20]

---

[13] R.E.S. Tanner, "The Theory and Practices of Sukuma Spirit Mediumship", in Beattie and Middleton (eds.), *Spirit Mediumship and Society*, p. 274.

[14] Ibid., p. 275.

[15] G. Lienhardt, *Divinity and Experience: The Religion of the Dinka*, Oxford: Clarendon, 1961, pp. 28f

[16] *Ibid.*, p. 31.

[17] *Ibid.*, pp. 32, 74.

[18] *Ibid.*, p. 74.

[19] *Ibid.*, pp. 76-77.

[20] *Ibid.*, p. 74.

The Shona of Zimbabwe, too, believe that God inspires individuals to heal the sick, prophesy and guide society to conform to traditional beliefs and values.[21] Where change has to be made, possessed individuals receive a word direct from God authorizing the move and the direction to be taken. For example, at the end of the nineteenth century when the Shona revolted against their colonial masters, it was the mediums of *Mwari* who encouraged the uprising.[22] They said *Mwari* was displeased with "his other sons" (the whites) who had assumed power in the household of their hosts. When the Shona and their Ndebele neighbours were defeated, mediums ceased referring to the Whites as the other sons of *Mwari*.

We have seen that although possession by God is resented in some traditions like with the Alur, and the Nuer, it confers oracular or other supra-human gifts on the possessed person in other traditions such as the Dinka and the Shona. The mediums are respected in society and are regarded as agents for social order, health and purity.[23] Possession by a deity, in this sense, affirms the realities of life on an ultimate level, for the transcendental spirit that uplifts the possessed person also lowers the person's potency.

Second, territorial spirits: These derive from dead chiefs and heroes. They possess certain mediums for the public welfare. Among the Nyakyusa, M. Wilson explains that there is a strong belief in the survival of the dead and their power over the living. As such, at the coronation of a new chief, the spirits of chiefs recently deceased are invoked to strengthen the new chief. The original chief is also believed by the Nyakyusa to live again in the new chief.[24] The line of former chiefs is considered important among the Nyakyusa. The authority of the present chief is dependent on this line and not on the personal qualities of the reigning chief.

Further, Wilson shows that different communities of the Nyakyusa were united through allegiance to royal spirits believed to have had influence over a wide area.[25] One such figure who became the centre of Nyakyusa worship was Kyala. Wilson says that Kyala was one of the original ancestors of the Nyakyusa. After a long period of being remembered in ritual, Kyala was divinized. His influence over the Nyakyusa was so great that in times of calamity, and in times of peace and prosperity, Kyala was worshipped and offered sacrifices. In

---

[21] M.L. Daneel, *The God of the Matopo Hills: An Essay on the Mwari Cult in Rhodesia*, The Hague: Mouton, 1970, pp. 22-25.

[22] *Ibid.*, p. 13.

[23] Lienhardt, *Divinity and Experience*, p. 35.

[24] Monica Wilson, *Rituals of Kinship Among the Nyakyusa*, London: Oxford University Press, 1957, pp. 3-4.

[25] *Ibid.* pp. 12-13.

his presence, the Nyakyusa celebrated their mystical dependence on their dead chiefs. Therefore, the Nyakyusa may be said to have found their unity in their royal spirits.

A more elaborate example of territorial spirits is presented by Schoffeleers. He shows that the M'bona cult in southern Malawi has remained an institution for a long time. With its central shrine at Khulubvi, it draws people from various ethnic groups.[26] According to Schoffeleers, M'bona was a man who was killed by chief Lundu for resisting him. M'bona's blood flowed forming a pool, a thing which alarmed villagers whose water supply was scarce. In order that people might have water, M'bona's spirit demanded that a shrine be built and a wife be given him.[27]

When the shrine was completed, many people visited it with their various petitions. M'bona's power grew as more people visited the shrine each year. Gifts of flour and meat were sent by the people to the shrine. At the restoration of the shrine, many people offered their services willingly. This resulted in many people recommitting themselves to M'bona and a closer unity among the people was fostered.

M'bona revealed himself through a medium. His manifestation was mostly during war or some disaster such as a severe drought. However, M'bona's medium was only possessed by M'bona when M'bona himself so wished. What M'bona said through his possessed medium was so important in the eyes of many that the M'bona cult became the national religion in Lundu's chiefdom.[28]

Lundu made sure that M'bona's messages were controlled and saw things in society the way Lundu wanted. This is an indication that the spiritual character of M'bona was a power Lundu had to reckon with in his territory. While Lundu used the M'bona cult to achieve his political ends, the cult and its shrine gained spiritual eminence in Lundu's country.

Among the Shona in northern Zimbabwe, Daneel notes that territorial spirits, *mhondoro*, developed from ancestors whose influence upon the people had continued to be felt long after they were dead. One such great *mhondoro* is

---

[26] Matthew Schoffeleers, "The Interaction of the M'bona Cult and Christianity, 1859-1963", in T.O. Ranger and John Weller, *Themes in the Christian History of Central Africa*, London: Heinemann, 1975, pp. 14-25.

[27] See also Matthew Schoffeleers, *Religion and the Dramatization of Life: Spirit Beliefs and Rituals in Southern and Central Malawi*, Blantyre: CLAIM, 1997, p. 45.

[28] Schoffeleers, "The Interaction between the M'bona Cult and Christianity", in T.O. Ranger and J. Weller (eds.), *Themes in the Christian History of Central Africa* London: Heinemann, 14-29

Chaminuka. He was regarded by the Shona as the greatest messenger and mediator between God and his people.[29]

As a *mhondoro* of the highest order, Chaminuka had come to be regarded by the Shona as the "son of Mwari".[30] Therefore, Chaminuka represented the voice of God himself; and any spirit medium possessed by the spirit of Chaminuka was highly regarded. Prayers and offerings were made to Chaminuka. Chaminuka in turn protected the people and assured them of rain in times of drought. On the political scene, the power of Chaminuka enabled the Rozwi chiefs to unite their people under regional *mhondoro*.[31]

The close relationship between the original *mhondoro*, Chaminuka, and God made it easy for the *mhondoro* cult to be joined with the Mwari cult of the southern Shona. However, this syncretism did not offer Chaminuka equal status with *Mwari*.[32] Chaminuka remained the highest *mhondoro* while *Mwari*, believed by the southern Shona to be transcendent, also became personal, communicating with his people through a spirit medium called "the Voice of Mwari".[33]

What has emerged is that territorial spirits played a mediatory role between God and the people. The territorial spirits were highly regarded. In their traditional background, the territorial spirits' concerns were for the welfare and prosperity of the community. Mediums possessed by such spirits carried social responsibilities they would not have had under normal circumstances.

Third, the ancestral spirits are generally associated with authority in the family. Fortes has pointed out that for Africans in general, the ancestor is not basically an entity representing the whole individual, in the way that a person is before death. The ancestor is rather to be conceived as a generalized personality or image of the authority of the role of the father. According to Fortes, all African fathers are authoritarian figures and all behave in the same way to their lineage.[34] This view of ancestors' authority emerges from the ancestor cult as generally presented by many writers. The authority of ancestors over their lin-

---

[29] M.L. Daneel, *Old and New in Shona Independent Churches*, Vol. 1, *Background and Rise of the Major Movements*, The Hague: Mouton, 1971, pp. 124f; also Daneel, *The God of the Matopo Hills*, pp. 24f.

[30] Daneel, *The God of the Matopo Hills*, pp. 24f.

[31] D.P. Abraham, "The Roles of Chaminuka and the Mhondoro Cults in Shona Political History", in E. Stokes and R. Brown (eds.), *The Zambesian Past: Studies in Central African History*, Manchester: Manchester University Press, 1966.

[32] Daneel, *The God of the Matopo Hills*, p. 25.

[33] *Ibid.*, p. 90.

[34] M. Fortes, "Some Reflections on Ancestors Worship in Africa", in M. Fortes and G. Dieterlen (eds.), *African Systems of Thought*, London: Oxford University Press, 1965, p. 40.

eage may best be viewed from the relationship which exists between the living and the departed.

Mulago insists that among the Bashi of central Kivu, Rwanda, and Burundi, an intimate ontic relationship exists with one another even where one member of the family is dead.[35] According to Mulago, death may bring change in the condition of existence, but relationships, status and interaction transcend the physical and biological limitations imposed by death. Hence a father remains a father to his son even after death. This is supported by Tempels when he says that even when the son has grown up he

> remains always for the Bantu man, a force, in causal dependence and ontological subordination to the forces which are his father and mother. The older force always dominates the younger. It continues to exercise its living influence over it. The world of forces is held like a spider's web of which no single thread can be caused to vibrate without shaking the whole network.[36]

Possession by an ancestral spirit thus entails a command, or conferment of punishment or approval within a household. Schoffeleers describes possession among the Mang'anja people of southern Malawi. He makes a fundamental distinction between spirits of the land and spirits of the household. According to Schoffeleers, possession by ancestral spirits or spirits of the household is for the well-being of the individual and his lineage.[37] Ancestral spirits possess only persons from their lineage over whom they have authority.

Among the Zinza of Tanzania, possession by ancestral spirits is generally regarded as advantageous. Through the medium, the departed ancestor is believed to revisit his skin, participating in their festivities and advising them on family matters such as marriage.[38] When the family has neglected the advice of the spirits and falls into misfortune, this is seen by the lineage as a result of the ancestor's displeasure. Further, where an ancestor seizes his descendant, bringing some disease or misfortune such as barrenness, this is regarded by the living as way of calling for attention. In this way the ancestor ensures that he continues to exist and have authority over his lineage.

Beattie finds a similar belief among the Nyoro. He reports that mediumistic rituals are performed in the context of the rites of passage of birth and marriage, and also after some misfortune which has been diagnosed as due to

---

[35]   V. Mulago, "Vital Participation", in Kwesi A. Dickson and Paul Ellingworth (eds.), *Biblical Revelation and African Beliefs*, London: Lutterworth, 1969, p. 138.

[36]   Tempels, *Bantu Philosophy*, pp. 40f.

[37]   M. Schoffeleers, "History and Political Role of the M'bona Cult", in T.O. Ranger and I. Kimambo (eds.), *The Historical Study of African Religion*, London: Heinemann, 1972.

[38]   Mulago, "Vital Participation", pp. 139-140.

family spirits.[39] After the spirit has possessed his medium, a communal meal is eaten by the lineage gathered. The medium puts some food in the mouths of the members of the family as a symbol of close attachment.[40] The possessed may also pronounce his blessings on the lineage in a tangible way, such as letting people sit on his lap.

What has emerged so far is that through possession, ancestors live on in their descendants and continue to exert their authority upon them. Their authority is carried on by the head of the household, the father. Further, through possession of one of its members by an ancestral spirit, the family is constantly reminded of its duty to adore and honour its ancestors through sacrifice and other acts. Thus family unity is enhanced.

Where an ancestral spirit possesses a medium outside its own lineage, it is essentially a malevolent power whose main activity is to cause various kinds of misfortune; it is thus difficult to control. Newell makes a distinction between the spirits identified with a particular family or clan, and the spirits which have no relationship with the family or the person it possesses.[41] The former are interested in the well-being of their lineage and possess only members of their own lineage for integrative purposes. The latter, on the other hand, afflict their host and disrupt the family by causing disease and death. Such alien spirits, according to Newell, represent evil and disorder in the society. For instance, among the Nyoro people,

> the more outside a ghost is, the more dangerous it can be. Thus unrelated ghosts of former domestic slaves, of blood partners (who are by definition of separate clans) and of wandering unnamed ghosts are among the most difficult to deal with.[42]

A similar belief is held by the Tonga of Zambia. As Colson says, "*Mashabe* represent alien humanity and are known by tribal rather than by personal names".[43] People possessed by such alien spirits act out certain characteristics of the invaders. For example, Daneel reports Shona people who were possessed by "European spirits".[44] In the trance state, the possessed person will dress in white man's clothes, request European food such as chips, and demand to be treated as a white man. Possession of this nature indicates res-

---

[39] Beattie, "Spirit Mediumship in Bunyoro", p. 160.

[40] Ibid.

[41] W.H. Newell, "God and Bad Ancestors", in W.H. Newell (ed.), *Ancestors: World Anthropology Series*, The Hague: Mouton, 1976, pp. 17-29.

[42] John Beattie, "The Ghost Cult of Bunyoro", *Ethnology*, Vol. 2/3 (1964), p. 24.

[43] E. Colson, "Spirit Possession among the Tonga", in Beattie and Middleton (eds.), *Spirit Mediumship and Society*, p. 71.

[44] Daneel, *Old and New in Southern Shona Independent churches* (Vol. 1), p. 134.

istance to foreign influences. It serves as a healing process where the possessed person and the community come to terms with alien spirits. They are given a name, identifying them and establishing a place for them within the old culture. This process also means that the old culture is renewed as it rearranges its structure to fit the new element.

The spirit world in Tumbuka tradition is similar to that among various ethnic groups in Africa as noted above. The Tumbuka view the spirit world in the same sense of the "unbroken circle" as described by John Taylor. The spirit world is inseparable from the physical world. However, in Tumbuka tradition, the difference between the spirit world and the physical is in the essence of life. One is lived in spirit and the other is lived in the flesh.[45] The spirit world in Tumbuka tradition is characterized by involvement. There is close and constant intercommunication between the spirit world and the physical. The spirit world makes its presence felt in the physical world through various means such as dreams, visions and possession. We shall deal with this point later. Here it is enough to note that the spirit world in Tumbuka tradition has a bearing on the physical world and that the two are held together as one.

Smith's general description of the spirit world in Africa comes closest to that of the Tumbuka. He places God, the Creator, above the spirit world. Under him are higher spirits, which Smith calls "founder spirits" of various clans. Then come lineage spirits which form a link between God and higher spirits on one hand, and the living on the other. In the Tumbuka spirit world, lineage spirits, better known as ancestral spirits, provide the base of religious expression. The departed and living members of the family are all involved in the welfare of the family. Meaningful communication with the ancestral spirits is effected through some form of manifestation such as possession. Great credence is attached to these spirits' manifestation as it is generally for the good of the household in question. At particular times when the family celebrates, e.g. an initiation, a birth, or a wedding, one member of the family may be possessed by a lineage spirit.[46] Even in sad times such as at death, there is communication with the lineage spirits. This close association of the lineage spirits with the living creates a religious atmosphere where the spirit world's presence is continuously felt.

The Tumbuka also believe that there are general spirits which have no genealogy. Donald Fraser describes these spirits as "spirits of the earth".[47] This

---

[45] A. Hetherwick, *The Gospel and the African*, Edinburgh: T. and T. Clark, 1932, p. 51.

[46] *Ibid.*

[47] Donald Fraser, *Livingstonia: The Story of Our Mission*, Edinburgh: Foreign Mission Committee of the United Free Church of Scotland, 1915, p. 29.

description corresponds to *"Fumu zapasi"* used by the indigenous people to refer to these spirits. Fraser connects the spirits of the earth with certain objects, presumably their supposed domain, e.g. spirits of large pools, forests, mountains etc.[48] Such spirits include spirits of forgotten people who lived an evil life and failed to join the ranks of the ancestors when they died. For example, a person regarded by the Tumbuka as a witch can not attain the position of an ancestor after death. His spirit is believed to roam in forests, caves, graveyards etc. These spirits possess people in order to afflict them.

THE SPIRIT WORLD IN RELATION TO THE PHYSICAL WORLD

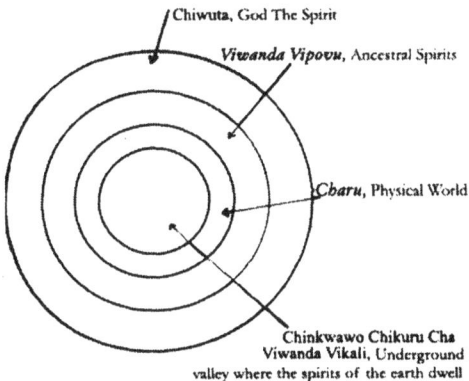

Chiwuta, God The Spirit

Viwanda Vipovu, Ancestral Spirits

Charu, Physical World

Chinkwawo Chikuru Cha Viwanda Vikali, Underground valley where the spirits of the earth dwell

Second are the spirits of deceased chiefs and village headmen. These correspond to the higher spirits, the founders, mentioned by Smith. In the Tumbuka spirit world, these royal spirits are regarded as the forefathers of the whole Tumbuka people. These spirits form a hierarchy by the order of their succession and achievements.[49] Their power is perpetuated in the ruling chief. While he is on the throne, the Tumbuka regard him as standing in the tradition of the departed chiefs and therefore as the embodiment of the royal spirits. The community expresses its political, social and religious identity by its allegiance to the ruling chief, the custodian of ancestral power.

Above the heroic spirits and the ancestors is *Chiuta*, God, who is the final authority. He too is conceived as a spirit, but in a category of his own. His involvement and communication with the living is magisterial, i.e. he communicates and acts through intermediaries such as ancestral spirits. *Chiuta* is regarded by the Tumbuka as too great to mingle in human affairs except in rare cases such as times of extreme need.[50] *Chiuta* completes the Tumbuka spirit world and is the ultimate spirit.

Committee of the United Free Church of Scotland, 1915, p. 29.

[48] *Ibid.*, p. 30.

[49] I owe this information on Tumbuka royal spirits to Mr P. Ndoni through personal correspondence.

[50] Mumba, "The Religion of my Fathers" in *International Review of Missions,* Vol 19 (1930), p.368.

THE SPIRIT WORLD IN COMMUNICATION
WITH THE PHYSICAL WORLD

Chiwuta, God The Spirit, Located somewhere
high in the sky above ancestral spirits

Viwanda Vipoou,
Ancestral Spirits (from above)

PHYSICAL WORLD

*Chinkwuuwo Chikuro Cha
Viwanda Vikali,*
Spirits of the earth (from below)

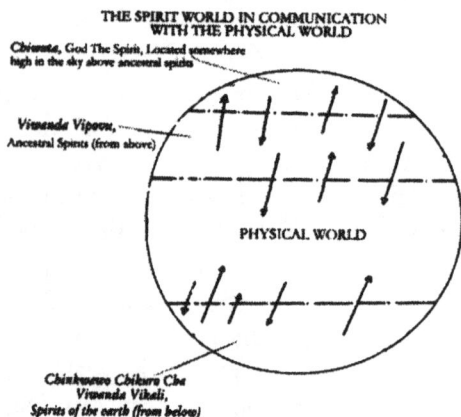

We see, then, that the spirit world in Tumbuka tradition is similar to that of many African peoples. Its reality is conceived in terms of its close link with the physical world. Whatever the community or individuals do or do not do, they are aware of the constant presence of the spirit world. The spirit world in Tumbuka tradition constantly communicates with the physical world thereby influencing people in various ways. This intercommunication between the spirit world and the physical world is a concept shared with people in many parts of Africa.

Possession as a world-wide phenomenon

Erika Bourguignon has made a survey of over four hundred societies with a view to establishing the existence of possession on a world-wide scale. The results of her study have shown that ninety per cent of the societies she studied had one form of possession or another. She terms this phenomenon "altered states of consciousness". This claim that possession is a world-wide phenomenon is echoed by other writers on the subject.[51] While Bourguignon points to the wide spread of possession, she does not imply that the phenomenon is universal. There are some societies where the phenomenon does not exist. For example, among the Maasai possession, until recently, was not known.[52]

---

[51] In his study of the religion of the Mbuti of eastern Zaire, E.M. Zuesse states: "Possession is very common in the Mediterranean area, European and Western cultures, and in south and east Asia." (E.M. Zuesse, *Ritual Cosmos: the Sanctification of the Life in African Religion*, Athens, Ohio: Ohio University Press, 1979, p. 186.) Sheila Walker says, "The phenomenon of spirit possession has existed through human history." (Sheila Walker, *Ceremonial Spirit Possession in Africa and Afro-America*, Leiden: E.J. Brill, 1972.)

[52] On how spirit possession came in and was used by Maasai women to achieve their conversion to Christianity, see Christel Kiel, *Christians in Maasailand. A Study of the History of Mission among the Maasai in the North Eastern Diocese of the Evangelical*

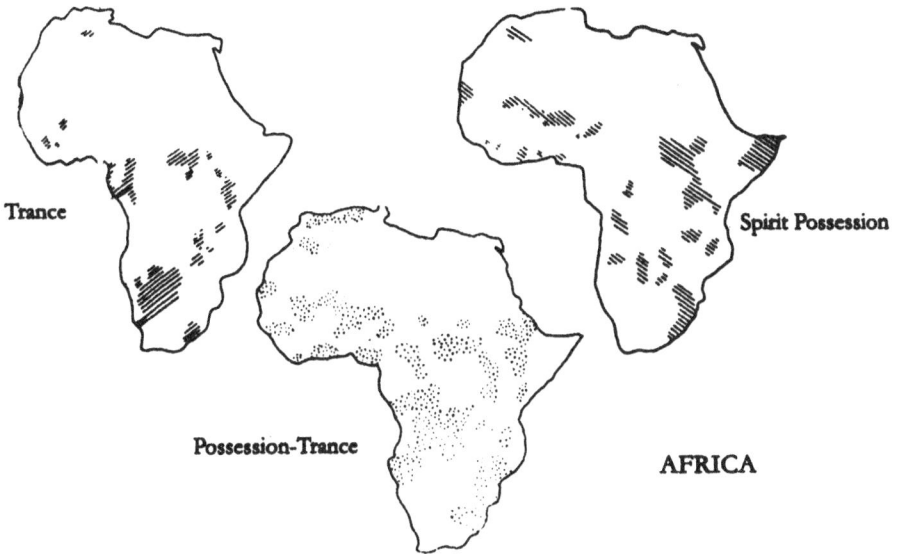

Distribution of Trance and Possession in Africa
from *Trance and Possession States*, R Prince (ed), by E. Bourguignon

Bourguignon makes a distinction between "possession trance" and "possession".

> We shall say that a belief in possession exists, when the people in question hold that a given person is charged in some way through the presence in him or on him of a spirit entity or power, other than his own personality, soul, self, or the like. We shall say that possession trance exists in a given society when we find that there is such a belief in possession and that it is used to account for alterations in consciousness, awareness, personality or other aspects of psychological function. [53]

We observe two points made by Bourguignon here. One is that the meaning of possession depends on the interpretation given it by the culture of which it is a part. The second point is that possession succeeds a physical event later interpreted in spiritual terms. In our study of possession among the Tumbuka, it is necessary to take Bourguignon's two points into consideration. Among the Tumbuka both possession trance and possession exist. This emphasizes the ambiguity of possession, as will be seen below.

Possession by and of a spirit: the ambiguity of possession

Irving Zaretsky has given a working definition of spirit possession. The definition is in two parts. First, he asserts, an individual is possessed when

> this external agent [a spirit] has inspired the individual to act in a certain manner, by means of having entered into or mounted him, thus taking over and or displacing the individual's own personality and acting in its stead.[54]

The possessed person's consciousness is so affected by the external agent influencing him that he loses his individuality. His individuality is possessed *by* the agent.[55] Prolonged illness usually precedes, and is symptomatic of,

---

[53] Erika Bourguignon, "Introduction: A Framework for the Comparative Study of Altered States of Consciousness", in E. Bourguignon (ed.), *Religion, Altered States of Consciousness and Social Change*, Columbus: Ohio State University Press, 1973, p. 7f.

[54] Irving Zaretsky, *Bibliography on Spirit Possession and Spirit Mediumship*, Evanston: Northwestern University Press, 1967, p. xii.

[55] John Beattie describes possession in Bunyoro and other cultures. He dwells on the individual's state of dissociation, and society's explanation of what it perceives as unusual behaviour resulting from the control of an outside agent. The agent either inspires the individual to act in a certain manner, or displaces the individual's personality and acts in its place. (John Beattie, *Other Cultures*, New York: Free Press of Glencoe, 1964, p. 229.) Similarly, among the Kalabari, individuals possessed by the spirit of *Oru Seki* lose their personality. When asked by Horton if they remembered their actions during the possession state, the answer was that they could not remember anything. (Robin Horton, "Types of Spirit Possession in Kalabari Religion", in Beattie and Middleton (eds.), *Spirit Mediumship*

possession by spirits. Also it takes a whole day or longer for the individual to come out of the possession state.[56] Possession *by* a spirit is welcomed by the community in that at the end of the day, the possessed emerges out of it renewed and made whole. Its suppressive nature is deplored.

The second part of Zaretsky's definition of possession reads:

> The agent acting through the individual communicates with varying degrees of coherence, a specific message pertaining to the life of the possessed individual, his illness or condition, the lives of others in general.[57]

We observed that the possessed individual displays a certain degree of control over his behaviour and shoulders more social responsibility than the average member of his society. According to Zaretsky, such "possession state is neither irreversible nor long-term".[58] The possessed person goes into trance and comes out of it with ease. He may be said to be possessed *of* a spirit. His influence upon the community is great.[59]

Common to both possession *by* and possession *of* a spirit, is a recognized change of behaviour "attributed by society to the control exercised by some external or transpersonal agent".[60] The difference between being possessed *by* and *of* lies in the quality of the possessing agent and the effect it has on the individual and his community. In the one the individual is overtaken by an agent and in the other he is inspired by an agent. Thus possession *by* and

---

and Society, pp. 17-18.)

[56] E. Colson, "Spirit Possession among the Tonga", in Beattie and Middleton (eds.), *Spirit Mediumship and Society*, pp. 87-88.

[57] Zaretsky, *Bibliography on Spirit Possession*, p. xiii.

[58] *Ibid.*

[59] In 1896 when the Shona launched a rebellion against white settlers, mediums who claimed to be possessed by the spirit of *Mwari* were at the heart of the rebellion. Their authority was beyond that of the chiefs (T.O. Ranger, "The Role of Ndebele and Shona Religious Authorities in Rebellions of 1896 and 1897", in Stokes and Brown [eds.], *The Zambesian Past*, p. 122). The authority of these possessed mediums was not limited to war times as Ranger points out: "The influence of the senior mediums was even in normal times more extensive than that of any secular authority, and could bring together for ritual purposes, even warring paramounts" (T.O. Ranger, *Revolt in Southern Rhodesia 1896-7: A Study in African Resistance*, London: Heinemann, 1967, p. 192). Among the Lugbara, Middleton found that for mediums revered by their community as doctors and operators of oracles, falling in possession was under their control. They were conscious of everything which went on in the ceremony to the extent of their directing the whole ceremony. Middleton even wonders if "real" possession counts much among the Lugbara (John Middleton, "Spirit Possession among the Lugbara", in Beattie and Middleton [eds.], *Spirit Mediumship and Society*, p. 226).

[60] A.F.C. Wallace, *Culture and Personality*, New York: Random House, 1961, p. 59.

possession *of* a spirit may be viewed, according to Zaretsky, as a psycho-pathological condition and socio-religious experience.[61] In the former, the personality of the possessed is diminished or taken over by the spirit whereas in the latter the personality of the possessed individual is elevated to a height of full humanity.

That an individual is possessed *by* or possessed of a spirit may be known to the community after the spirit's appearance in the possessed. This stresses the ambiguity of possession and accounts for the mixed treatment, be it respect, caution or fear.[62] The reason for this ambiguity is that the possessed individual is regarded by his community to be endowed with both power to heal and to kill. Further, evil spirits as well as benevolent spirits are known to possess individuals.[63] Naturally, the unpleasant side of possession has made it very suspect in the "Western world". However, modern social analysts and writers on the subject have repudiated the popular view that possession is demonic or schizophrenic. The positive factors underlying possession are cause for recent interest in research on the subject.

Modern studies and explanations of possession

I.M. Lewis, an anthropologist, has considered the phenomenon of possession from a sociological perspective. He treats separately peripheral cults and what he terms, "main morality possession religions",[64] i.e. religions where possession is central to the customs and beliefs of the people. Again, Lewis makes a further division in the latter between religions that place importance on ancestral spirits and those where possession is founded on spirits which were never human.

Possession and authority

Lewis sees authority within a cult as closely connected with authority within the social system. He expresses the relationship between authority and possession in terms of dominance, i.e. one powerful group dominating a weaker group

---

[61] Zaretsky, *Bibliography on Spirit Possession*, p. xiii.

[62] M.F.C. Bourdillon, *The Shona Peoples: An Ethnography of the Contemporary Shona, with Special Reference to their Religion*, Gweru: Mambo, 1976, p. 188.

[63] Robert Gray has shown that among the Segeju people, a diviner-healer can heal disease. At the same time, he can cause death. (R.F. Gray, "The Shetain Cult among the Segeju", in Beattie and Middleton (eds.), *Spirits Mediumship and Society*, pp. 183-184). The belief is shared by many people in Africa including the Tumbuka of northern Malawi.

[64] I.M. Lewis, *Ecstatic Religious: An Anthropological Study of Spirit Possession and Shamanism*, London: Penguin, 1971, p. 34.

within a given society.[65] Lewis says that the fact that more women than men get possessed is an indication that they are deprived and are without social status. By being possessed, the weaker group achieves a kind of freedom and power denied them in normal circumstances.[66] They achieve this freedom by directing their possession, during which they express their grievances, to the authorities. Therefore, possession is seen as a technique through which society allows dissatisfied members to act out their grievances without disrupting the order.

Possession as a sensor in religion

A further point Lewis makes is that possession enables individuals to raise their social status. When possessed persons master possession techniques, they become diviners recognized by both authority and citizenry. Consequently, their active role as diviners elevates them to a social status higher than they had before.[67] This rise in status puts the individual in a privileged position, giving them a closer relationship with the dominating group.

In situations where the phenomenon of possession has a central position in religion, Lewis says that possession is a preservative of social order. In this case usually religious leaders belong to the same social strata as some political leaders. This state of affairs makes possession exclusive, i.e. possession becomes the monopoly of the dominating group. Lewis writes, "in certain exotic religions that allow ecstasy to rule most aspects of their adherents' lives, all the evidence indicates that the more strongly based and entrenched religious authority becomes, the more hostile it is towards haphazard inspiration".[68] In this sense, possession functions as a sensor by which society preserves its tradition. The community expects those possessed to be competent inter-preters of social events and to be able to detect and deal with social impurities when they arise.

Possession as a unifying factor

Sheila Walker, like Lewis, views possession from an anthropological point of view. She attempts to uncover the importance of the phenomenon to both individuals and communities.[69] Walker looks at possession through a wide lens, seeing its different aspects and its complexity. She states that possession fosters

---

[65]   *Ibid.*, p. 88.
[66]   *Ibid.*
[67]   *Ibid.*, p. 303.
[68]   *Ibid.*, p. 34.
[69]   Sheila Walker, *Spirit Possession in African and Afro-American Forms, Meanings and Functional Significance for Individuals and Social Groups*, Leiden: E.J. Brill, 1972, p. 11.

social unity. She cites Haitian society. There, possession ceremonies draw together communities to celebrate in dance the presence of a spirit embodied in the possessed individual.[70] In the process, the community discovers its identity and thereby is solidified.

Another interesting point Walker makes is that possession suspends social inhibitions, allowing all those present to become equals irrespective of their social status in ordinary life.[71] The significance of possession in this case is that it gives importance to the possessed individual. At the end of the ceremony the individual is integrated and the community is made whole.

Possession as entertainment

Walker further points out that possession provides entertainment for people whose normal lives are marked by hard labour. She writes, "the phenomenon of ceremonial possession is very important for the functioning of the society of which it is part. One valuable role it plays is in providing entertainment".[72] Within ritual occasions, possession dances may be partly religious and partly social. The occasion provides people with an opportunity to meet, chat and laugh and enjoy themselves as they watch the dancers.

A.M. Ludwig explains possession according to how it occurs physiologically, its general characteristics and its functions. He, like Bourguignon, refers to possession as "altered states of consciousness".[73] These altered states of consciousness (ASC) include daydreaming, hypnosis, hysterical states of dissociation and depersonalization etc.

When does possession occur?

Ludwig points out that ASCs occur when a multiplicity of subjective experiences such as fear, rage reactions, joy etc. stimulate the brain waves. The stimulation is regulated by a gauge-like mechanism. This gauge varies with every individual. When the level of the stimuli falls below or above the gauge, the person is liable to an altered state of consciousness.[74] In Ludwig's terms, possession can be entered into by any normal person provided sufficient external stimuli is induced on the individual's brain waves.

---

[70] *Ibid.*, p. 97.
[71] *Ibid.*, p. 103.
[72] *Ibid.*, p. 97.
[73] A.M Ludwig, "Altered States of Consciousness", in R. Prince (ed.), *Trance and Possession States*, Montreal: R.M. Bucke Memorial Society, 1968, p. 69.
[74] Ibid., pp. 69-70.

The characteristics and function of possession

According to Ludwig, an individual in an ASC is subject to disturbed time sense, alternations of thinking, loss of control of himself, change in emotional expression etc.[75] The individual's psychological experience in the ASCs is preoccupied by a mental process at a level more intensive than is usual. This impairs the individual's sense of reality and hence the deviation.

Ludwig divides the states of consciousness into two classes, viz. the unpatterned states and the patterned states. The former include hypnosis, sleep state, and sensory deprivation state.[76] He considers that individuals in this category fall outside a socially recognized pattern. Therefore their ASCs are private. However, the meaning of a state the individual may be in can be religious or secular. Ludwig says that the meaning is given by the individual experiencing the change.[77] The latter category includes "religious conversion and healing trance experiences during religious revival meetings, spirit possession states, either by the holy Ghost or tribal spirits, panic states and rage reactions".[78] Ludwig points out that this category falls within the institutionalized forms or pattern. States within this category may be given secular or religious meaning within the culture in which they are found. The difference between these two is that the latter is institutionalized and concerns the community, whereas the former is subjective and affects only the individual.

It is evident that modern writers on possession stress the diverse elements found in the phenomenon. They reveal that the subject of possession has many sides to it and therefore is better understood when seen through separate disciplines, i.e. from psychological, anthropological, biological, religious angles and so forth. This calls for those people concerned with the religious side of the phenomenon to approach the subject aware that other disciplines provide light in the dark corners of the subject otherwise left out of an approach from one perspective.

In Lewis' and Walker's views of possession, we have seen that the phenomenon contributes to the social welfare of the community, providing a socially accepted outlet for individuals deprived of social power. Lewis, unlike Walker, advances a theory of possession which subordinates the lower class to the ruling class of society. In such a theory, possession, given secular or religious meaning, is seen as a means for satisfying the needs of the poor.

---

[75] Ibid., p. 79.
[76] Ibid., pp. 71-72.
[77] Ibid., p. 72.
[78] Ibid., pp. 72-73.

Power is one of those needs taken to be compensated in religious ceremonies involving possession. Can it be that there is more to possession than the arrangement of power? Among the Tumbuka where social strata are not clearly defined, as we shall see in Chapter Two, Lewis' theory does not apply. Authority among the Tumbuka lies within individual households and any grievances that arise are directed to the head of the household.

There is a general agreement among writers that possession stabilizes and solidifies the community. During possession ceremonies among the Tumbuka, different villages gather together to celebrate the healing of the possessed individual who would otherwise be on the fringe of society. In the process, relationships are enhanced and oneness fostered.

Among the Tumbuka, possession is generally not entered into through mechanical means. The Tumbuka do not deliberately seek to be possessed, but they are "seized" or "touched" by the spirits. They dread the initial possession because it is the one which reduces the ego of the possessed. This state of affairs comes about because of the inexperience of the possessed. In such a situation, possession may be viewed as perhaps maniacal. However, possession among the Tumbuka is not merely a subjective experience which sinks the human personality. Raymond Prince asserts that where possession is institutionalized, it is a means for individuals to transcend social structures.[79] The possessed becomes an innovator within society. We shall see this point in Chapter Three. Here it is enough to say that possessed individuals cannot simply be treated as maniacs. The true character of their condition must be measured by their contribution to society.

As a religious factor, possession among the Tumbuka represents a breakthrough, the undertaking of priesthood and a new way of life.[80]

Among the Nguni, Judith Gussles shows that *isangoma*, an individual possessed by spirits, is regarded by Nguni as "reborn", i.e. a new being. He assumes priestly functions and bears more responsibility in society than before.[81]

---

[79] Raymond Prince, "Psychotherapy as the Manipulation of Endogenous Healing Mechanisms: A Transcultural Survey", *Transcultural Research Review*, Vol. 2/4, Montreal, (October 1976), p. 15.

[80] Prince has argued that possession is used in initiation ceremonies into priesthood as a symbol of genuine calling. It is also used as an aid in the priest's religious duties, ibid., p. 121.

[81] Judith D. Gussles, "Social Change, Ecology, Spirits Possession among the Southern African Nguni", in Bourguignon (ed.), *Religion, Altered States of Consciousness*, pp. 111-114.

Another example is given by P. Verger. He says that among the Nago-Yoruba, possession is one important means for recruiting priests. An individual possessed by unidentifiable spirits is regarded as called by *Orisha* or *Vodum*.[82]

In Tumbuka tradition the possessed individual reflects an atmosphere of religious worship. He becomes totally controlled by the spirit of a deity. In this state, the possessed individual is "mediator between the people and deity".[83] The possessed individual carries the deep religious desires of the community and their own. In his or her dance they point to the fact that there is in human life a point where rationality ends. This is when the divine fills or possesses the human. At such a point, all that the human can do is to act out that experience.

Further, possession among the Tumbuka can represent evil wrought in society by antisocial activities such as witchcraft and foreign elements which threaten the social fabric. These are conceived as spirits which possess people in order to torment them. For example, in South Africa, Sundkler records epidemics of influenza and malaria in the early period of this century. These caused numerous deaths, believed by the Zulu to have been the work of witches. This precipitated widespread possession occurrences. The spread of possession coincided with the opening up of mines in South Africa and the influx of labourers from neighbouring countries. *Amandawe*, a new type of possession developed. It was attributed by the Zulu to those foreigners. Those possessed by *Amandawe* often spoke a foreign language and barked like dogs. To remedy the situation, possession ceremonies connected with *Amandawe* were held. The possessed publicly declared their innocence and danced out the afflicting spirits under the direction of an expert medium.[84]

As possession in South Africa represents unwelcome influences, so too among the Tumbuka. As we shall see later, there was proliferation of possession when the Tumbuka were invaded by Ngoni. Until much later when Tumbuka accommodated the Ngoni into their society, they regarded the newcomers' influence as counterproductive. However, the point we want to make here is that this form of possession is the other side of the phenomenon which we saw above.

---

[82] P. Verger, "Trance and Convention in Nago-Yoruba Spirit Mediumship", in Beattie and Middleton (eds.), *Spirit Mediumship and Society*, p. 51.

[83] R. Firth, "Problems and Assumptions in an Anthropological Study of Religion", *Journal of the Royal Anthropological Institute*, Vol. 89/2 (1963), p. 141.

[84] B. Sundkler, *Bantu Prophets in South Africa*, Oxford: Oxford University Press, 1961, pp. 23-25.

The effects of possession on the individual and the community

Possession as a religious factor among the Tumbuka has implications for both the individual and the community. First, the individual achieves a new spiritual fulfilment and security denied to him in ordinary circumstances. This view was summed up by Andrew Lang long ago:

> In philosophy of animism and in the belief of many peoples, savages and civilized, spirits of the dead or spirits at large can take up their home in the bodies of living men. Such men or women are spoken of as "inspired" or "possessed". They speak in a voice not their own, they act in a manner "alien natural" to their character, they are said to utter prophecies and to display knowledge which they could not normally have acquired, and in fact do not consciously possess in their normal condition. All these and similar phenomena the savage explains by the hypothesis that an alien spirit - perhaps a demon, a ghost, or a god - has taken possession of the patient. The possessed, being full of the spirit, delivers sermons, oracles, prophecies and what Americans call "inspirational address" before he returns to his normal consciousness.[85]

Leaving aside the contemporary use of the word "savage", Lang describes the height to which an individual may be elevated in possession. This is true in Tumbuka tradition. A possessed individual is expected to transcend his inadequacies and enter into a deep spiritual condition which benefits him and the community. In the state of possession, the individual may intercede for an epidemic to cease or for his own relation to gain health.

Second, to the community, possession among the Tumbuka provides collective opportunities for purification. Impurities such as grudges and jealousies, harboured in everyday life and guarded by rules and restrictions, are suspended during possession. For example, Evans-Pritchard indicates that among the Nuer, when spirits possess certain individuals, the whole community comes together renewing their relationships and giving support to the possessed. The community has a sense of belonging together and shares a common sense of equality because the community is influenced by numerous spirits known to all.[86] This applies to the Tumbuka. Possession ceremonies are times when different lineages come together and celebrate their togetherness. This celebration gives hope to the community for a more meaningful life characterized by harmony in both the physical and the spiritual world.

A further point is that in Tumbuka tradition, possession provides the community with an opportunity to commune with the divine. The people who direct possession ceremonies are recognized by the community as religious

---

[85]   Andrew Lang, *The Making of Religion*, (2nd ed.), London: Longman, 1900, pp. 139.
[86]   Evans-Pritchard, *Nuer Religion*, pp. 158-159.

leaders. Their presence and prominence in the proceedings creates a worshipping atmosphere. In this situation the spirits of the departed are invoked and appealed to. The possessed individual is in a trance and dances. Now the community is concerned to know which spirit possesses him or her. This practice by the Tumbuka is similar to that of the Kalabari who also place importance on identifying the spirits which possess them.[87] Therefore, among the Tumbuka, possession sets the community on a spiritual level where it communes with a deity.

Possession, we have noted, is explained by modern writers in various ways. It is explained in terms of its social, psychological, religious implications and so forth. In itself, possession is neither good nor bad. It is what Ignatius Pambe calls "symbolism".[88] Its implications and symbolism belong to, and are best understood by, the possessed and the community in which possession is found. Among the Tumbuka, the phenomenon occurs as a religious factor and therefore has religious implications.

Some influences on the Livingstonia missionaries

From what has been said above, the Tumbuka world-view is similar to that of other peoples in Africa. But the Livingstonia missionaries who went out from Scotland to work among the Tumbuka did not share that view of the world. As we shall see later, the missionaries found the Tumbuka world-view strange, especially the spirit force made to bear on the lives of the living. They also found possession practices of the Tumbuka, which are linked with the spirits, very strange. The missionaries' world-view was influenced by many years of Christian history which had pushed any manifestation of the spirit into the background, and by concepts of rationality in European culture deeply suspicious of such phenomena.

Irvingism and its significance to the missionaries

In 1827, four decades before the Livingstonia missionaries set sail for Malawi, Edward Irving challenged the Church of Scotland's teaching or lack of teaching about the Holy Spirit. He also challenged the Church's rigid and formal modes of worship.[89] Gordon Strachan has argued that Irving's teaching about the gifts

---

[87] Horton, "Types of Spirit Possession in Kalabari Religion", in Beattie and Middleton (eds.), *Spirit Mediumship and Society*, p. 43.

[88] Ignatius Pambe, "The Symbolism of Spirit Possession", *Service Orientation*, Vol. 5 (1983), p. 11.

[89] Detailed biographies on the life of Irving have been written by W. Washington, W. Jones, M. Oliphant, A.L. Drummond and others. Here it is enough to say that Irving was

of the Spirit, speaking in tongues and prophecies, was a result of Irving's sincerity towards biblical teaching. He believed that the words, "you shall receive the Holy Spirit" mentioned in Acts 2:38-9 did not only mean the inward holiness and fruitfulness, but also the outpouring of the Spirit, giving power to believers. Irving was convinced that this gift of the Spirit was extended to the present believers in the same manner as it had been at Jesus' baptism and at Pentecost.[90]

Irving's teaching about baptism of the Holy Spirit found practical support when outbursts of the Spirit were reported in the West of Scotland in 1828. A number of people, including James Macdonald who later became a lay preacher, were reported to have been converted through the power of the Spirit.[91] M. Campbell, who was working in this area where the outburst of the Spirit was experienced, shared Irving's view about the gifts of the Spirit. When Irving heard about these incidents, which were also confirmed by some of the members of his congregation who were in personal touch with the West of Scotland, he went there to see for himself. From what Irving saw, he believed that the gifts of the Spirit had not ceased with the end of the Apostles. He talked to individuals filled with the Spirit and participated in prayer groups where speaking in tongues was part of the order. Irving concluded that if the church was not experiencing the gifts of the Spirit it was because of its unbelief more than anything else. From there Irving wrote his book, *On the day of Pentecost,* in which he argued his case about the need to go back to the Apostolic times when the Spirit was central in Church activities. Irving went

---

born in a place called Annan in Scotland in 1792, and came from a well-to-do family, which provided him with good educational opportunities. At the age of thirteen he was at Edinburgh University where he proved himself a genius when he graduated in mathematics with honours. After his studies, Irving taught briefly as a school master in Haddington. He did his theological studies at Divinity Hall in Edinburgh and was licensed in 1815. In 1822 he was ordained and worked in Glasgow as Dr Chalmers' assistant for two years before he accepted a call by Caledonian Church, Regent Square, London. His congregation, which he found with only fifty members, soon grew so large that a new sanctuary to seat over a thousand people had to be built. Irving drew large crowds, filling the church every Sunday. Commenting on Irving's power to draw many people into his church, Oliphant writes, "it was not genius or eloquence alone, but something infinitely greater. A man all visible in those hours of revelation, striving mightily with every man he met in an entire personal unity which is possible to very few" (M. Oliphant, *The Life of Edward Irving*, Vol. 1, London: Hurst and Blackett, 1862, p. 135). See also Jean Christie Root, *Edward Irving. Man, Preacher, Prophet*, Boston, 1912).

[90] Gordon Strachan, *The Pentecostal Theology of Edward Irving*, London: Darton, Longman and Todd, 1973, pp. 55-66.

[91] Robert Norton, *Memoirs of James and George Macdonald of Port Glasgow*, 1840.

further. In his preaching both in London and Scotland, every time he went there, he emphasized the spiritual gifts and the church's need to receive those gifts.

> I will not cease to use the withdrawal of these gifts as an argument of our being under the judgement and wrath of God; while I regard that account of the matter with which we content ourselves - that the extraordinary have been withdrawn from us, but the ordinary remain as a poor shift to remove the blame off our shoulders, and as making an unworthy use of the Divine purpose and intention.[92]

Irving preached with such conviction that many came to share his views. He believed that every believer was baptized into the Spirit and should receive the gifts of the Spirit. Failure to receive the Spirit derived from the Church being under God's judgement for its unbelief. This teaching was new to Irving's hearers. Thus crowds of people went to hear him wherever he preached. In Edinburgh the church was so packed that people had to stand outside:

> He reached Edinburgh in Assembly Week in May. So as not to interfere with meetings he arranged to preach in St Andrew's Church at 6 a.m. By that hour the whole of George Street was packed. This continued when the next day he moved to the West Kirk (St. Cuthbert's), and hundreds could not gain admission.[93]

At this height of success many churchmen criticized Irving's preaching, particularly his doctrine of incarnation which later was found to be heretical.[94]

In 1831 when Irving failed to attend the General Assembly in Edinburgh as his wife had just given birth to a son, Martin, he conducted regular prayer meetings which were well attended by members of his congregation. The purpose of the meeting was to pray for the General Assembly which was in session at the time. Unfortunately, the Assembly which had heard about Irving's activities, condemned his writings, especially on the Incarnation, and ordered his Presbytery to try him for heresy. He was also to be debarred from ever preaching in Scotland. When Irving heard about the hostility towards him in Scotland, he nevertheless continued with his prayer meetings. But instead of praying for the Assembly, the group prayed for the manifestation of the Spirit.[95] Soon after that, the gifts of the Spirit began to appear among the members of the prayer group. Some members shook while others spoke in tongues. Irving

---

[92] Edward Irving, "The Dealing Virtue of Baptism", Homily 11, Homilies on Baptism, *Collected Writings*, Vol. 2, 1829, p. 277.
[93] H.C. Whitly, *Edward Irving: An Interpretation of his Life and Theological Teaching*, Edinburgh: New College, 1953, p. 237.
[94] The trial of the Rev. Edward Irving, M.A., before the Presbytery of Kirkcaldy at Annan 1833.
[95] Oliphant, *The Life of Edward Irving*, pp. 305-306.

believed, as he had always preached, that this experience of the Spirit was the result of God himself. Later, Irving accepted the manifestation of the Spirit and speaking in tongues in church worship on Sunday. He was criticized by both his own Board of Trustees and the Presbytery in London. They accused him of violating the ecclesiastical order of worship as laid down by the National Church. When Irving's case was referred to his Presbytery in Scotland, he was found guilty of teaching heresy.[96]

Irving's teaching emphasized the baptism of the Spirit and the gifts of Spirit, elements which had been pushed into the background by the Church since the second century. Irving himself did not speak in tongues although he allowed it within the church. It was because of his conviction about the continued experience of the Spirit in the present believers, together with his teaching on the Incarnation, that Irving was deposed in 1834. However, his memory was kept fresh by the Catholic Apostolic Church which emerged immediately after his deposition. In its decision to depose Irving, the Church of Scotland firmly established that orthodoxy, sobriety and orderliness in worship would guide all her ministers and members at all times. The first generation of Livingstonia missionaries shared the same fundamental perception of Christianity with those who had condemned Irving.

The reaction of the Livingstonia missionaries to their experience among the Tumbuka, at least in the initial period, suggests a concern to avoid emotionalism or stress on the work of the Spirit and Spiritual gifts. They preferred to provide intellectual teaching of the Christian faith. Converts had to spend many years learning the Gospel truths before they could be baptized. The missionaries refrained from hurried baptisms, seeing these as unfruitful. When they did baptize, they made sure that converts were literate and intelligently understood their new religion.

The question here is, coming from a background where the spirit world and the manifestation of the Spirit was de-emphasized, were the Livingstonia missionaries to act in concert with a spirit-oriented Tumbuka? Or were they to oppose it? The question is here simply put and does not do justice to the complexity of the problem. In this book about the contact between the Livingstonia missionaries and the Tumbuka, I hope that justice will be done to the lively but complex exchange which took place. It is also my hope that, through this study, the Livingstonia Synod, and indeed the whole of the Church of Central Africa Presbyterian (CCAP), will regard pastoral concern for the possessed as an important part of its mission.

---

[96] *Ibid.*, p. 307.

The Livingstonia missionaries who brought the Gospel to the Tumbuka were people of European origin. Their world-view was completely different from that of their converts. While in the missionary world-view spirits and possession were marginal, in the Tumbuka world-view spirits were real, and possession was institutionalized and central to their religious system. When the Tumbuka converted to Christianity, they broke away from their old religion. However, their possession history became a fertile ground for a favourable response to the Christian teaching, especially about the "indwelling spirit", when this was presented to them. This conflicted with the first missionaries' beliefs as they preferred sound teaching and intellectual understanding of the Christian truths to religious experience of the Spirit.

Chapter 2

Tumbuka History 1780-1904

Their origins

The historiography of Malawi reveals that one cannot speak of one ethnic group without being entangled in other groups. As L. Vail says, "the peoples of Central Africa are mixed peoples with mixed cultures having mixed histories".[1] Religious changes in Tumbukaland in the 19th century resulted from a complex process of interaction of practices and institutions of diverse ethnic groups knitted together by historical events.

Mlowoka's dynasty and the Ngoni rule were determining factors in the religious changes of the Tumbuka in initial and subsequent years of the contact with the Christian faith. Both these powers brought intense religious conflict among the Tumbuka. This does not imply that before these powers impinged upon the Tumbuka there were no religious, social or political changes. The inroads made by various groups of people into Malawi between the 16th and 19th centuries, and the shifting of local people from one part of the country to the other, had already set in motion religious changes later stimulated by Mlowoka, the Ngoni and the missionaries.

The northern region of the present republic of Malawi has been the home of many peoples. Among those mentioned by Portuguese writers Gaspar Bocarro and Barretto in the 17th century were the Tonga, the Nkhonde and the Tumbuka.[2] The Tumbuka, the dominant group in the region, comprised the Phoka, the Henga, the Nkhamanga, the Siska, and numerous related groups.[3] Gamitto described the Tumbuka as follows:

> They are tall and robust, with small features, and the same kind of agate colour.
> They are warlike and turbulent; they are frequently involved in internecine

---

[1] Leroy. Vail, "Religion, Language and Tribal Myth", in J.M. Schoffeleers (ed.), *Guardians of the Land: Central African Territorial Cults*, Gweru: Mambo, 1979, p. 210.

[2] The primary sources for information about Malawi in the 17th century are given by Gaspar Bocarro and M. Barretto, reproduced by G.M. Theal, *Records of South-Eastern Africa*, 9 Vols., 1898-1903.

[3] T. Cullen Young, *The History of the Tumbuka Kamanga Peoples*, London: Frank Cass, 1970. pp. 27-29.

> warfare, in which the Chewa never take part. They are very prolific, but their
> population is greatly diminished by the wars they have among themselves.[4]

The incessant internal strife among the Tumbuka may account for their lack of
social and political unity. It also left the group vulnerable to outside invaders.
Their aggressive tendencies were released in fighting amongst themselves
which weakened their ability to fight organized foes. In the south of
Tumbukaland lay a long belt of the Maravi people whose confederation
provided a much needed balance of power with the Tumbuka. Further south
and along the lake were the Yao.

T. Cullen Young, one of the first Scottish missionaries among the Tumbuka,
attempted to reconstruct their past. Though his work remained in note form, it
is invaluable to us. Most writers agree that these northern region peoples are
Bantu who migrated from the north, possibly south of Lake Victoria. Both
Young and Marwick agree that the Tumbuka once formed part of the Luba
empire in the Mumba around the Congo.[5] It is not clear why the Tumbuka
migration took place. The most likely supposition is that the exodus was caused
by some conqueror, as was the case later with the Ngoni. What is clear, then, is
that these peoples north of the Dwangwa river share the same origin.
According to Young, the Tumbuka occupation of northern Malawi dates back
beyond the 15th century. In 1932 he wrote:

> In these two names we have the Nkhamanga and the Senga people who today
> occupy the same territory as did their ancestors of three hundred and fifty years
> ago. Moving further north from the great river (Zambezi) into territory that is
> now Nyasaland, records give indisputable evidence of the early existence upon
> their present ground of tribes who are well known today.[6]

Land settlement

The area inhabited by the Tumbuka in 1870 stretched from the Songwe river in
the north to the Dwangwa river in the south, from Lake Malawi in the east to
the Luangwa valley in the west.[7] Both Tew and Young think that the wide area
occupied by the Tumbuka indicates that their entry into Malawi was in trickles.
Some clans and families went in through Chitipa while others entered by a
more western route through the Luangwa valley following an easterly

[4] A.C.P. Gamitto, *King Kazembe*, trans. I. Cunnison, Lisbon: Junta de Investigaçoes do
Ultramar, 1960, Vol. 1, p. 63.
[5] Young, *The History of the Tumbuka Kamanga Peoples*, p. 26; also M.G. Marwick,
History and Tradition in East Central Africa, London: Longman, 1963.
[6] *Ibid.*, p. 17.
[7] Gamitto, *King Kazembe*, p. 70.

direction.[8] Gamitto suggests that the Tumbuka did not have land of their own, but that they settled in areas which were already peopled:

> The Tumbuka are a distinct tribe, and live as colonies on the Chewa lands, in villages of their own situated among Chewa villages; and in many of the latter there are some Tumbuka inhabitants also.[9]

Gamitto's statement was made after his short stopover at Kasungu - a border between Tumbukaland and Chewaland. Thus he had seen only those Tumbuka who had drifted southwards and settled among the Chewa having failed to find new lands. The only inhabitants who may have been the original owners of the land north of Dwangwa were the Akafula, popularly known as *Mwandionera kuti*. Most writers agree that the Tumbuka settlements were scattered over a large area. Their uncoordinated trek and settlement were later to be reflected in the decentralized socio-political and religious structure of these people.

Political unity

Tumbuka influence stemmed from their numbers rather than from a centralized authority. Among some of the oldest Tumbuka clans, like Mkandawire, Kachali or Harawa, were independent chieflets who were contented with micro-village politics.[10] This state of affairs facilitated the peaceful settlement of newcomers such as the Nyirongo, Chipofya, Nyanjagha and others. By the same token, smaller groups like the Lambya and the Phoka were absorbed into the Tumbuka communities. The Tumbuka influence extended into Kasungu district, as observed in Young's words: "Old men in the district of Mwasi's Kasungu, who have a hazy childhood memory of Livingstone, have told me that they were at one time Tumbuka and spoke Chitumbuka."[11] It is possible that some Tumbuka drifted south in search of new land and settled in Kasungu. Young's writing about Tumbuka families and chiefdoms gives no suggestion that there was ever a united and extensive Tumbuka state. When David Livingstone passed through the northern region in 1859, he found the people divided into independent chieftaincies. What united the Tumbuka was a shared culture, as Young points out: "It was a state of matter involving the presence of many family divisions without any federating centre beyond the possession of a common type of language."[12] From the preceding analysis, it

---

8   Young, *The History of the Tumbuka Kamanga Peoples*, **pp. 23-24.**
9   Gamitto, *King Kazembe*, p. 71.
10 Young, *The History of the Tumbuka Kamanga Peoples*, **pp. 42-44.**
11 *Ibid.*, p. 24.
12 *Ibid.*

would not be too much to conclude that Tumbuka political organization was open-ended. Its strength was in its flexibility and ability to accept new groups of people along with their religious beliefs. At the same time, this uncoordinated existence rendered it an easy prey to aspirants to power such as later were to be seen in Mlowoka ,and the militarily organized Ngoni.

Trade

Long before the white men arrived in Malawi, trade and contact with the coastal lands such as Kilwa and Zanzibar had been established. "Many years before the discovery of Lake Nyasa by Europeans, its existence and position were known to the Arabs of Zanzibar, and a more or less constant traffic was in progress between the coast and an area called Nkhamanga."[13]

Ironwork in the 19th cenury: bow stand, double gong, battle axe with decorated tang, awe and hoe.
From History of Central Africa, by P.E.N Tindall.

Dr Laws was later to be impressed by the economic developments which existed among the Tumbuka. He saw that the people were agriculturists well geared to their hilly terrain, canoe builders, ivory carvers, blacksmiths, herders of few cattle and many goats.[14] In fact, it was their industriousness and potential wealth in Tumbukaland which

---

[13] *Ibid.*, p. 15.
[14] Robert Laws, Talks and Addresses given by Dr Robert Laws (L/1/4/2 MNA) n.d.

gave hope to Livingstone for inaugurating a Christian mission.[15] However, Tumbuka traditional trade was not fully exploited until after 1780 when Mlowoka penetrated Tumbukaland. Before examining Mlowoka's influence, let us look at the Tumbuka social structure.

Social structure

The Tumbuka were a matrilineal people who found themselves sandwiched between the patrilineal/virilocal peoples such as the Lambya, Nkhonde, Kinga and Nyakyusa to the north, and the matrilineal/uxorilocal people - the Chewa, Yao and Lomwe to the south.[16]

Diversity in marriage customs among the Tumbuka, as they found themselves placed, was inevitable. In the north they mixed and intermarried with Nyakyusa and others, while in the south they mixed with Chewa and Yao. Consequently the northern Tumbuka pattern of descent and inheritance became virilocal and patrilineal. South Tumbuka remained uxorilocal and matrilineal because their Chewa compatriots in the south were also matrilineal and uxorilocal. Both monogamy and polygamy were accepted as normal. Young maintains that local patterns of culture were altered as newcomers from the eastern side of the lake came in and established quasi-chiefdoms.[17] With such a variety of cultural elements finding their way into Tumbukaland, northern Tumbuka grew apart from southern Tumbuka, but the two remained united linguistically.[18] Their beliefs and spirit possession practices, though with some variations, basically remained the same.

Mlowoka's reign and politics

Mlowoka, who acquired his name from the fact that he crossed from one country into another (kulowoka), was a coastal African whose contacts with the Arabs had made an impact upon him. For example, he dressed like an Arab. After settling at Nkhamanga in 1780, he encouraged the Tumbuka to trade in ivory, iron ore and animal skins .[19] It was easy for Mlowoka to win the confidence of the people as a new resident because he displayed wealth and splendour and made the local people aware of the value of ivory, leopard skins

---

[15] David and Charles Livingstone, *Narrative of an Expedition to the Zambezi and its Tributaries*, London: Ward, Lock and Co., 1927, p. 68.
[16] Mary Tew, *Peoples of the Lake Nyasa Region*, London: Oxford University Press, 1950.
[17] Young, *The History of the Tumbuka Kamanga Peoples*, pp. 44-47; also Vail, "Religion, Language and Tribal Myth", p. 211.
[18] Vail, "Religion, Language and Tribal Myth", p. 212.
[19] Young, *The History of the Tumbuka Kamanga Peoples*, p. 51.

and other valuables. This made the already existing but insignificant trade between the Nkhamanga people and the people on the coast and in Zanzibar grow. Mlowoka himself grew in wealth and power, and he rose to the position of a paramount chief without strife.[20] His rule through representatives enabled him to control a large territory, and certainly his marriages with daughters of various heads of clans, such as the Mkandawire and Kachali, strengthened his position. By these steps, Mlowoka secured recognition for Nkhamanga as the centre of authority. Thus he successfully weakened the already uncoordinated political system of the Tumbuka. Mlowoka's centralization of all authority united the Tumbuka in a way unknown before. Chieflets, such as Katumbi in Hewe, Chipofya at Mwazisi, Chiwurunta in the south of Nkhamanga and Mwachirwa further south of Nkhamanga, had to pay tribute to Mlowoka.[21] By the same method of persuasion, Mlowoka affected the Tumbuka religious beliefs, as we shall see later.

When Mlowoka died in around 1795, the chieftainship changed hands in quick succession, leaving the whole chiefdom in a state of political fluidity.[22] Moreover, while the Chikulamayembes, as Mlowoka's dynasty was later known, were trying to maintain their position, the Ngoni warriors from South Africa, under their leader Zwangendaba, entered Malawi in 1840 through Mchinji, conquered the Chewa and pushed their way north. They marched through the lands of the Tumbuka, Tonga and Nkhonde into present day Tanzania. After Zwangendaba's death, they returned to settle as the dominant power in much of the north eastern Regions of Malawi. The Chikulamayembe title was to be revived only by the British administration which reinstated Chilongozi Mlowoka in 1907.[23] This reduced Mlowoka's chieftaincy to that of a mere vassal to the British. The political centre of Chikulamayembe was never to see the glory it had enjoyed in the past.

---

[20] *Ibid.*, pp. 27-28.
[21] *Ibid.*, pp. 43-44.
[22] Margaret Read, *The Ngoni of Nyasaland*, London: Oxford University Press, 1956, p. 52.
[23] W.A. Elmslie, *Among the Wild Ngoni: Being Some Chapters in the History of the Livingstonia Mission in British Central Africa*, London: Oliphant, Anderson and Ferrier, 1899, p. 292.

The Tumbuka and their neighbours

The Yao

More disruption entered the scene with the arrival of the Yao. In the 1850s, Yao people, mainly of the Amachinga and Amangoche sub-groups, began to appear in Malawi from the east.[24] Duff MacDonald mentions some of their early settlements along the lake shore and in the Shire Highlands.[25] While a large contingent dominated the Shire Highlands, a sizeable group placed itself under Jumbe at Nkhotakota in the north-east of the central region. In about 1840, like Mlowoka earlier in the north, Jumbe arrived at Nkhotakota with a retinue of slave followers, an impressive display of guns and a lot of cloth. He came in peace and friendship. The Yao collaborated with Jumbe in his ivory and slave traffic to the coast. The Yao went into the interior as far as Kasungu and the southern part of the northern region armed with guns. They raided the villages and captured slaves whom they marched to the lake shore at Nkhotakota. Jumbe built large dhows and sent trade caravans filled with human cargo across Lake Malawi to the east coast.[26]

Jumbe and his Yao collaborators did not directly affect the Tumbuka socio-political and religious life in the highlands. It is highly probable, though, that their activities at Nkhotakota and in the hinterland caused a number of ambitious chieflets to raid and sell their neighbours as slaves in exchange for the much coveted calico, beads, salt and guns.

This point is strengthened by the fact that in 1863 David Livingstone found some of the lake shore trader agents as far as Luangwa Valley in Bisa country.[27] It was during this same period that many coastal Arabs pushed westwards to eastern Congo, opening new slave sources.[28] Placed in the middle of this commercial enterprise, the Tumbuka religious system was open to external

---

[24] Yohanna B. Abdallah, *The Yaos: Chikala cha waYao*, 2nd ed., ed. and trans. Meredith Sanderson, London: Frank Cass, 1973, p. 6 (Zomba: Government Press, 1919).

[25] Duff MacDonald, *Africana: the Heart of Heathen Africa*, London: Dawsons of Pall Mall (Reprint) 1969 [1882], Vol. 2, pp. 30-33; also Young, *The History of the Tumbuka Kamanga Peoples*, p. 84.

[26] R. Codrington, "The Central Angoniland District of the Protectorate", *Geographical Journal*, Vol. 5 (May 1898), pp. 509-522.

[27] David Livingstone, *Missionary Travels and Researches in South Africa*, London: Ward, Lock and Co., 1857, p. 79.

[28] George Shepperson and Thomas Price, *Independent African: John Chilembwe and the Origins, Setting and Significance of the Nyasaland Native Rising of 1915*, Edinburgh: Edinburgh University Press, 1958, p. 11.

influences. The Ngoni established in the north undoubtedly deterred the Yao slave hunters from doing as much harm as their strength would have allowed.

On several occasions Dr. Robert Laws spoke to Jumbe, trying to persuade him and his Yao group to stop indulging in the slave trade. But Jumbe would only stop trading in slaves if missionaries gave him other means of transporting his ivory to the east coast.[29] Of course the missionaries could not meet that demand. As a result, Jumbe and his Yao helpers continued with their activities until 1895 when the British put an end to Jumbe's reign and took over the administration of Nkhotakota.[30] The Yao remained at Nkhotakota, which over the years grew to be the largest Muslim village in Central Africa. Its population, which included many freed slaves from the inland, became fishermen; they related to the Chewa and Tumbuka neighbours through legitimate trade under one colonial master.

The Nkhonde

To the north of Nkhamanga lived the Nkhonde people. They apparently entered Malawi through the north-west corner of Karonga district in around 1790.[31] They may have been a small group and probably found a very small indigenous population which offered no resistance.

Prior to the coming of the Nkhonde, the area must have been sparsely populated by Lambya in the upper Songwe and Sukwa in the middle Songwe, a group of Simbombwe at Mpata near Karonga, and some Nyika around the Nyika plateau. These seem to have been only family groups without any political cohesion.[32] Consequently they have long been absorbed into the larger Nkhonde and Tumbuka communities.

Under their chief, Chawara, the Nkhonde lived side by side with the Tumbuka, but without affecting each other. As Young points out:

> In physique and in habits, in temperament and in speech, the Henga (Tumbuka) and the Nkhonde differ completely. They rarely inter-marry and carry on their contrasted lives without any sign of the wish to cooperate or share.[33]

The reason for such lack of integration is not clear. However, a peaceful treaty between Chawara, the Nkhonde chief, and Mlowoka of Nkhamanga was signed in a tangible way. Young wrote; "To seal this arrangement, Chawara sacrificed

---

[29] David Livingstone, *Missionary Travels*, p. 80.
[30] *Ibid.*, pp. 252-253.
[31] Young, *The History of the Tumbuka Kamanga Peoples*, p. 57.
[32] *Ibid.*
[33] *Ibid.*, p. 56.

an ox while Mlowoka slew a man."[34] Thus a cordial and lasting relationship was established.

Young suggests that, judging from the relative values of the two offerings, Chawara recognized the Nkhamanga authority as supreme.[35] Chawara's self-subordination may have only been out of respect as Mlowoka's influence never extended beyond the Songwe river.[36] In fact, Chawara's self-subordination paid off. He gained more land for his people without bloodshed, and avoided antagonism with his Tumbuka neighbours. The Ngoni invasion in the 19th century caused unrest among the Nkhonde and the Tumbuka, and Nkhonde history became entangled with that of the Tumbuka.

> The disturbances which in the 19th century broke up the Nkhamanga power had a certain influence among the Nkhonde also, but not as completely to interrupt the succession in the reigning family. The break up of Nkhamanga, on the other hand, served to detract from the importance of the Mlowoka's house in comparison with the apparently unbroken authority of Mphande.[37]

However, the Nkhonde continued to be separate mainly because their chiefly line was undisturbed even after the arrival of the Ngoni.[38]

The Tonga

Another influence on the Tumbuka was from the lakeshore Tonga. There is much to suggest that on the grounds of affinity in race, language and religion, the Tonga and the Tumbuka are one people with the same origins. Thus to speak of one is to speak of the other. According to Young, the Tonga, like the Tumbuka, came from the north following the same routes as had been used by various Tumbuka groups:

> Some hundreds of years ago, people of different clans seem to have been moving from North to South. In those days they were moving slowly, getting here and there until they came to Wemba country... from there two big clans left Chitimkwu and began to go south to look for land to dwell in.[39]

If these people were complete strangers to the Tumbuka, they would not have traversed Tumbukaland to settle along the lake shore without being checked.

---

[34] *Ibid.*, p. 59.
[35] *Ibid.*, p. 61.
[36] *Ibid.*
[37] Tew, *Peoples of the Lake Nyasa Region*, pp. 90-91.
[38] See also Shadreck Billy Chirembo, "Colonialism and the Remaking of the Chikulamuyembe Dynasty, 1904-1953", History Paper, Chancellor College, Zomba, 1993.
[39] Young, *The History of the Tumbuka Kamanga Peoples*, p. 90.

Second, the family names of the Tonga, though with slight variations, are consistent with familiar names.

> Clans that came later were the following: some more of the Bandas and also of the Nkhomas; the Miyala, the Chirwa, the Chunga, the Saka, the Nyarwanga and the Kunyinji.[40]

Third, the area settled by the Tonga duplicated the Tumbuka zone and no resistance again seems to have arisen from the Tumbuka. This, however, does not imply absence of strife as is natural in a growing family.

> Kanyenda marked the boundary between himself and Baza Nyirongo who had arrived later, probably along with other Nyirongos in Nkhamanga, and Luhangas and others. The boundary was somewhere at Mzimba, near the Vipya ... and so they did, giving double portions to those who gave articles of much value and small portions to those who gave goods of small value.[41]

Inequality of land distribution did breed internal strife, as was the case between Chisumphi and Longwe. These two men received land from Kanyenda. But Longwe received a smaller portion than did Chisumphi. Although the quarrel did not result in a battle, it brought hatred between the favoured and the unfavoured. Like the Tumbuka, the Tonga were matrilineal, uxorilocal community. Intermarriage between the two groups was common.

> It is quite certain that long ago people from Tongaland were going to Nkhamanga and Marambo because their relatives were there. And all Nkhamanga people were keeping the line inheritance as the Tonga, the Chirwa, the Wemba and all Marambo people were doing - that is to say that the children belonged to the mother's side. But Chikulamayembe broke through this rule.[42]

Even though Chikulamayembe's influence never extended to the Tonga along the lakeshore, their marriage system changed at the same time as that of the Tumbuka under Chikulamayembe.[43]

Linguistically the Tonga language is close to Tumbuka. The proximity of these two peoples makes it very easy for them to mingle. Through micro-migrations and intermarriage, blending or blurring across linguistic lines was effected. In this same way, it would be true to say that religious ideas of such adjacent peoples, like other aspects of culture, got blurred to a certain degree.[44]

Although the Tonga think of themselves as separate from the Tumbuka, their socio-political and religious structures are so similar to those of the

[40] *Ibid.*, p. 94.
[41] *Ibid.*, p. 93.
[42] *Ibid.*, p. 96.
[43] *Ibid.*
[44] Tew, *People of the Lake Nyasa Region*, p. 66.

Tumbuka that they have united the two groups, enabling them to live peaceably over many centuries.[45]

The Maravi

Stretching from Kasungu down to the Zambezi River in the south, and from the east shore of Lake Malawi to north west of the Luangwa River in Zambia, lived an agglomeration of peoples called the Maravi. They comprised three main groups - the Nyanja, the Chewa and the Mang'anja.

There is disagreement among writers about an ethnic group called Senga. Duff includes them among the Chewa.[46] Mary Tew suggests that they may have been close to the Chewa, but lost their cultural identity and became a separate group. Tew suggests these people came from the Petauke district in Zambia and entered Malawi through a northerly route.[47] T.C. Young first thought the Henga and the Tumbuka were the same people and he used the composite title, Tumbuka-Henga, to denote a people he assumed were the owners of most parts of the northern region. Young soon discovered that there was another group of people called Senga who had entered northern Malawi from Zambia. Instead of referring to the Henga and the Senga separately, Cullen Young wrote about the two groups as if they were one ethnic group.[48]

From personal knowledge of the people under discussion, I would suggest that the Henga Tumbuka and the Senga are two ethnic groups. The Senga originated, and are still found, in eastern Zambia; and the Henga, as Young first suggests, are a section of the Tumbuka found in the Henga valley east of the Tumbuka Nkhamanga area. The Senga people, about whom Duff MacDonald may have been writing, should not be confused with the Henga. The Senga inhabited the country west of Chipata in Zambia.[49] These indeed shared a common culture with the Maravi, especially with the Chewa.

---

[45] For the Tonga, see also J. van Velsen, *The Politics of Kinship: A Study in Social Manipulation among the Lakeside Tonga of Nyasaland*, Manchester: Manchester University Press, 1964; David Kapenyela Mphande, "On the Use of Tonga Myths, Folktales and Proverbs in Moral Education", PhD, University of Malawi, 1998.

[46] H.L. Duff, *Nyasaland under the Foreign Office*, London: George Bell, 1903, pp. 50-67.

[47] Tew, *People of the Lake Nyasa Region*, pp. 30-32.

[48] Young, *The History of the Tumbuka Kamanga Peoples*, pp. 6-7.

[49] An ethnographical map in W.V. Brelsford's *The Tribes of Northern Rhodesia*, (Lusaka: Northern Rhodesia Government Press, 1956), shows that the Nsenga inhabited the area which stretched from Chipata to the north bank of Zambezi River; the Senga people occupied Luangwa Valley and the Henga occupied an area called Henga Valley east of Nkhamanga in northern Malawi.

The Senga who came to northern Malawi deserve a special note because in their land of refuge among the Tumbuka they, together with the Bemba-Chibisa, introduced Virombo spirit possession.[50] Here suffice to say that the Senga no longer exist in northern Malawi as a separate group. They were absorbed into Tumbuka-Ngoni culture through intermarriage and cohabitation.

Among the Maravi there is a tradition which says that God created the couple on the mountain Kamphirintiwa.[51] The Maravi believe that they are descendants of this primal couple. This legend legitimizes the Maravi people as the original owners of most of what is known as Malawi today. However, writers such as Lane Poole, John G. Pike and others think that the Maravi emigrated into the present Malawi from the north as did the Tumbuka.[52] Poole suggests that the Maravi entered Malawi in 1500.[53] We observe that the Maravi entered Malawi almost at the time as the Tumbuka and share the same tradition. Though separated by language, the Maravi and Tumbuka are linked by a common origin and are both of Bantu stock.

The political unity of the Maravi before the European era needs to be studied thoroughly before any kind of definitive picture can be drawn. A.J. Willis' contribution may be helpful to this end:

> The Portuguese at Tete believed that the Maravi formed a great empire in the triangle between the Luangwa, the Lower Zambezi and the Lake but this conception was exaggerated. There is no evidence that any Chief became paramount over a powerful kingdom such as had once existed south of Zambezi.[54]

On his first journey of exploration through Malawi, David Livingstone found a peaceful atmosphere among the Maravi, but the people lived under independent chieftaincies bearing different clan names. However, Livingstone was of the opinion that some sort of political unity among these people had existed in the past. Gamitto, who passed through the Maravi country before other white men, wrote about the possibility of the existence of a Maravi confederation.[55] As to the nature of that unity we are left to guess.[56]

---

[50] Tew, *People of the Lake Nyasa Region*, p. 53.

[51] This creation myth, and a comment on it, can be found in Schoffeleers, *Religion and the Dramatization of Life*, pp. 10f.

[52] E.H.L. Poole, *The Native Tribes of the East Province of Northern Rhodesia*, Livingstone: Government Press, 1938, pp. 35-37; also A.H. Pike, "A Pre-colonial History of Malawi", *Nyasaland Journal*, Vol. 8/1, Zomba: Government Press (1965), pp. 13-20.

[53] Poole, *The Native Tribes of the East Province*, p. 37.

[54] A.J. Wills, *The History of Central Africa*, London: International Africa Institute, 1965, p. 138.

[55] Gamitto, *King Kazembe*, p. 50; also David and Charles Livingstone, *Narrative of an*

The probability is that the Maravi people came to Malawi in a small group, possibly a clan under one recognized leader. This type of immigration was equally found among the Tumbuka and Tonga. Upon arrival, the Maravi found the Akafula, who were wandering hunters and gatherers in that region. Through intermarriages, the Maravi may have absorbed the Akafula, swelling their numbers until eventually they broke into several chieftaincies. Another possibility is that there arose a leader whose power united the Maravi; we do not know. For our purpose it is enough to know that the Chewa Maravi influenced much of the southern Tumbuka religious beliefs.

H.H. Johnston included the Tumbuka Nkhamanga among the Maravi.[57] Also Manterio, in 1831, counted the Tumbuka as part of the Maravi confederation.[58] How far this is true is a matter of speculation. What is certain is that the two peoples were divided by language but shared many cultural elements.

Like the Tumbuka before 1780, the Maravi were a matrilineal society. Inheritance was through the mother's line. A male guardian (nkhoswe), guided all matters concerning his female matrikin. He also was the guardian of the offspring of his mbumba.[59] The ankhoswe were generally marriage sureties - an important function in establishing a legitimate marriage.[60] The Maravi kinship system was very similar to that of the Yao and the Tumbuka before Mlowoka and the Ngoni.[61]

The nature of the country in the 19th and early 20th century period was in a state of political fluidity. No one group of people had successfully imposed their rule in Malawi. An attempt to establish an empire combining Malawi and some parts of Tanzania, Mozambique and eastern Zambia was to be made by a new group - the Ngoni, but with much disturbance.

The Ngoni

In the last decades of the eighteenth century Dingiswayo, united a number of Nguni clans into a militarily based chieftaincy in what is now northern Natal.

Expedition, p. 25.

[56] See Kings M. Phiri, "Chewa History in Central Africa and the Use of Oral Tradition 1600-1920," Ph.D., University of Wisconsin, Madison, 1975.

[57] H.H. Johnston, *British Central Africa*, London: Methuen, 1897, p. 360.

[58] Gamitto, *King Kazembe*, p. 53.

[59] T. Cullen Young and Hastings K. Banda, *Our African Way of Life*, London: Lutterworth, 1946, pp. 13, 73-83.

[60] *Ibid.*, pp. 14-18; also A.G.O. Hodgson, "Notes on the Achewa and Angoni of the Dowa District of the Nyasaland Protectorate", *Journal of the Royal Anthropological Institute of Great Britain and Ireland*, Vol. 63 (1933), pp. 123-164.

[61] W.P. Johnson, *Nyasa the Great Water*, London: Humphrey and Milford, 1922, p. 105.

He was succeeded, at the beginning of the nineteenth century, as leader of this formidable power by Chaka, head of a small clan called Zulu. Despite the insignificance of the clan, Chaka's ferocious policy of conquest and raiding caused many neighbouring Nguni groups to leave the area. Some left in organized parties marching northwards like the Shangana and the Ndebele of Mzilikazi, others like the Mfengu fled westwards as refugees to their fellow Nguni, the Xhosa people of what is now the Eastern Province of South Africa.

One organized party was led by a very able chief, named Zwangendaba, who had for a time served as a *nduna* under Chaka. His Nguni faction were eventually to settle in Malawi and became known as the Ngoni. Their royal clan was that of Jere, a clan name still to be found among the Mfengu.

On their way north, the Ngoni passed through Sochangane's country from whence they recruited many people who may have been dissatisfied with Sochangane's rule. Some joined Zwangendaba's trekkers through marriage.[62] In fact, Zwangendaba himself married Thonga women in Sochangane's country after his Nguni wives had been murdered by Sochangane's army which tried to prevent Zwangendaba's advance northward. From these Thonga women were born Mbelwa, Mtwaro and Mperembe, who later succeeded their father and laid a strong foothold among the Tumbuka in Malawi.

In Zimbabwe, Zwangendaba further reinforced his group by assimilating some Karanga people who gave little resistance to the Ngoni intrusion. However, a fierce battle broke out between Zwangendaba's people and Nqaba's group which had also moved north.[63] The result of the fight was that Zwangendaba was defeated, forcing him to cross the Zambezi river. Stories of how Ngoni crossed the Zambezi were later told by Magwengwe Nkosi.[64] These stories point to the beliefs of the Ngoni. One story is that when the Ngoni came to the river where there was much water, making it hazardous to cross, Zwangendaba washed himself with medicine, *muti*, procured by Sobantwapa - a medicine-man and priest responsible to the paramount chief. As the chief washed with the medicine, the water began to run low, and while he was washing, the people crossed to the other side until the last person was over. The second tale is that Zwangendaba, like Moses, struck the water with his staff and people crossed on dry land. Since these stories were told at a much

---

[62] A.T. Bryant, *Olden Times in Zululand and Natal: Earlier Political History of the Eastern Nguni Clans*, London: Longman, 1929, p. 82.

[63] H.P. Junod, *Bantu Heritage*, Johannesburg: Hortors, 1938, pp. 415-425; listed in E.A. Walker, *A History of South Africa*, London: Longman, 1940.

[64] Yesaya M. Chibambo, *My Ngoni of Nyasaland*, London: Lutterworth Press, 1942, pp. 11-13.

later date (1934), it is no wonder the latter resembles the biblical story of the Israelites crossing the Red Sea.

Having crossed the Zambezi, the Ngoni passed through Senga country in Zambia pressing on northwards as far as Lake Victoria, where Zwangendaba died. Some of them then retraced their steps and finally settled in the present northern and central regions of Malawi.[65] One section under Gama broke away and joined the Ngoni Maseko who followed a more north-east route. Part of this group settled on the east shore of Lake Malawi and became better known as the Magwangwara. The other part of the Ngoni Maseko settled between Ntcheu and Dedza.[66]

It is ironical that the Ngoni, who had left their home country in South Africa in search of peace, became one of the disruptive forces in Malawi, then a comparatively peaceful region. Under their *Inkosi* Mbelwa I, from around 1850, the Ngoni raided the Tumbuka on the high plateau, the Tonga on the Lake shore and the Nkhonde beyond Nyika plateau.[67] In militaristic fashion, they also marched to Nkamanga and devastated Chikulamayembe's centre and his power was drastically diminished. Thereafter, the scattered Tumbuka chiefs who had not been slaughtered or compelled to flee were deposed and replaced by Ngoni *nduna*; if left in their positions, they were attached to the Ngoni paramount chief.[68] Young men of fighting age were recruited into Ngoni army units. They were drilled in Ngoni warfare and were promoted by merit. Courageous young Tumbuka warriors such as Mlolo were able to acquire positions of influence and responsibility within their overlords' society. By raid after raid, the Ngoni soon subjugated the whole of northern Malawi and even extended their empire into eastern Zambia. Within seventeen years of Ngoni presence in Central Africa, they had colonized various peoples covering three countries.

The interaction between Ngoni and Tumbuka produced a variety of social changes. These changes resulted from conflicting attitudes in political and social organization. First, the Ngoni militaristic life and detachment from the land conflicted with claims of the agrarian Tumbuka to ownership of the land. The Ngoni thwarted any competing claims of political control by constantly raiding their neighbours right into the 1880s.[69] Second, the Ngoni imposed their patrilineal system of marriage along with *lobola* on matrilineal Tumbuka society. *Lobola* consisted of a number of cattle which were given to the wife's

---

[65] J.K. Rennie, *The Ngoni States and European Intrusion in the Zambesian Past*, pp. 302-331.

[66] *Ibid.*, p. 315; also Elmslie, *Among the Wild Ngoni*, p. 28.

[67] Elmslie, *Among the Wild Ngoni*, pp. 27f.

[68] Young, *The History of the Tumbuka Kamanga Peoples*, p. 27.

[69] Mzimba District Residence's Report Book, Vol. 1, 1879-1902, MNA.

parents. When a sufficient part or the whole *lobola* was paid, the wife left her home to join her husband in his village. As *lobola* became the basis for a legitimate marriage, inheritance through the father's line as practised by the Ngoni was also forced on the Tumbuka.[70] In the Ngoni patrilineal society, the male children were the transmitters of what T. Cullen Young calls "the life stream".[71] When they became of age, they fulfilled their function of fathering, and supplied their community with a new generation of Ngoni members. Most important was that these young men became the backbone of the Ngoni army. The Tumbuka wanted their young men on the fields as new farmers. As the Tumbuka accepted both monogamy and polygamy, the introduction of the *lobola* may have reduced polygamy due to shortage of cattle. But that it disrupted Tumbuka agriculture is evidenced by the numerous wars which went on between 1850 and 1880. To an onlooker, it would appear as if the foundation of Tumbuka political and social structures as known in Chikulamayembe's time had been scrapped. However, the ferocious and destructive habits of the Ngoni were not as barbarous as they have generally been portrayed. The expansion of their *impis* through assimilation of conquered subjects and the attachment of tributary chiefdoms, and marrying of local women, left their own society open to influences by the subject peoples.[72]

When the Ngoni settled among the Tumbuka, they became colonial masters whose politico-socio system made a great impact on the lives of the Tumbuka. But this was short-lived.

Arrival of the Europeans

A party of Scottish missionaries, who had landed at Cape Maclear under the leadership of Ed Young in 1875 to fulfil David Livingstone's desire to transform the Malawi region through Christianity and commerce,[73] came into direct contact with the Tumbuka when they settled at Bandawe in 1881. Once in the field, the missionaries' vision of their task was not representative of Livingstone's understanding. Some wanted to replace local structures with Western structures. We shall deal with the Mission influence in Chapter Four. At present it is enough to say that the Livingstonia Mission joined the socio-political and spiritual power struggle which was already in the air in Tumbukaland. The declaration of a protectorate over part of Malawi in 1889 by the

---

[70] Further south, in the Dedza area, the Ngoni adopted the matrilineal system of the Chewa.
[71] T. Cullen Young, *Contemporary Ancestors*, London: Lutterworth, 1934, p. 71.
[72] P.E.N. Tindall, *History of Central Africa*, London: Longman, 1968, p. 63.
[73] David Livingstone, *Missionary Travels*, p. 28.

acting consul, Buchanan, who was later succeeded by Harry H. Johnston, hindered the establishment of Malawi society around one militarily strong ethnic group. In 1904 Johnston annexed the northern region to the rest of the British Protectorate thereby frustrating further independent African political initiatives. This new white man's power transformed the country and its people in a totally different way than would have happened under an African paramount. It provided missions with a familiar atmosphere in which to work. Tumbuka traditional society, hitherto fertilized by socio-politico systems and practices of many surrounding people, came to include Western elements which broadened its basis of appeal.

The Tumbuka were and are a hardworking and hospitable people as Gamitto witnessed long ago:

> This morning we continued our march S.S.E. and after going three leagues we began to come across small Tumbuka villages. Thanks to Providence that we now believe ourselves to be free of the frightful scourge of hunger.

However their socio-political condition was constantly changing. Their scattered communities had been engaged in interminable internecine warfare which left them very vulnerable to powerful outsiders. Thus they lived under a variety of 'colonial' powers in the century before the coming of British colonial authority. In this time they were constantly absorbing new elements into their society and this was their strength. They were never a coherent nation yet they had the flexibility to survive with their Tumbuka identity intact.

Chapter 3

A Religious History of the Tumbuka since 1780

Concepts of God

The year 1780 was the last the Tumbuka ever lived as a homogeneous group. The self-imposition of Mlowoka at this period and later the Ngoni, the influence of the neighbourhood and the presence of the missionaries, as already noted, not only undermined the socio-political system of the Tumbuka, but also challenged their religion. In his book, *Contemporary Ancestors*, Young underlines some of the Tumbuka beliefs. Concerning God, he says that they saw him as a "Rain Maker".[1] As such, God was viewed by the Tumbuka as a moving and life-giving force. Young writes:

> We know from tradition that a common form of 'religion' was shared over a very wide area before that invasion [by the Ngoni]. "God moved," the tradition has it, "to and fro from Mangazi to Chekang'ombe [Chikhangombe]." ... On the mountain-top itself, God was approached by representatives of the people with votive gifts when prayers were made for rain.[2]

This territory was inhabited by the Tumbuka before Mlowoka arrived in 1780.[3] Apart from being beacons for the Tumbuka borders, the two hills Mangazi and Chikhangombe were regarded by the local people as 'holy mountains' on which God made himself especially known. The mountains were a symbol of God's eminence and care. The rains always seemed to start from one of these mountains. Being an agrarian community, living close to nature as the Tumbuka did, it is not surprising that their knowledge of God was primal and ecologically linked with the earth and its fertility.

As to how far such an idea of God, expressed in its "sacred mountain sanctuary", and its priests and priestesses, can be said to have developed by 1780, no clear evidence is available. Nevertheless, after examining the surrounding people's belief about God and finding strong traces of that belief, Young admits that:

---

[1] Young, *Contemporary Ancestors*, p. 25. This book is not directly on the Tumbuka although much reference is made to them. It is a general book with an overview of African religions. Young was influenced by social anthropologists such as E.W. Smith and others.
[2] *Ibid.*, p. 128f.
[3] *Ibid.*

the idea of a 'great god' does in fact underlie African thought to an extent which has so far been under-rated, and that direct approach, through something to which the name of 'prayer' may legitimately be given, is considered possible. The fact that the rain, the sun, and probably the earthquake are in various areas chosen to symbolize the 'mighty one', does not mean polytheism. It means that little, non-communicating, isolated groups of human beings all recognize equally one great fact – the fact of an Over-Ruler.[4]

Undoubtedly, the Tumbuka concept of God was at that time confined within its own borders, giving it a small base. But that the Tumbuka considered God a great spirit who manifested himself in the experience of life can be seen from the cult of Chikhangombe which flourished during Mlowoka's reign, will be seen below. Here it is enough to note that Chiuta's power to give rain, the fundamental element of life, was at the base of the Tumbuka concept of him.

Young maintains that the Tumbuka regarded God as the creator and source of everything. He further says that the distance between God and the world of men is a technical one. He writes:

The world of men was bounded on all sides at the farthest horizon by the coming together of earth and sky, but it was not a sealed chamber. All round this circle the 'Owner' (Mwenecho) had placed pillars of the hard ironwood tree, and upon these pillars the sky rested.[5]

Young indicates that the Tumbuka were aware of, and recognized, God's lordship over them and over the earth. Accordingly, the Tumbuka lived in God's presence. An incident told by Young illustrates this point:

As a certain African headman once remarked to his people after a passing traveller had derided the local missionary for teaching that there is a God, "What kind of a fool is this? He sees and yet is blind."[6]

God's existence and his creative power were matters of fact to the Tumbuka.

The personality of God, as conceived by the Tumbuka, was characterized by power. God's power was unique. By it he created and sustained the whole of creation. This tremendous power of God made him both transcendent and immanent in Tumbuka religion, so that God was seen as far removed from humans, and at the same time close to them.[7] This quality of God made him, in

---

[4]   *Ibid.*, p. 130. In recognizing the Tumbuka knowledge of God through God's own divine initiative, Young shares the Apostle Paul's dictum: "What can be known about God is plain ... For since the creation of the world God's invisible qualities - his eternal power and divine nature - have been clearly seen, being understood from what has been made." Romans 1:19-20.

[5]   *Ibid.*, p. 131.

[6]   *Ibid.*, p. 127.

[7]   Hetherwick describes the personality of God as follows: "We note that this word

Tumbuka understanding, invisible and spiritual, and placed him in a class of his own.

Further, the Tumbuka held a monotheistic view of God. God was the Ultimate Controller of all things, the Ultimate owner of life and Ultimate determiner of human destiny.[8] Although the Tumbuka believed in ancestral spirits and other lesser deities, they regarded Chiuta as the final authority. The ancestral spirits and other intermediary spirits were appealed to up to a certain point. When all other means of solving human suffering failed, the Tumbuka final hope was in God.[9] This dynamic personality of God is further explained in the names they gave him.

Names of God

There are three names of God used among the Tumbuka. *Leza, Chiuta* and *Mulungu.* The original concept of God derived from the usage of these names in the pre-1780 period is not known.[10] Historians of religion, and anthropologists who have written about the Tumbuka concept of God, approached the subject from an etymological viewpoint. This approach does not necessarily bring out their understanding of God. Its value is in explaining the root and formation of words expressing an idea.[11]

Mulungu etymologically carries with it no idea of personality. It belongs to that class of nominatives which denote qualities or attributes, things conceived in the abstract. It is never either grammatically or in common speech associated with personality." Hetherwick, *The Gospel and the African*, p. 69.

[8]   Mumba insinuates the finality of God when he says, "we believe in a Supreme Being whom we recognize as the Creator of all things. He has laid down laws which His creatures must obey; the breaking of some of the laws is punished by earthly rulers; for others, local to the family or clan, the punishment is approved by ancestral spirits through non-assistance by intercession, the Supreme Being preserving His prerogative, mainly showing Himself in general manifestations of disapproval by bringing down such punishment as pestilence, smallpox and other destructive diseases." Levi Mumba, "The Religion of my Fathers", *International Review of Missions*, Vol. 19 (1930), p. 368.

[9]   Lienhardt has described the Dinka experience of God as represented in realities such as drought, childbirth etc. He finds that in the Dinka culture, a considerable development of the conception of God was achieved. This applies to the Tumbuka. G. Lienhardt, *Divinity and Experience: The Religion of the Dinka*, Oxford: Clarendon, 1961, pp. 147ff.

[10]   Dr P. Ellingsworth, a modern linguist, suggests that in order to perceive the meaning of God in a given cultural setting, it is necessary to study the usage and meaning of the name(s) of God as people apply them. As that generation of the Tumbuka is long gone, it is not possible to get firsthand information. Personal interview with Dr P. Ellingsworth, University of Aberdeen, 5 April 1984.

[11]   Ernst Dammann, "A Tentative Philological Typology of some African High Deities", *Journal of Religion in Africa*, Vol. 2 (1969), pp. 94-95.

Ernst Dammann interprets the name *Leza* in different ways. He believes that *Leza* may have been conceived by the Tumbuka as a lunar deity, the giver of rain or may have been an ancestor.[12] E.W. Smith says that the name *Leza* with its derivations *lesa*, "to care for", and *lera*, "to nurse" has a filial connotation. It implies that like a mother, God nurses his people.[13] The name of God, *Leza*, as described by both Dammann and Smith, gives a fertility dimension of God, the motherhood of God. This fits well the Tumbuka agrarian society and their matrilineal system of marriage and inheritance before the 1840 Ngoni invasion.

Second, concerning *Chiuta*, another name of God among the Tumbuka, Dammann suggests that it was associated with the sky and is a personification of the power connected with it.[14] According to Dammann, *Chiuta* means the rainbow and also the hunter's bow. Dammann notes that by using *Chiuta* as the name of God, the Tumbuka identify Him with the sky or hunter's bow. *Chiuta* was conceived as "the great one of the bow".[15]

Kauta Msiska describes the derivation and usage of *Chiuta* in similar terms as Dammann. He says, "The root meaning of *Chiuta* is the same everywhere. *Chi* always shows size or quality. If the "bow" is small, it is *kauta*; if it is medium, it is *uta*: but if it is extraordinarily large, as the sign of power it is *chiuta*."[16] The Tumbuka may have conceived *Chiuta* as the creative power behind the created order. He revealed Himself to them in elements of creation such as the rainbow.[17]

---

[12]   Ibid., p. 90.

[13]   W.G. Robertson, in E.W. Smith (ed.), *African Ideas of God*, (Edinburgh and London: Edinburgh House Press, 1950) p. 113, an early missionary of Livingstonia, describes the use of the name *Leza* among the Tumbuka. He says that *Leza* was derived from the Tumbuka experience of God. God cared for them. God made lightning flash as a sign of rain and therefore of fertility. W.G. Robertson, "The Native Idea of the Divine Being", *The Aurora: a Journal of Missionary News and Christian Work*, Vol. 2/9, Livingstonia (1898), p. 21. Hetherwick, another early missionary, also shows that *Leza* was used by the Tumbuka to denote God. Hetherwick, like Robertson, connects the use of this name of God with the agrarian life of the Tumbuka. Hetherwick, *The Gospel and the African*, p. 68.

[14]   *Ibid.*, p. 90.

[15]   *Ibid.*, pp. 86-87.

[16]   Stephen Kauta Msiska, *Golden Buttons: Christianity and Traditional Religion Among the Tumbuka*, Blantyre: CLAIM, 1997, p. 24.

[17]   Young analyses the name *Chiuta* as follows: Chi- (big, fullness, huge) - uta (bow) means "the great bow". This bow was associated with the rainbow. The rainbow may have been regarded by the Tumbuka as resulting from God's activity. It implies according to Young, "the power upon whose reliability the changing seasons and all human food activities depend". Young, *Contemporary Ancestors*, p. 127; see also Hetherwick, *The Gospel and the African*, p. 69.

The third name, is *Mulungu*. Dammann thinks that this name originally expressed the idea of "place". Later it evolved into a third class noun. He says:

> Locative ideas are probably at the back of a certain number of designation for the High God. One of these is *Mulungu*. Probably *Mulungu* was originally in the eighteenth noun class of Bantu languages and designated the dwelling place of the ancestral spirits. From there it seems to have migrated into the third noun class, to express its magical power, or because it had the characteristic of spirit.[18]

Although Dammann's theory seems plausible, it assumes uniform linguistic and historical development among the various Bantu ethnic groups. This is unlikely to have happened. In fact , *lungu*, interpreted by Dammann kinship in Tumbuka, means "rightness" or "undeviating direction".[19]

Levi Mumba describes *Mulungu* as God-Spirit.[20] According to Mumba, *Mulungu* is the Greatest Spirit and is in a class of his own. He is the originator of all life and the created order.[21]

When Tumbuka trade with the east coast increased between 1780 and 1830, the Tumbuka understanding of *Chiuta* also expanded. Another factor which widened the Tumbuka concept of God at this period were inroads made by the Yao, the Tonga, Nkhonde, the Ngoni and later the missionaries.

Venturing Tumbuka merchants crossed their own boundaries between Chikhangombe hill and Mangazi, where Chiuta's influence was much felt, into regions occupied by the Makua and other peoples whose God may not have

---

[18] Dammann, "A Tentative Philological Typology", p. 88.

[19] Young, *Contemporary Ancestors*, p. 127.

[20] Mumba, "The Religion of my Fathers", p. 365.

[21] A helpful explanation of the name *Mulungu* is given by Robertson. "Mu- (the one who) -lenga (creates), and with its derivation *longa* means to arrange or to put neatly, to pile up in an orderly fashion. Robertson in E.W. Smith (ed.) *African Ideas of God*, p. 21. Hetherwick found that among the Maravi people south of Kasungu, the name *Mulungu was also used as a generic* term in addition to its reference to God: "The word *Mulungu* is used with various significances. (1) It is applied to the spirit of an individual in substitute for the more common term *mzimu*.(2) It is applied to anything connected with God Himself, Divine Worship, the Church Building, the Bible, the Minister's Robes, the Church Bell, etc. (3) Seeing the white man's week began on Sunday, the people round Blantyre called the week itself by the same divine term. (4) It is also used to signify "fate", or "fortune" – good or ill. In fact, anything that is unusual or whose origin cannot be accounted for is "God". (5) To worship any spirit of the dead is "to worship God"." Hetherwick, *The Gospel and the African*, p. 69.

been known to the Tumbuka. Upon their safe return home, they would attribute their success to *Chiuta*.[22]

Further contact with the coastal Arabs and some of the Swahili whose religion was Islam which preaches about God as monotheistic and universal, injected new meaning into the Tumbuka perception of *Chiuta*. From a *Chiuta* who cared for the Tumbuka within their geographical boundaries only, *Chiuta* was now understood to exercise a wider influence in an area that extended beyond Chikhangombe hill and Mangazi.[23]

From their many years of peaceful association with the Lakeside Tonga whose God was also *Chiuta*, the Tumbuka conception of God was confirmed. The name *Chiuta* in both Tonga and Tumbuka is identical. Its designation of God as "the greatest one", the creator of all things and humans, the giver of rain and the most powerful one, can be found in both groups. Both the Tonga and the Tumbuka worshipped *Chiuta* on special hills; both had priests and priestesses responsible for the ceremonies. The Tonga, however, also believed that *Chiuta* protected them while fishing on the lake. This protective power of *Chiuta* on the lake came to be included in Tumbuka worship, especially by those who often crossed the lake on their way to the east coast.

The Nkhonde *Kyala*, God, did not find a place in Tumbuka vocabulary. Among the Nkhonde, *Kyala*, it is thought, may have been an ancestor. After a long period of time, he was deified giving him the highest position above all ancestors.[24] There is no trace in their worship of *Chiuta* that the Tumbuka thought of him as an ancestor. For the Tumbuka *Chiuta* was Spirit, "and those who worshipped him worshipped him in spirit", to use the words of the writer of the fourth Gospel. What was also different between *Kyala* and *Chiuta* is that until 1955 *Kyala* "was living in the underworld in the realms of the shadows, not 'up'".[25] *Chiuta* was transcendent and his power was unparalleled. It appears that, in the main, the Tumbuka rejected the concept of God as held by the Nkhonde. This, however, did not lead to a total rejection of Nkhonde ideas about God.[26]

---

[22] McCracken has argued that when Malawians traveled far and wide, their conception of God radically altered to fit with their changing world. McCracken, *Politics and Christianity*, p. 120.

[23] Vail notes that the influence of Chikhangombe, the mediating spirit between *Chiuta* and the Tumbuka, expanded as far south as Nsanje. To the west his influence extended into Zambia. Vail, "Religion, Language and the Tribal Myth", p. 221.

[24] Dammann, "A Tentative Philological Typology", pp. 89-90.

[25] Ibid., p. 92.

[26] Mackenzie explains that the *Nkhonde* believed in God, *Kyala*, Creator and Owner of all things. Mackenzie, *The Spirit-Ridden Konde*, London: Seeley, 1925, p. 178. This notion of

In 1840 the Tumbuka were invaded by the Ngoni whose vocabulary and conception of God contrasted with that of the Tumbuka. Environmental changes make people emphasize or de-emphasize certain aspects of their religion. In the case of the Ngoni whose original home is South Africa, *Unkulunkulu*, God, had been replaced by a royal cult. Their many years of wandering in the wilderness knitted them together under one leader, and their military power which won them many battles gave them self-confidence. Their notion of God appeared to diminish as a result.[27] By the Ngoni impact, the Tumbuka monotheistic belief in *Chiuta* was blurred. They had to accept a hierarchical deity epitomized by the Ngoni paramount Mbelwa. This situation went on until 1881 when the missionary enterprise challenged this and further introduced a new understanding of God. We shall examine this point further in the following section. Here it is enough to say that the Tumbuka notion of *Chiuta* was not obliterated by the Ngoni imperial power. It survived in the scattered Tumbuka communities and continued to be a means of Tumbuka identity in the face of pressures from the Ngoni aristocrats.[28]

Enormous changes in the Tumbuka conception of God were wrought by the Christian Church. First, was the dissolution of the Ngoni colonial rule. In 1878, Livingstonia Mission established two observation stations in the northern province while its headquarters were still at Cape Maclear. One station was at Bandawe in the heart of Tongaland, and the other post was at Kaningina on

---

God was in agreement with Tumbuka understanding of *Chiuta*. It strengthened the Tumbuka concept of God as Creator, all powerful and owner of all things.

[27] Komba has suggested that a branch of the Ngoni who settled in Tanzania after Zwangendaba had died, regards its success in conquering the land as the work of the ancestors. Consequently, they worshipped and venerated their ancestors without any reference to God. According to Komba, this emphasis on the ancestors removed the notion of God in this people. He writes, "And so when a tribe is conscious of its power to conquer other tribes and rule them, it puts undue confidence in itself and tends to forget higher principles". J.J. Komba, "God and Man", Ph.D., Pontifical Urbaniana University, Rome, 1956, p. 66. By "higher principles" Komba implies the notion of God. Margaret Read shows a similar trend among the Ngoni of northern Malawi. She says, "It was clear that the attitude of the living towards the dead was one of respect and honour, but predominantly one of avoidance and fear as among some of the neighbouring tribes", *The Ngoni of Nyasaland*, p. 163.

[28] Rau interprets the religious interaction between the Ngoni and the Chewa south of Kasungu. He says that the Chewa were affected by the Ngoni social and political changes. However, the Chewa maintained their identity by stressing on the activities of Chisumphi, their high God. In order to avoid the puzzles in Chewa religion and to legitimize their presence in Chewaland, the Ngoni aligned themselves to the Chisumphi cult. W.E. Rau, "Chewa Religion and the Ngoni Conquest", in Schoffeleers (ed.), *Guardians of the Land: Essays on Central African Territorial Cults*, pp. 142f.

the border between Tongaland and Ngoniland.[29] This second post was at a strategic point. It enabled the missionaries to check the Ngoni attacks on the Tumbuka and the Tonga. Bandawe station, exclusively in Tongaland, where most missionaries lived and worked from 1881, became the envy of the Ngoni. When the Ngoni saw the advantages the Tonga were having from the mission's presence, the Ngoni begged the white men to leave the Tonga at the lake and settle with the Ngoni on the plateau.[30] The missionaries agreed to open up schools in Ngoniland, but also explained why it was important for them to remain at Bandawe: "We explained to them that our Mission was to bring the gospel to every creature."[31] Of course, the other reason why the mission needed Bandawe was to use it as a port for bringing in supplies. Through diplomacy and confidence in a God of love, the Livingstonia Mission succeeded in keeping peace between the Ngoni on one hand, and the local people on the other. Mission schools and evangelistic activities spread in all the land controlled by the Ngoni. The effect of mission activities was that many young people chose to follow the church's teaching when their Ngoni leaders would have had them go to raid neighbouring ethnic groups.[32] Consequently, the Ngoni military power was weakened further. The Ngoni aristocrats were losing in every direction. Their subjects deserted them. The Tonga had a reliable source of calico and other goods at the mission station established in their country. This development was enough to undermine the supremacy of the Ngoni. It is, therefore, not surprising that in 1904, the Ngoni aristocrats accepted the British flag to fly at Mbelwa's headquarters in the Mzimba district. The Ngoni had resisted this move for more than a decade[33] and now realized the material benefits they would gain by subjecting themselves to the power. Consequently, the Ngoni overlordship in Tumbukaland and in the northern region ended for ever. At last the Tumbuka were redeemed and their conception of God had a new opportunity of being redirected to its original form.

---

[29] Annual mission statistics 1879-1898 (L1/9/1 MNA). One year after these two stations had begun, Bandawe became the principal station. Albert Namalambe, the first Livingstonia Mission convert at Cape Maclear and David Madzango were put in charge. William Koyi and George Williams were in charge of the post at Kaning'ina. In 1879 Koyi and Williams arrived in Mbelwa's own village. Later that same year Dr Laws, in the company of Koyi and a few others went to visit Mbelwa with the view to start schools and evangelize the area. But the chief would not see them as he was angered by many Tonga who had broken away from the Ngoni *impi* and fled back to their homes.

[30] Elmslie, *Among the Wild Ngoni*, p. 221.

[31] *Ibid.*

[32] *Ibid.*, pp. 222-252.

[33] Donald Fraser, *Winning a Primitive People*, London: Seeley, 1914, p. 245.

From 1881 onwards, the Christian church established itself among these people, and challenged the hierarchical system brought to the Tumbuka by the Ngoni in the 1840 to 1879 period. First, the missionaries taught that God is known and should be approached through Jesus Christ.

> We are here as missionaries seeking, in the first place, the conversion of the natives to Christ, and the building up in them of Christian characters, reflecting the image of Christ in their daily lives. For carrying out our commission many methods may be employed, differing in efficiency in different places, and among different peoples, but all must be subservient to the great end in view, helpful to it, or given up as useless if not doing so.[34]

The conversion experience brought through such teaching caused a re-adjustment in the Tumbuka conception of God. Jesus Christ now stood in the place of ancestral spirits and the heroic chiefs who mediated between God and man. In the presence of Jesus, the conqueror of death and the power above all spirits, the spirits of dead chiefs and ancestors no longer mattered. However, there was no wholesale abandonment of the old in favour of the new. What the missionaries achieved was the introduction of Jesus through whom God was to be known. This encouraged the reordering of the world within the Tumbuka tradition.

Second, missionaries taught that God was only one. Laws, like most of the missionaries, believed that the effective way of bringing the local people to a knowledge of this one God was through education. He wrote, "We must organize and persist in attacking the kingdom of darkness. Real light on the problems comes with opening of the Institution [i.e. Overtoun Institute]".[35] By "the kingdom of darkness", Laws implies ignorance stemming from lack of knowledge of God. As seen by the missionaries, this "kingdom of darkness" would melt away when the Tumbuka received enough education. The effect of the missionary education on the local people was that the Tumbuka scale of God was enlarged. They now understood God as a God of history and of salvation. At the same time, the monotheistic view of God present in Tumbuka tradition was restored.

Third, the name of God used in the Tumbuka Bible translation emphasized the traditional belief.[36] By 1891 the Tumbuka language had been reduced to

---

[34] Robert Laws, *The Aurora*, Vol. I/II, Livingstonia (1 February 1897), p. 9.

[35] Robert Laws, "Mission Report", *The Aurora*, Vol. 6/1, Livingstonia (1 August 1897), p. 5.

[36] When at Cape Maclear, Dr Laws translated Mark's Gospel into Nyanja. After the book was printed in 1880 at Lovedale, the whole consignment of over one thousand copies was destroyed in the Lower Shire in a war between the Mang'anja and the Portuguese. Dr Laws then translated the Gospel of John. This was published by the National Bible Society of

writing.[37] This rescued the Tumbuka language from being submerged by that of the Ngoni which had become the official language in courts and in public places. Laws translated the Gospel of Mark at Khondowe. For the name of God, he adopted *Chiuta*, a name he found widely used among the Tumbuka to denote God. Similarly, Donald Fraser translated the Gospel of Matthew at Embangweni. His use of the name *Chiuta* confirmed the use of the name as discovered by Laws. By 1929 a whole New Testament bearing the name God in the Tumbuka language had been sent to the Christian Literature Society in Durban for printing. In 1930 over 5,000 New Testaments were circulating in Tumbukaland.[38]

A Tumbuka convert, S.C. Hara, took upon himself to translate the whole Old Testament in the Tumbuka language.

> A native brought a pile of notebooks containing a complete translation of the Old Testament carried out by himself. He is a Christian, educated at Livingstonia, later in Government service in Rhodesia, who is now back in the Loudon area. He has undertaken this translation entirely on his own initiative, from a desire that his own Tumbuka people might have the whole Bible in their own tongue.[39]

This translation was found by W.Y. Turner to be sound. It formed the basis of the present Tumbuka Old Testament. The name of God used in the translation was also *Chiuta*. The use of this name by these early writers helped restore the monotheistic view of God held by the Tumbuka before the Ngoni disruption. It also reflected the spirit world as conceived by the Tumbuka in the old order. On the other hand, the missionary preaching about this God altered the Tumbuka understanding of him. He was now given Christian meaning and a new perspective.[40]

Scotland in 1881. The Mission then moved from Cape Maclear to Bandawe. There Dr Laws completed translating the whole New Testament in 1886. (Anonymous paper on revised Nyanja Bible, n.d., file on Nyanja Bible translation, National Bible Society of Scotland archives.) The name of God, *Mulungu*, used in this translation was used by the Nyanja speakers, today referred to as Chewa. For the first ten years of their work among the Tumbuka, the missionaries used the Nyanja Bible translation with *Mulungu* as the name of God. The Chewa language, being allied to the Tumbuka language, drew the two peoples closer together by using the name *Mulungu*. However, the Tumbuka maintained their own language.

[37] D. Fraser, *Livingstonia*, pp. 32-34. Cf. Donald Fraser, *The New Africa*, London: Edinburgh House Press, 1927.

[38] National Bible Society of Scotland archives, file No. 100, 1929.

[39] W.Y. Turner to G.A.F. Knight, 21 October 1929, NBSC archives file 100.

[40] For the effect of this new conception of God among the Tumbuka, see Chapter 4, "The Mission and the Conversion".

Worship and shrines

In the scattered settlements the Tumbuka lived in, worship had originally centred around individual families.[41] Heads of families acted as priests in their household worship. This is evidenced by the fact that when Mlowoka arrived in Tumbukaland, he found no established shrine except that at Chikhangombe hill. Even then, worship and the survival of the shrine seem to have depended on the occurrence of drought rather than on the desire for fulfilment from communal ritual or on an interested chief like Lundu in the case of M'bona.

In the family, no particular time was set apart for worship. Many writers note that worship and prayer were spasmodic and mostly held in times of great need such as illness, drought and other misfortune. It is true that certain times heightened the need for prayer and worship. Hetherwick points out that:

> The great events of the daily life of family or village community are still related to those who, in the spirit world, remember those alive or are by them still remembered. The planting, hoeing and harvest seasons, a birth, a marriage festivity, a hunt on a large scale, a journey to the coast with slaves or ivory are all events in which the paternal or ancestral spirits are supposed still to have an interest, and in consequence their favourable recognition is sought.[42]

Meanwhile, if a member of a family undertook a solitary journey, he first informed the head of his family who directed him to the chief of the village. Often, but not always, the chief would be related to the whole village. The chief prayed for the traveller in the following manner:

> My son has come, he goes on a journey, enlighten his eyes, preserve him on his journey, escort this child, may he return with his head unscathed. Please, please, let him undertake the journey, and be very successful.[43]

---

[41] In his observation of the Mang'anja people of southern Malawi, Schoffeleers has made a fundamental distinction between spirits of the household and spirits of the land. The former were invoked for the well-being of individuals and the lineage section only, and the latter for the territory and the population as a whole. The worship connected with both classes of spirits, according to Schoffeleers, was trifacial and at two levels. The first was in the family where the spirits were venerated; the second, at the village level where the spirits of dead chiefs and elders of a village were worshipped; and third, whole chiefdoms assembled to worship God when such was required by circumstances. J.M. Schoffeleers, "History and Political Role of the M'bona Cult", in Ranger and Kimambo (eds.), *The Historical Study of African Religion*, pp. 75-76. This worship pattern is so much centred on shrines that it appears as if no worship took place outside the shrine. Applied to our area of study, Schoffeleers principle contrasts with the worship pattern developed in Tumbukaland.

[42] Hetherwick, *The Gospel and the African*, p. 58.

[43] MacDonald, *Africana*, p. 76.

This prayer was recognized by the family and was given together with an offering of flour or chicken. If no bad omen occurred before the trip, the sojourner took his leave with the assurance that his whole family would remember him while he was away. It is observable here that family worship was always connected with an immediately past event or an imminent event.

Kavuwa (spirit temple).
From *Our Mission in Livingstonia* by D. Fraser.

What brought together a whole village for worship was a common sense of danger. Codrington describes how some villages had huts for the spirits of dead chiefs and heads of families. Sacrifice and worship to God through the ancestral spirits was made, in these huts. In other villages, Codrington says that worship was held under *msoro* trees.[43] This suggests that the Tumbuka had always had a decentralized system of worship. However, Codrington was writing after Nkhamanga had been plundered by Ngoni and worship at Chikhangombe had subsided. Therefore it would not be surprising if worship at the village level had intensified. First, the Tumbuka had to group together in their village worship to check the Ngoni intruders. Second, it may have been that as more and more people settled in Tumbukaland, patterns of worship and the old order changed. It expanded from caring for the family to meeting the needs of whole villages and those of the entire chiefdom.

Much of village worship and prayers were on behalf of the whole community. This is best illustrated by a prayer said during a drought period:

We beseech you to hear us. We have come to greet you, and visit you who are with God. We have brought you a little gift so that we may ask for rain; the children will all die of hunger, the sun is too cruel. Hear us, Nampanda, O che Kawina ... there where you are at rest, assemble in your power and give us rain.[44]

Like most other prayers, it was preceded by a short introduction, why worshippers had come, clapping of hands to honour them that are nearer *Chiuta* and, indeed, *Chiuta* himself; and then invocation of the spirits followed and finally the prayer was concluded by clapping of hands.

---

[43] Codrington, "The Central Angoniland District of the Protectorate", pp. 514-515.
[44] Abdallah, *The Yaos*, p. 21.

The cult of Chikhangombe

In the period between 1780 and 1830 there flourished a cult of "the sub-god Chikhangombe" among the Tumbuka.[46] The name Chikhangombe, according to Fraser, denotes a hill north west of Nkhamanga and was also applied to a spirit snake, Chikhangombe. He [the spirit snake] was believed by the Tumbuka to have had the mane of a lion on his head.[47]

As a spirit, Chikhangombe was ahistorical, in the sense that he never was a human being. Chikhangombe's influence extended between Chikhangombe hill and Mangazi. This afforded Chikhangombe to claim adherents from distant places.[48] Chikhangombe's main significance was in providing the people with much needed rain:

> He [Chikhangombe] is the god of the rains which come to the Henga people, and he sits among the mists that creep about the summit and in the wild cataract which rushes through the gorge below.[49]

The elevated dwelling place of Chikhangombe on hilltops and in impassable abysses set him apart as the undeviating and upright spirit. His power to give rain was observed by the Tumbuka in the strong winds they believed Chikhangombe rode on when travelling. Chikhangombe's connection with humans was through representatives who went up Chikhangombe hill to ask for rain and to make other community petitions.

In various places where the spirit of Chikhangombe was worshipped, a wife for the spirit was provided.[50] It was this wife, regarded as the prophetess, who from time to time was possessed by the spirit of Chikhangombe. When there was need for rain, the prophetess went up Chikhangombe hill in the company of two elders, and one 'unspoiled' virgin who bore the torch used later to light a fire once the group reached the summit. On the mountain-top, the prophetess offered a sacrifice of a black goat and some maize flour. In the process of praying, the wife would be possessed by the spirit of Chikhangombe. This was regarded by the Tumbuka as a sign of effective communication with the spirit Chikhangombe. Coming down the mountain following a different route from

---

[46] D. Fraser, *Livingstonia*, p. 24.

[47] Ibid., cf. Young, *Contemporary Ancestors*, p. 129; also Vail, "Religion, Language and the Tribal Myth", pp. 220-222.

[48] D. Fraser, *Livingstonia*, p. 25; Young, *Contemporary Ancestors*, p. 128f.

[49] D. Fraser, *Livingstonia*, p. 26. Chikhangombe is at Njakwa, a mountainous area with high peaks in Rumphi District.

[50] Personal interview with Mr Chiziwa Gondwe, a 76 year old grandchild of Mlowoka, Bangalala village, Rumphi, 15 February 1983. cf. Vail, "Religion, Language and the Tribal Myth", p. 218.

the one used first, the prophetess and her entourage wore black cloths on their heads. (The colour symbolized black clouds of rain.) They did not look back as they descended. Doing so would have brought misfortune either to the party or to the whole group waiting at the foot of the mountain. When they arrived back in the village, they were welcomed by drum beating, dancing and beer.[51] If rain fell, as was expected, the Tumbuka regarded it as a result of the prayer and sacrifice given on the mountain-top. If on the other hand no rain fell, a "Jonah" was sought and made to pay a ransom.

The place of possession, during the early period, i.e. about 1780, was linked with Chikhangombe priest and priestesses scattered in Tumbuka settlements. Elders of each family also acted as the religious leaders of their kindred. But in times of community crisis, people united to find a common solution through one individual. This person's authority was recognized if he demonstrated, through possession, his uprightness and ability to communicate with the Divine.

When Mlowoka arrived at Nkhamanga in 1780 and took over the reins, he attempted to unify Tumbukaland by building a political authority based on trade.[52] At the same time, he endeavoured to bring the worship of Chi-khangombe under his control. He succeeded in controlling *mwavi*, the poison cup, widely used by Tumbuka as a means of obtaining justice.[53] But that he left the priesthood of Chikhangombe cult untouched meant that worship of this spirit snake ran very much the same way as before. Local priests and priestesses who conducted worship such as Kachali in Nkhamanga were possessed by the spirit of Chikhangombe without much reference to Chikulamayembe. Other places of worship far removed from Nkhamanga, such as Phwezi in the Henga Valley, Mwandama in Hewe, Mvula in Usiska, Mhango and Chipoka ba-wori near Rumphi[54] directed their worship through other spirits rather than Chikhangombe. Further, the communities in these areas tended to pay more allegiance to their local chiefs than they did to the Chikulamayembe dynasty. While this weakened the force of the cult of Chikhangombe, it also frustrated Chikulamayembe's scheme to unite the Tumbuka on a pattern similar to that at Nsinja, as described by Schoffeleers.[55]

Chikulamayembe's commercial and political activities had another side to them. They enabled him gradually to expand and exert his political authority

[51] Interview with Mr Laiton Chiziwa Gondwe.
[52] See Chapter Two, "Tumbuka History 1780-1904".
[53] Elmslie, *Among the Wild Ngoni*, p. 62.
[54] Personal interview with Rev. S. Kamanga, moderator of Livingstonia Synod, formerly a pastor in the Henga Valley, Ekwendeni, 14 February 1983.
[55] Schoffeleers, "History and Political Role of the M'bona Cult", p. 72.

over the Tumbuka by mutual agreement rather than by military conquest. In times of extreme drought, people travelled from distant places such as Usiska, Mbalachanda and other places to go to Nkhamanga to worship and offer their sacrifices at Chikhangombe hill.[56] Attracted by trade activities which flourished in this area, some chiefs married their daughters to Chikulamayembe in order to gain his favour. One such chief was Chifusi in the Henga Valley.[57] Chikulamayembe would, in turn, give protection to villages from which the girls came. As such, his authority became recognized widely. This also meant that Chikulamayembe entered into a number of lineages with the result that he strengthened worship at Nkhamanga as well as encouraging local spirit worship. Thus the importance of shrines and territorial cults which dominated the religious life of the Chewa as described by Schoffeleers did not arise in the Tumbuka pattern of worship. A decentralized model prevailed in Tumbukaland.

This situation was reinforced by the arrival of the Ngoni in 1840. In that period both Chikulamayembe's dynasty and worship of the spirit snake Chikhangombe were at their lowest ebb. Mlowoka's death in around 1795 had eroded the political and religious glory Nkhamanga had enjoyed for many years. The one Ngoni raid on Nkhamanga, soon after their arrival, erased what political power was left;[58] the priests and priestesses of Chikhangombe were scattered. The Ngoni paramount Chief Mbelwa I became the sole ruler and did not tolerate gatherings which had nothing to do with his praise - be it religious or otherwise.[59]

The reaction of the Tumbuka to Ngoni overlordship was to form a new religious movement. According to Vail, this new movement was characterized by *vipili* spirit snakes.[60] Vail suggests that *vipili* was a carry-over of Chikhangombe worship. This assumption makes sense when the character and effect of *vipili* on the Tumbuka is examined.

Mpili (vipili - plural) is an adder, a gentle snake when unprovoked, but deadly when it strikes. The Tumbuka saw themselves as gentle people who had allowed the Ngoni conquerors to settle in Tumbukaland unopposed and sack their major centre of worship in Nkhamanga. To recapture their past, local priests and priestesses possessed by *vipili* spirit snakes, incited the Tumbuka to

---

[56] Personal interview with Mr Solomon Vitendwe Gondwe, a 76 year old village elder, Livili village, Bolero, 15 February 1983.

[57] Ibid.

[58] Elmslie, *Among the Wild Ngoni*, p. 28.

[59] *Ibid*.

[60] Vail, "Religion, Language and the Tribal Myth", pp. 222-223.

revolt against their Ngoni masters.[61] In 1880 the Tumbuka rebelled against Mbelwa. The result was that the Tumbuka were defeated at Mount Hora.[62] Once again, the Ngoni had demonstrated their military strength and the superiority of their spirits. The Tumbuka had to learn to live with the Ngoni on their backs.

With the shaking of the old order and the opening up of a new pluralistic world, an influx of new elements brought confusion in Tumbukaland. Various spirit beliefs which came with the Ngoni, and different peoples who had found a home among the Tumbuka at this time, had not been accommodated in Tumbuka culture. Relationships between people were unclear and the future was unclear. Witchcraft and the use of *mwavi*, the poison ordeal, to cleanse society of impurities, were widespread.[63]

When in 1905 epidemics of influenza and smallpox swept over the northern region and many people died,[64] the Tumbuka blamed it on foreign spirits and other enemies of society. To remedy the situation, witch eradicators engaged in witch hunting and protected people by giving them root medicine. The effect of these witch eradicators was weakened by missionaries whose presence in Tumbukaland was then strong. They denounced the eradicators as impostors and asked the people to arrest them.[65] The Tumbuka dared not do such a thing as they believed that witch eradicators would kill them with their power. As a result, the use of *mwavi* continued underground, but at a lower level than before.

Belief about death

The Tumbuka considered death to have both natural and preternatural causes. Young concludes that "the foundation belief on death was that it should not occur. Except in the very old and the immature, death is a hostile blow from outside."[66] The blow from outside, Young mentions, was regarded by the Tumbuka as "the result of spirit or mystic influences - the work of invisible and intangible agencies".[67] The Tumbuka believed that these spiritual forces emanated from the enemies of society such as *mfwiti*, witches, strangers and

---

[61] Vail suggests that *vilipi* was a residue of Chikhangombe worship. Vail, "Religion, Language and the Tribal Myth", p. 222.

[62] Elmslie, *Among the Wild Ngoni*, p. 275.

[63] Vail, "Religion, Language and Tribal Myth", p. 223.

[64] Njuyu Minute book, 4 November 1906 L1/1/3/22 (MNA); also Elmslie, *Among the Wild Ngoni*, p. 310.

[65] Elmslie, *Among the Wild Ngoni*, p. 311.

[66] Young, *Contemporary Ancestors*, p. 169.

[67] Hetherwick, *The Gospel and the African*, p. 76.

spirits ill-disposed to humans.[68] Consequently the question asked when death occurred was: *Who* has caused the death? and not *What* has caused it? This attitude still prevails in some parts of the country. Young says that at death the Tumbuka believed that the spirit left the body and continued to live separately from matter.[69] This is supported by D.C. Scott when he says:

> Many of the Malawi people held the view that the spirit lived inside the body and was capable of living without the body. For most of them taking of one's photograph was extracting one's spirit from the body and was highly resented.[70]

With the Tumbuka, the spirit was immaterial and had a peculiar power whose influence on humans was immense; hence they feared the spirit's unfriendly return if proper burial ritual was not accorded the dead.[71] For this reason it was important that good relationships with the spirit of the departed be maintained. This was done through annual remembrance ceremonies when libations were poured at the graveyard and when, in the village, festivity was conducted.

The spirit of a dead member, especially that of an older member, assumed a higher role than before.[72] For instance, if a grandfather died, his leadership role in his lineage was taken over by his eldest son. However, the son always exercised his authority over the household in reference to the grandfather now dead. Consequently the dead continued to exist in spirit, affecting their kin and offspring.[73] The Tumbuka perception of death is that of releasing the spirit

---

[68] The ferocious treatment given to witch suspects indicates the degree of the crime witches were allegedly accused of. See Elmslie, *Among the Wild Ngoni*, pp. 59, 153, 160; Agnes Fraser, *Donald Fraser*, London: Hodder and Stoughton, 1934, pp. 191-195.

[69] Elmslie, *Among the Wild Ngoni*, p. 59.

[70] D.C. Scott, *A Cyclopedic Dictionary of the Mang'anja Language*, Edinburgh: Foreign Mission Committee of the Church of Scotland, 1892, pp. 415f.

[71] Young, *Contemporary Ancestors*, pp. 169.

[72] *Ibid.*, p. 170.

[73] John Manda died away from his home while working in Blantyre. Before he died he had wished to see his folk for the last time. He never did as he died after a short illness. John's feeling must have been shared by his relations at Bandawe, his home. Although John was given a proper burial at Bandawe, his death was not easily taken by his family who had looked to John for their financial needs. After a year had elapsed since his death, Victoria Manda, his niece, became possessed by John's spirit. She spoke in John's deep baritone voice. When she spoke, no one who knew John doubted that it was him now speaking through his niece. One of the spirit's demands was that meat be prepared and given to it. The voice threatened death of the possessed niece if its demands were not met. A feast on behalf of John's spirit was held whereupon Victoria lived a more sober life than before. She is now a medium of repute. What spirit is guiding Victoria in her new career in not our concern here. The point is that a spirit has radically affected and influenced Victoria's life. Personal interview with Rev. W. Manda, c. 58 years old minister of Livingstonia Synod, Bandawe Mwase, 25 January 1983.

which continues to exist apart from the body. The meaning of the spirit depends on the affection the dead person inspires or the strength of personality.

Young maintains that burial rites of the Tumbuka varied according to the social class one belonged to in life. Slaves were never given proper burial. Their bodies were either left in the forest to the delight of hyenas or cast in shallow graves.[74] As their lives were less regarded in the physical world, so their spirits did not count for much in the Tumbuka spirit world.

The death of free persons brought great sorrow and a sense of loss to the Tumbuka, especially if the dead person was a woman. Womanhood was regarded as a symbol of life.[75] Therefore bearers of such sad news as the death of a woman carried their lives in their hands as:

> The messengers were dispatched to the parents and friends carrying with them a hoe or a fowl, for if they came empty handed they would be in danger of being killed. When they announced their sad news they laid down their gift, and fled for their lives.[76]

This custom may have enabled the woman's lineage to assert their authority over their dead who had spent much of her lifetime away in her husband's village. It may also have been a sign of their claim of her spirit back to their village. However, spirits of dead men were considered by the Tumbuka to have more influence on the living than the spirits of women.

In preparation for burial, bodies of either sex were prepared by old women.[77] They bathed the corpse, applied oil to it and wrapped it in cloth. The body was then laid on the mat upon which death occurred. The role played by the old women was an important one. It symbolized the continuity of life as epitomized in the long life of these old women.

Preparation of the grave was done by young men called *bazukulu*. They dug the grave to a sufficient depth and then made a cleft in the side of the grave at the bottom.[78] The young men who dug the grave became close friends of the bereaved family. They also were considered "grandchildren" of an elderly dead person even if they were not related to him.[79] The dead man was buried with his belongings such as clothes, pots, spear, walking stick and so forth. A chief was buried together with his wives and slaves.[80] For example, Chief Chikuse in

---

[74] Young, *Contemporary Ancestors*, p. 170.

[75] *Ibid.*, p. 170-171.

[76] D. Fraser, *Livingstonia*, p. 156; cf. Young, *Contemporary Ancestors*, pp. 169-170.

[77] Young, *Contemporary Ancestors*, p. 170

[78] Personal interview with Mr S. Moyo, c.82 years old, Tumbuka elder, Bangala village, Rumphi, 15 February 1983.

[79] Young, *Contemporary Ancestors*, p. 172.

[80] *Ibid.*, pp. 176-177.

the south of Tumbukaland was buried with "seven of his wives while thirty persons succumbed to the poison ordeal".[81] This shows that the Tumbuka appeared to believe that the dead would need the material things and some human company on their journey to the land of the spirits. It also shows that the Tumbuka view of the life hereafter was that of continuance. We see now that the Tumbuka believed that, when death occurred, an enemy had caused it. Death deprives the person of their body, everything else continues as before. The spirit of the dead could return to life and possess the living to bless them if they fulfilled the burial rites or to torment them if they had neglected the rites.

Personal immortality and eschatology

Among the early missionaries to Central Africa, Alexander Hetherwick developed some understanding of the Malawi peoples' concepts of immortality and eschatology. He observed that for Malawi people immortality was an integral part of life. Death was a transition from one form of life to another. This shift did not entail any change in the structure of human society. Hetherwick asserts:

> It can be said with every certainty that death brings no change in the status or character of the soul as it leaves its earthly tenement and passes into the unseen the chief in this world is still the chief there with all his wants and all his retinue about him; and the slave is still the slave, bound to his master as when on earth.[82]

To achieve personal immortality, the dead person depended on the living members of his lineage who knew him. They remembered him and shared gifts of food with him. While those who knew those now in the land of the spirits continued to exist, constant communion between them was maintained.

> Thus communion with the spirit of the dead is sought and obtained in the common sacrificial meal. Just as in life they sat around the food plate or shared in one beer pot, so still they sit as it were in each other's presence, and partake of the same food in an act of fellowship and friendship.[83]

This bond between the living and the dead expressed in a common meal gave assurance of the immortality of the departed members.[84]

---

[81] The District Commissioner's report book, Kasungu District, 1902-1927 (N/P/3/2/27 MNA); also Livingstonia, *ibid*, pp. 254f.

[82] Hetherwick, *The Gospel and the African*, p. 50

[83] Young, *Contemporary Ancestors*, p. 182.

[84] But with the span of time and the passing away of people who knew those now dead, the spirits lose their identity, a stage Mbiti calls the *zamani*. Mbiti, *African Religions and Philosophy*, p. 162.

Second, Hetherwick found that the idea of a final consummation was present among the local people. He says that the people believed that this world was unending, *muyira-yira*.[85] According to Hetherwick, the word *muyaya*, unending, found among the Tonga was the closest one to the English word "eternal". The word *muyaya* is also currently used among the Tumbuka people and with the same significance as in the Tonga language. The view of the Tumbuka about an unending world was thus shared by their neighbours. As their eschatology envisaged only a present reality without a future end, i.e. consummation, it may be that the Tumbuka concentrated on trying to strike an equilibrium in the present life between the spirit world and the physical.

With the understanding of an unending world as drawn above, it makes sense that punishment and reward in the life after death were not part of the Tumbuka eschatology. This was clearly expressed by an early Tumbuka convert, Levi Mumba:

> We do not believe in a future hell of any kind after death to be reckoned with in the spirit world. Man is amply punished for his sins in this very world. He knows quite well that he has to pay for his misdeeds in this same world. If a man leaves a matter unsettled at his death, then his living relatives settle it for him. So the spirit of the departed enters the spirit world without anything against it.[86]

There was no write-off of bad debts. Retribution by the spirits and by one's neighbours was part of the punishment one got for conducting a bad life. The Tumbuka linked misfortune and wrongdoing. Crop failure, premature death, illness and other misfortunes were interpreted as the result of some wrongdoing. To heal the situation, proper rituals had to be performed.

What Hetherwick got out of the view of the local people on immortality seemed fertile ground for the Gospel. He therefore concludes:

> We are thus able now to realize in some small measure how much there is in native belief and thought already cherished by him, to which the Gospel can at once make an appeal. The cardinal truths of belief in spirit, in a spirit world, in a Supreme Spirit in some form or another, in communion with the spirit world through prayer and sacrifice, these the messenger of the Gospel finds ready to his hand – to make the path of the preacher easier to the heart and conscience of the African tribesman.[87]

How much the missionaries were able to draw from this Tumbuka traditional view of life after the grave needs a thorough investigation of its own.

---

[85] Hetherwick, *The Gospel and the African*, pp. 51-52.
[86] Mumba, "The Religion of my Fathers", p. 366.
[87] Hetherwick, *The Gospel and the African*, p. 109.

Religious influences from the neighbours of the Tumbuka

The Tonga

We have already noted how close linguistically and socially the Tonga were to their next door neighbours, the Tumbuka. This had a bearing on their religious beliefs. A.G. MacAlpine, a missionary who worked among the Tonga at Bandawe, shows that the Tonga beliefs did not differ greatly from those of the Tumbuka. They believed in *Chiuta* - a name for God carrying the same meaning in both communities.[88] For both the Tonga and the Tumbuka, *Chiuta* meant the Giver of rain, Creator and Source of all life.

In their worship of *Chiuta*, the Tonga used the *msoro* tree and certain hills, as the Tumbuka did. MacAlpine points out hills in Marenga and Mankhambira' where the Tonga believed *Chiuta* had his abode.[89] These hills were replicas of Chikhangombe, Chipokawawoli and other "holy hills" in Tumbukaland. In 1885, when drought struck the northern region, Tonga chiefs sent messengers to Chikhangombe in Tumbukaland to ask for rain.[90] Rain fell later that year proving to the Tonga the combined effort of their prayer to *Chiuta* at home and in Tumbuka country.

A shared frustration during this same period 1882-1885 aroused a corporate Tonga - Tumbuka religious-political response. Mbelwa I had brought many Tumbuka and Tonga chiefs to their knees and effectively occupied their land. This triggered ethnic consciousness among the subjected peoples. The Tonga - who had been recruited into the Ngoni *impi* on the high land-began to return to their home.[91] Their example was followed by the Tumbuka. The result was that the Ngoni paramouncy began to lose ground. Inspired by the new form of spirit possession - *vipili* - which spread like bush fire in both Tongaland and Tumbukaland, as we have noted already, the Tonga rebelled against their Ngoni masters in 1880 and successfully defeated the Ngoni *impi* sent down to the Lakeside to teach the rebels a lesson. Encouraged by the success of their Tonga brothers, the Tumbuka mobilized their own army trusting that *vipili* spirit snakes would bite their foes. Although the Tumbuka were thoroughly crushed by the Ngoni, they had demonstrated their will to stand by the graves of their ancestors - if that could prove that they were the owners of the land. At the

---

[88] A.G. MacAlpine, "Tonga Religious Beliefs and Customs", *Journal of the African Society*, Vol. 5 (1905-1906), pp. 25-26; Vol. 6 (1906-1907), pp. 3-12.
[89] Ibid.
[90] MacAlpine, "Mission Report", *The Aurora*, Vol. 1/1, Livingstonia Mission (1 February 1897), p. 4.
[91] Elmslie, *Among the Wild Ngoni*, p. 99.

same time, the Tumbuka and the Tonga rebellions show the religious and political solidarity which prevailed between the two groups.

The Nkhonde

From the north, the Tumbuka were influenced by the religion of the Nkhonde. D.R. Mackenzie in his book, *The Spirit-Ridden Konde*, demonstrates how spirit beliefs of the *Nkhonde* were close to those of the Tumbuka. First, he says that the *Nkhonde* believed in *Kyala* - an equivalent of *Chiuta* in Tumbukaland. They believed that *Kyala* was the greatest spirit found everywhere - *chikulu ku nsi*; and owner of all things *Tenende*; the undying one, *ndorombwike*, and the only Creator.[92] The only point where the *Nkhonde* differed from the Tumbuka was in the use of the name for God. The *Nkhonde* use of *Kyala* was also applied to persons in whom the deity was believed to dwell[93] whereas the Tumbuka use of the word *Chiuta* was exclusively applied to God. What is interesting in the *Nkhonde* usage of the *word Kyala* is that they believed that humans are carriers of God's spirit and, when they are filled with that spirit, they become "little gods". It is, however, recognized that this *Nkhonde* concept can be interpreted to mean that these people acknowledge more than one God. But MacKenzie's conversation with a *Nkhonde* elder on this point reveals otherwise:

> An old man with whom I was conversing on the subject recently, looked at me with surprise when I brought the conversation round to 'other gods'. "There is only one *Kyala* (God)", he said with great emphasis, and other old men gave the same decided reply.[94]

This is a concept which would be accepted by the Tumbuka as it enhanced their understanding of *Mulungu or Chiuta*.

A second point of agreement between the *Nkhonde* and the Tumbuka was in their beliefs in spirits. The *Nkhonde* called spirits *basyuka*[95] meaning those who rise from dead. This is close to the *mizimu*, spirits, as held by the Tumbuka. The *Nkhonde* believed that when a person died his *unsyuka*, spirit, went to the land of the spirits from where the spirit might return to exert itself on the living.[96] The spirits returned to earth for two main reasons, according to MacKenzie. The first was to "assure themselves that they still have descendants

---

[92] MacKenzie, *The Spirit-Ridden Konde*, pp. 178-179.
[93] *Ibid.*
[94] *Ibid.*, p. 183.
[95] *Ibid.*, p. 191.
[96] *Ibid.*, p. 192.

on earth", and second, "the spirits returned to make sure that they are not forgotten by the living, for the spirit to whom no attention is paid by the living becomes of no account in the underworld".[97]

When spirits returned they were believed to take the form of harmless serpents. Only chiefs' spirits entered into lions, going about to see how the people were behaving. Among the *Nkhonde*, the chief was regarded as closest to the spirits. As such, it was he alone who could speak to spirits and to *Kyala* on behalf of everyone. However, the chief had an official called *unyago*.[98] His duty was to present offerings at the grave where the last chief was buried. This man, who may be called a priest, also went with the chief to pray, and he knew all required rituals. It was also he who taught new chiefs the ritual. When a chief died the *unyago* was possessed by the spirit of the dead chief but without him becoming an acting chief. He was regarded by the *Nkhonde* as the "holder of the sceptre". The spirit which possessed the *unyago* was controlled by means of powerful medicine immediately after possession occurred. This practice was not found among the Tumbuka.

What seems to have brought the *Nkhonde* closer to the Tumbuka was belief in foretellers called by the Tumbuka *nchimi* and by the *Nkhonde abakomwa malago*.[99] The *Nkhonde* believed that these people were possessed by the spirit of some hero and through that the spirit foretold the future. In 1785 chief Mwenemisuku was warned by a woman prophetess that a lion would kill many people that year. The chief obeyed the caution given and protected his people; none of them was killed, though the total killed by a lion that year in neighbouring villages was put at forty.[100] To the *Nkhonde*, as it would have been to the Tumbuka, there was no difficulty in connecting the prediction and the fulfilment. To them the inspiration of the spirit-possessed foreteller was genuine.

At about the same time (1785) when the Chikhangombe cult flourished in Tumbukaland, the *Nkhonde* established their own shrine at Mbanda hills.[101] On these hills the *Nkhonde* priests and priestesses prayed for rain and were possessed by an intermediary spirit. With such similarities, *Nkhonde* religious beliefs influenced the Tumbuka and went on unhindered by the political and social differences which existed between the two ethnic groups.

---

[97]   *Ibid.*, p. 195.
[98]   *Ibid.*
[99]   *Ibid.*
[100] *Ibid.*, p. 223.
[101] Young, *Notes on the History of Tumbuka-Nkhamanga Peoples*, p. 60.

The Maravi

From the south of Kasungu, the Tumbuka were influenced by Maravi religious beliefs. Schoffeleers presents a comprehensive study of the 19th century Maravi religion. He shows that it was divided into two segments, the Chewa cult centred on a god, Chisumphi; and the Mang'anja cult around a divinized human being, M'bona.[102] It was the Chisumphi cult whose influence on the Tumbuka was felt most.

According to Schoffeleers, Chisumphi was believed by the Chewa to have been a spirit which rode on strong winds. Its function was to provide rain. Ntara says that Chisumphi had a wife, Makewana (mother of all people) whose role was to intercede for rain. This role gave Makewana so much respect among the Chewa that the cult of Chisumphi was popularly known by her name.[103]

The central cult object was *thunga*, a spirit snake represented by one of the senior Mbewe officials. Both Schoffeleers and Ntara point out that the main shrine of Chisumphi was Kaphirintiwa in the Dzalanyama mountains.[104] Chidzorizi, a Phiri clan leader, was the founder of this shrine. Minor shrines were established in most parts of the country occupied by the Chewa. Priests and priestesses in these shrines were appointed by the holder of the Makewana title at Kaphirintiwa. This elevated the importance of the shrine at Kaphirintiwa. Further, Makewana became a powerful figure to reckon with.[105] Ntara suggests that in addition to their religious office, these "wives", i.e. the priestesses, also held political authority. Some of them were chiefs, as in the case of Chirenje and Mankamba. The ascendancy of the Phiri to chieftaincy in the 1830s, and the Ngoni invasion in the 1850s, put an end to female leadership.[106] This shift from female to male dominance was reinforced when the British regime took over the reins in 1891. This meant that, in the Chisumphi cult, males replaced females as Chisumphi's "wives". As a matter of

---

[102] Schoffeleers (ed.), "The Chisumpi and Mbona Cults in Malawi: A Comparative History", *Guardians of the Land: Essays on a Central African Territorial Cult*, Gweru: Mambo, 1979, p. 149.

[103] Samuel Josiah Ntara, *Mbiri ya Achewa*, Zomba: Government Press, 1950, p. 6.

[104] *Ibid.*, p. 13; also Schoffeleers (ed.), "The Chisumpi and Mbona Cults", p. 151.

[105] Schoffeleers (ed.), "The Chisumpi and Mbona Cults", p. 152.

[106] For a similar partial change from female to male religious leadership in the Lower Shire, see Schoffeleers, *Religion and the Dramatization of Life*, chapter 4, especially pp. 89f.

fact, these male priests continued to be referred to as "wives" long after the women had been replaced by men.[107]

Possession practices characterized office bearers in the Chewa shrines. The spirit wives were possessed by the spirit of Chisumphi. In that state they transmitted Chisumphi's messages.[108] At a much earlier date, around 1750, Gamitto had observed that prophet figures called "the children of Chisumphi" resorted to possession in the performance of their duties.[109] It may be the "children" were later referred to as wives.

In the Chisumphi cult, striking similarities with the Chikhangombe cult in Nkhamanga emerge. Vail observes that Chikhangombe was recognized as a rain giver deep in the Chewa country and was believed to have a spirit wife Mangazi at Nsinja.[110] Conversely, the Chisumphi cult was influential among the Southern Tumbuka. Mangadzi, conceived by the Tumbuka as a female spirit, was appealed to at times of birth to bless newly-born babies. Further, Mangadzi was associated with the south winds which brought rain.[111] According to Vail, both cults lacked a central organization and used local hills as centres of worship. In addition there was a similar conception about Chewa Thunga and about Tumbuka Chikhangombe.[112] Both Thunga and Chikhangombe were believed to be spirit snakes who had power to give rain and travelled riding on strong winds. By sharing of cults over a long period, without the sort of political disruption which occurred when the Ngoni arrived on the scene, the Tumbuka religion grew closer to that of the Chewa. Immigrants into southern Tumbuka from Maravi country took over local shrines and moulded them in the same pattern as in Chewa country. For instance, the Katumbis of Hewe took over control of the shrine at Mwanda Hill without provoking the local people.[113] It may also be that with Tumbuka migrants entering Chewa country, similar changes occurred unifying the Tumbuka and the Chewa.

---

[107] For more information on Makewana, Chisumphi's wife, see Isabel Apawo Phiri, *Women, Presbyterianism and Patriarchy: Religious Experience of Chewa Women in Central Malawi*, Blantyre: CLAIM, pp. 26-32. Also see her article, "African Traditional Women and Ecofeminism: The Role of Women at Chisumphi Cult in Preserving the Environment", *Religion in Malawi*, Vol. 6 (1996), pp. 14-19, for the present state of Makewana.

[108] Schoffeleers, "The Chisumphi and Mbona Cults", p. 153.

[109] Gamitto, *King Kazembe*, p. 341.

[110] Vail, "Religion, Language and the Tribal Myth", p. 218.

[111] Ibid.

[112] Ibid., p. 220.

[113] Ibid., p. 221.

The Yao

Further influence on the Tumbuka religion in the 19th century came from the Yao. As already noted, the Yao entered Malawi in the first half of the 19th century from Mozambique and settled along the west coast of Lake Malawi. Through trade in slaves and ivory, their raids as well as their religious influence penetrated deep into Tumbuka and Chewa country south of the Dwangwa river.[114]

According to Duff MacDonald, the Yao religion was centred around the worship of spirits which can be divided into three classes: family spirits, chiefly spirits, and *Mulungu*, God - considered by the Yao as the Supreme Being.[115] In the family, spirits of dead members were invoked in times of birth, puberty, marriage, illness and death. The Yao considered the family spirits nearer to *Mulungu* and therefore best suited to intercede for the family. The head of the family also acted as priest in his household.[116] In the family spirits, the Yao asserted their own identity. Being a matrilineal society, the important family spirits were from the mother's side.

The chiefly spirits were connected with the rulers who had died, but were considered to be still actively involved in the welfare of the people. The Yao believed that their living chief, standing in the tradition of past chiefs, was endowed with the power of the immediate past chief. At the same time, they believed that the chief was the clan priest who approached *Mulungu* on behalf of all the people.[117] Clan worship was conducted under a *msoro* tree. The times for worship were marked by significant events such as drought, clan funerals etc.[118]

When Yao entered Malawi, their belief in *Mulungu* strengthened that of their new neighbours - the Tumbuka - who also worshipped Mulungu. "Holy hills" as Chikhangombe, Mangazi and others where the Tumbuka believed *Mulungu* made his presence specially felt also became sacred to the Yao. The Yao also sanctified other hills such as Namisimu. There they worshipped *Mulungu* in times of drought. Further, the Yao regarded the spirits of dead Tumbuka and Chewa chiefs as still powerful, as they had regarded their own chiefs when in Mozambique. For instance, the Yao chief Kapeni prayed at

---

114 Young, *Notes on the History of the Tumbuka-Nkhamanga People*, pp. 37-38.
115 MacDonald, *Africana*, pp. 59-75.
116 *Ibid.*, p. 65.
117 *Ibid.*, p. 67.
118 Abdallah, *The Yaos*, p. 19.

Mang'anja shrine of Kang'omba on Mount Soche well after the Mang'anja had been ousted by the Yao invasion.[119]

Another point of agreement was sharing of family spirits. Many commentators on the Yao present them as ruthless slave-drivers who had no regard for life and no wish of a settled life. A Yao historian, Yohanna B. Abdallah, shows that this was not always the case. As a matrilineal people, the Yao met with other matrilineal people such as the Tumbuka and the Chewa. The Yao intermarried with the local people and increased in number.

> Right from the hilly country near the Lake across to the Lujenda, near the Walolo country; from the south near Chikala and Lake Chilwa and Mandimba (i.e. Machinga), right up across the Rovuma to Chingoli, the Achingoli and Wamwela country - the whole of this area was covered with villages; the people filled it completely like the gruel in that plate. They were extraordinarily fertile; one woman would have sixteen or seventeen children or more.[120]

This increase in population resulting from mixed marriages opened up avenues for sharing in family spirits. Children born of mixed marriages regarded with respect spirits from both the mother's and father's side. Consequently a favourable relationship between the newcomers and the owners of the land developed especially after the decrease of slave trade in the 1870s.[121]

However, the religious picture of the Yao was complicated by their assimilation of Islam. When they settled at Nkhotakota between Tumbukaland and Chewaland, their allegiance was to Jumbe, a chief trader with the east coast, whom they kept well supplied with slaves. To him, the Yao also looked for religious leadership. A Muslim himself, Jumbe encouraged the spread of Islam through trade by his Yao agents. Young reports that in 1878, the Yao had made a convincing impression on chief Mwase of Kasungu on the need to open up trade links with Jumbe and about the power of Islam. Consequently, some agreement had been reached about a trade centre at Kasungu from which slaves would be driven to Nkhotakota and Islam spread north into Tumbukaland.[122] Had Mwase not turned his back on the Yao and aligned himself with the Ngoni paramount Mbelwa to avoid the threat he had posed against Kasungu, the Yao influence on the local people in the interior would have been considerable. MacDonald remarks that when the Yao embraced

---

[119] MacDonald, *Africana*, pp. 68-69.
[120] Abdallah, *The Yaos*, p. 25.
[121] *Ibid.*, p. 29.
[122] Young, *Notes on the History of the Tumbuka-Nkhamanga People*, p. 38. David Bone has satisfactorily argued this point. See David Bone, "Islam in Malawi", *Journal of Religion in Africa*, Vol. 13 (1982), pp. 128-129.

Islam, their attitude towards other peoples became antagonistic.[123] Constantly, the Yao raided peaceful villages and carried captives away to slavery. The Yao tendency to raid conflicted with the attitude of the more settled agrarian Tumbuka and Chewa communities. The result was their rejection of the Islamic beliefs of the Yao. On the other hand, the long exposure of the Yao to Arab traders at Kilwa and Zanzibar had afforded them a sophistication envied by their neighbours in Malawi. Impressed by the Yao Arabized modes of dress and religion, marginal Tumbuka drifted from their homes and settled at Nkhotakota where they became Muslims.

What seems to have prevented Yao direct Islamization of Tumbukaland was the check offered by Ngoni dominance. When the Yao had demonstrated the power of the gun by putting down many Chewa chieflets, including one of Mbelwa's own generals, the Ngoni reinforced their *impis* by arming them with guns. Thus the Yao were thwarted from further advance northward into Tumbukaland. Chief Mwase's timely diplomatic association with the Ngoni further prevented Yao influences in the north.

The Ngoni

Yet another influence on Tumbuka religion came from the Ngoni. Before 1820 when the Ngoni broke away from the Kingdom of Chaka, their religion was the same as that of the other Nguni. Significant changes occurred in Ngoni religion on their march northward. They adopted conquered peoples into their *impis* who brought in new spirit beliefs. When the Ngoni finally settled in Tumbukaland, their form of religion, modified on the way, mixed with that of the Tumbuka. This amalgamation took the form of superimposition of the Ngoni hierarchy upon the local population. The result was that the Tumbuka worshipped both the Ngoni spirits of royal ancestors as embodied in *Nkhosi ya Makhosi* hierarchy and their own *Chiuta*. On their side, the Ngoni had to come to terms with local spirit beliefs in order to manage and be accepted by the local people.

Background

According to Monica Wilson, ancestor cult was the main feature of Nguni religion in AD 1700. The Nguni believed that their ancestors were the owners of the land. It was the ancestors who passed on the land to the present generation. For this reason, the spirits of the departed, *amadlozi*, had great

---

[123] MacDonald, *Africana*, p. 31.

influence over the living.[124] When a person died, the Nguni believed that his spirit, *idlozi*, separated from the body and floated around the grave where the body was buried. After a period of one or two years, the spirit then joined the council of ancestors in the underworld.[125]

The surviving spirit, separated from the body, was believed by the Nguni to be an exact copy of the dead person.[126] When the spirit appeared to one of the members of the lineage through dreams or visions, he appeared as in physical life. Not all dead people became ancestors when they died. Heads of families, village headmen, chiefs and such figures are the ones who became ancestors. They continued to enjoy the authority they held on earth. Spirits of women, children and slaves did not become ancestors. Their spirits continued to lead a life similar to that in the physical world.[127] Among the living, they were represented by chiefs and village headmen.

The Nguni believed that ancestors conferred blessings upon their descendants and protected them from households outside their lineages. Therefore, the power of the ancestors over the living was restricted. Willoughby writes,

> Although they [the ancestors] have found enlargement of power through release from the restraints of the body, are not omnipotent; nor can they read the secrets of human hearts, though they know all that their children do, say or suffer. They are as interested as ever in their descendants who remain "out on the earth", but indifferent to members of other communities, unless they owe them some grudge or have to hinder them from hurting their protégés.[128]

Because ancestors were exclusively interested in the affairs of their descendants, worship directed to them was limited to within their own lineages. Even their worship was only to "those who are something more than a name to the living members of the family group".[129] Worship took the form of a prayer said by the priestly head of the family. Sacrifices of food were offered on certain occasions such as at rain ceremonies.

---

[124] M. Wilson, "The Nguni People", in M. Wilson and L. Thompson (eds.), *The Oxford History of South Africa*, Oxford: Oxford University Press, 1969, pp. 75-130.

[125] A.T. Bryant, "The Zulu Cult of the Dead", *Man*, Vol. 95 (1917), pp. 65-66.

[126] Ibid., p. 67.

[127] Ibid.; also W.C. Willoughby, *The Soul of the Bantu*, London: SCM, 1928, p. 57.

[128] Willoughby, *The Soul of the Bantu*, p. 88. When a Zulu king, Cetshwayo, was asked in 1883 if he believed in spirits he said, "Yes, the *idhloni*. These are merely the ghosts of the departed ... they look after their relations who are living." C. Webb and J.B. Wright (eds.), *A Zulu King Speaks: Statements Made by Cetshwayo on the History and Customs of his People*, Pietermaritzburg: University of Natal Press, 1978.

[129] *Ibid.*, p. 6.

Ancestral spirits revealed themselves to their descendants, "to warn them of danger, or to disclose new medicines to a magician of their line. More usually their visits are to demand a sacrifice, or to reproach the living for some breach of custom".[130] There are three ways in which the ancestral spirits manifested themselves among the Nguni. "Often enough, the ancestor spirits appear to the living in dreams."[131] Like most Bantu speaking peoples, the Nguni believed that dreams are a form of revelation through which a sleeping person may communicate with the spirits of the living dead. Second, they also believed that ancestral spirits appeared in the form of a snake, usually harmless, commonly found in flowers and bushes around homes.[132] When these snakes appeared, they were regarded as ancestral spirits coming home to visit their descendants. Consequently, the snakes were left to wriggle around the home without being molested. Third, ancestral spirits possessed certain individuals. This form of revelation had two major functions; it served as a way for becoming a diviner, and as an authentication of prophecy.[133] Possession was an effective means of religious experience among the Nguni.[134]

---

[130] W.M. Eiselen and I. Schapera, "Religious Beliefs and Practices", in I. Schapera (ed.), *The Bantu Speaking Tribes of South Africa: an Ethnographical Survey*, London: Routledge and Kegan Paul, 1937, p. 251.

[131] Ibid., p. 253.

[132] Eileen J. Krige, *The Social System of the Zulus*, London: Longman, 1936, p. 285.

[133] Sundkler describes three types of spirit possession among the Zulu. First, is the *isangoma*, an ancestral spirit which manifests itself through the initiation of a diviner. The word *isangoma* is applied to the spirit of an ancestor as well as to the diviner who possesses that spirit. The second type of possession is the *amandiki*. According to Sundkler, the Zulu believed that *amandiki* are spirits of deceased migrant labourers who died in South Africa. Because they died so far away from home, their families might not hear about their death. For this reason proper burial rituals were not performed at their death. Their spirits were not integrated with the main body of their ancestral spirits, thus they cause illness to local people. *Amandiki* is a fairly new type of possession which emerged at the end of the 19th century. Its purpose, as seen above, was to deal with foreign spiritual forces. If the Zulu were perplexed by calamities of which they did not find the cause among themselves or among their ancestral spirits, they looked for cause from outside their own borders. For example, the outbreak of influenza in 1919 to 1920 and malaria in 1933 were believed by the Zulu to have been caused by these foreign *amandiki*. Consequently there was a rapid spread of *amandiki* possession. *Itshanusi* also known as *inyangai*, is the third type of possession described by Sundkler. He says that *itshanusi* were professional people who entered their role through their knowledge of herbs and ability to cure illness. Both men and women could become *itshanusi*. An *itshanusi* gained knowledge of herbs through possession by an ancestral spirit or through dreams. First, the *itshanusi* acquired his knowledge of herbs through possession. He invoked one of the spirits of his ancestors to inspire and direct him to find the proper medicine to cure an illness before him. The ancestor appealed to, was held to have been an expert *itshanusi* during his life time who now continued an interest in

Less intimate, but nevertheless recognized in Nguni religion was God. J. Hodgson says, "he [God] is typically the background god of a nature religion".[135] According to Hodgson, the Nguni ascribed all existent life and the whole of the created order to God. The various praise names of God used by the Nguni reflect their conception of him.[136]

Unkulunkulu, "the great one" was the most prominent praise name of God among the Nguni.[137] The literal translation of *Unkulunkulu* conveys the sense of timelessness or being extremely old.[138] Some writers think that he was one of the ancestors of the Nguni. Through evolution, he was deified and became associated with the sky, his place of abode.[139] Such an opinion is difficult to verify.

---

the profession through his descendants. When the *itshanusi* invoked this spirit he entered into a possession state believed by his people to be under the influence of his ancestor expert. Under possession, the *itshanusi* procured medicine and healed disease. In this case the *itshanusi* was in control of possession. He came out of it without much ado. For *itshanusi*, possession legitimized his practice; and for his audience, it was a sign of power drawn from the ancestors they believed to be the guardians of tradition and trustees of spiritual forces. Sundkler, *Bantu Prophets*, pp. 22-28.

[134] This is illustrated by an event which took place in a congregation where Sundkler was pastor. "A prayer woman, Saulina, in our Ceza congregation suddenly disappeared from our church services, and it was reported that she was about to *ukwethwasa* (i.e. be possessed by a spirit). I went to the Kraal and tried to persuade her to abandon such an idea, but both she and her pagan husband had definitely resigned themselves to her fate. 'Leave me for some years, *mfundisi*' (teacher or preacher), she said. 'I can do nothing about this possession ... My *idhlozi* wants me. But after, perhaps two years, I will be back again.'" *Ibid.*, p. 23. Sundkler could not persuade the woman to break her conviction. In the woman's mind, the Christian faith and her *idhlozi* possession were two religious systems. Each one of them made demands on her. Her solution to the tension caused by dual membership was to take leave from one of them in order to satisfy the vacuum left by the other. The pastoral problem raised in Saulina's story finds many parallels among Tumbuka Christians. We shall deal with the pastoral problems of possession in chapter six. What is important for our study here is that the Zulu, from whom the Ngoni originated, believed in spirit possession. By it, they coped with social and religious changes in their society. When the Ngoni contact with the Tumbuka brought similar responses among the local people, it was not strange to the Ngoni. Their cousins in South Africa had corresponding beliefs, as already noted.

[135] J. Hodgson, *The God of the Xhosa: A Study of the Origins and Development of the Traditional Concepts of the Supreme Being*, Cape Town: O U P, 1982, p. 41.

[136] *Ibid.*, pp. 43-50.

[137] *Ibid.*, p. 54.

[138] Krige says that *Unkulunkulu* is not known "for he is said to have died so long ago that no one knows his praises", Krige, *The Social System of the Zulus*, p. 281.

[139] Cf. H. Callaway, *The Religious System of the Amazulu*, Springvel: John Blair, 1870, pp. 50-51; and W. Wanger, "The Zulu Notion of God According to the Traditional Zulu God-names", *Anthropos*, Vol. 19/1-2 (1923-4), pp. 656-657.

The fundamental concept behind the name *Unkulunkulu* may be in what C.M. Doke calls "the Supreme Deity" and "the Progenitor of human race, the great ancestor and ancestral spirit of mankind, who is believed to have created all things around him".[140] As the originator of all created things, the source of human life, *Unkulunkulu* may have been, symbolically, the greatest ancestor in the Nguni world view. It may also be that God's creative capacity, in the Nguni understanding of him, removed God from the ranks of ancestors derived from dead ordinary human beings.[141] However, what seems certain is that *Unkulunkulu* was the ultimate spirit whose power was manifested spasmodically through nature.

The other praise name of God among the Nguni is *uMvelingqangi*. Hodgson says that this name "is derived from *ukuvela*, to come forth from, to originate; and *nqangi*, first in point of time".[142] The Nguni used the name to denote the origin of creation, that its cause was God. Contained in this name is also the idea of God being at the beginning of time.[143] Many writers think that after *uMvelingqangi* had created the world, he moved away into the sky leaving the ancestral spirits in charge except in extreme cases such as disasters.

Until 1800 the Nguni continued to direct their worship to God occasionally as was done in the past. This worship was connected with nature's threat upon human life. Hodgson writes: "All the awesome and more dangerous aspects of nature, such as drought, thunder, lightning, hail, violent rain and wind, were attributed to the supreme being and were often personified by *iZulu*."[144] The Nguni saw lightning as emanating from God. Any person struck dead by it was

---

[140] C.M. Doke and B.W. Vilakazi, *Zulu-English Dictionary*, Johannesburg: 1953, p. 580. In his definition of high God, Dammann asserts, "in many parts of Africa ... besides the spirits and deities there is an isolated deity, quite independent from and not related to other deities, solitary and unknown origin, without dependents, neither wife nor family". Dammann, "A Tentative Philological Typology", p. 86.

[141] W. Wanger argues that the notion of creativity among the Zulu was ascribed to *Unkulunkulu* alone. No human being shared this quality. He writes, "no Zulu will consciously predicate *Ukudala* (to create) of a human being". W. Wanger, "Zulu religion", *Anthropos*, Vol. 21/3-4 (1926), p. 356.

[142] Hodgson, *The God of the Xhosa*, p. 53.

[143] Callaway discovered that *uMvelingqangi* among the Zulu was associated with kingship. A young chief who succeeded his father on the throne was referred to by the Zulu as *uMvelingqangi*. Callaway, *The Religious System of the Amazulu*, p. 99. However, that the name was also applied to God as the originator of human life and all creation made its use special.

[144] Hodgson, *The God of the Xhosa*, p. 47.

regarded by the people as having breached some custom and therefore to have been taken away by God's wrath manifested in the lightning.[145]

According to Hodgson, worship of God among the Nguni consisted of a prayer and sacrifice. A priest offered sacrifice of a cow and prayed to God when lightning had killed a person.[146] This was to appease God so that such misfortune would not occur again. Natural disasters did not occur always. Consequently, worship directed to God precipitated by natural disaster was occasional. This put *Unkulunkulu* or *uMvelingqangi* on the periphery of Nguni worship.[147]

The emergence of Chaka as the chief of the Zulu in 1802, and his warfare against the rest of the Nguni peoples, not only disrupted their political and social infrastructure, but it also disturbed their religious life.[148] First, the chiefs regarded by the Nguni as both rulers and priests of the first order were killed by Chaka. Others fled for their lives, while those who remained were deposed. Thus the important link between the ancestral spirits and the living provided by the chiefs was removed. This damaged the existing worship pattern among those ruled by Chaka.

Worse still, Chaka's raids uprooted many people from their homes causing them to leave behind their land closely connected with the ancestral spirits, and the sites of their shrines. They also left behind possessions of cattle, goats and sheep which constituted valuable sacrifice. By 1820 when Chaka was at the height of his power, Nguni religion was at its lowest ebb in what is now Natal. It was at such a time that Zwangendaba, one of Chaka's generals rebelled and led a group of people northward.

When the Ngoni, under the leadership of Zwangendaba, moved out of South Africa in 1820, they broke from Nguni religion. Their worship, formerly centred around ancestral spirits was replaced by a royal cult embodied in Zwangendaba himself.[149] Surrounded by his *ndunas*, Zwangendaba became, to the Ngoni, a human god moving among his people and leading them to a virgin land they hoped for. There the Ngoni would live in peace. Meanwhile, their

---

[145] Callaway notes that the people who were killed by lightning were regarded by the Zulu as unclean. Therefore, they were not given proper burial. Callaway, *The Religious System of the Amazulu*, pp. 117-118.

[146] Hodgson, *The God of the Xhosa*, p. 51.

[147] Most writers on Zulu religion think that God was a forgotten being. He was never worshipped as his influence on the Zulu was marginal. Cf. Krige, *The Social System of the Zulus*, p. 281; and Callaway, *The Religious System of the Amazulu*, p. 101.

[148] On Chaka's political and military activities, see chapter 2.

[149] See Rau's argument in "Chewa Religion and the Ngoni Conquest", noted in Chapter 3 above.

religion became a religion of promise, without cultic sites and without territorial borders. Their religion was bound together with the experience and possible goal of the journey now before them.[150] This contrasted sharply with the Nguni religion left behind where ancestors, particular localities and seasons of the year were central in worship. The cyclical seasons, seed and harvest time which guided the settled Nguni no longer applied to the Ngoni who now endured the test of a long journey.

In about 1830 Zwangendaba and his *impis* passed through Swaziland and the High Veld absorbing Nguni and non-Nguni recruits and marrying their women. It was from such groups that the Ngoni religion received new elements thereby altering even further original spirit beliefs.[151] Zwangendaba himself married a Thonga woman opening the royal cult to a wider influence hitherto unknown to the Ngoni.

The Ngoni were pushed further north by military pressure from the Boers and other African groups behind them. The Ngoni crossed the Limpopo river in 1825. For a short period, they camped among the Shona they had defeated. But once again they moved, this time across the Zambezi river in 1835. As they moved further north they absorbed Shona and Karanga young men and women. These new members injected into Ngoni religion yet another element. Consequently, Ngoni religion altered further.

As a result of the Ngoni exodus from South Africa with their march through the wilderness, their assimilation of foreign people into their ranks and the undaunting loyalty to Zwangendaba, their religion changed too. Now their religion was bound up in future battles where Zwangendaba and his ancestral spirits would lead them. The priests who emerged among these wayfarers served the chief. Before the *impis* went out on their raids, they gathered under the feet of Zwangendaba and were "doctored for war" by the priests, i.e. given protective medicine which would strengthen them in battle. As already noted, one such priest responsible to Zwangendaba was Sobatwapa Nyawu who assisted the Ngoni to cross the Zambezi river in a miraculous way.[152] Other

---

[150] There is a close parallel to this in the Exodus story when the Israelites marched out of Egypt, Exodus 1-36. However, the difference is that the Ngoni exodus had no religious connotations whatsoever.

[151] Pachai has argued that once the Ngoni moved away from their Nguni roots in South Africa, political and social changes happened very quickly and "the external intrusions brought about side-effects". Bridglal Pachai, "Ngoni Politics and Diplomacy in Malawi: 1848-1904", in Pachai (ed.), *The Early History of Malawi*, London: Longman, 1972, p. 179. By "side-effects" Pachai implies the new forms of social and political structures which emerged. This applies to the religion of the Ngoni as well.

[152] See Chapter two.

priests, known as *itshanusi* who received "second sight", were responsible for detecting defaults believed by the Ngoni to be injurious to the army. We shall examine this point later.

What happened when the Ngoni and the Tumbuka interacted with each other in their religion was affected by elements arising from the social and political situation. First, the Ngoni depended on their military muscle epitomized by their *inkosi ye pansi*, Mbelwa, i.e. the king of the earth. This was in contrast with the traditional *inkosi phezulu*, the king of the sky and giver of rain.[153] In Nkhamanga, the Ngoni assaulted and sacked the cult centre of Chikhangombe, disrupting the foundation of the Tumbuka religious authority as known in Chikulamayembe's time. The fall of Nkhamanga in 1845 was enough to challenge their old order. In place of the democratic and decentralized religious organization which existed before was put a Ngoni hierarchical structure centred around paramount Mbelwa.[154] The Ngoni self-assertion impaired the monotheistic belief which existed among the Tumbuka. For the Ngoni, their unbending unity under their paramount had become a faith to live by.

Intermarriage between the Ngoni and the Tumbuka, and their adopting of a settled life, gradually disorientated both the Ngoni and the Tumbuka as it brought confusion of ancestors and therefore of spirits. The offspring of Ngoni-Tumbuka marriages were possessed by either spirits from their Ngoni fathers or from their Tumbuka mothers. It was not feasible for *inkosi* Mbelwa or his successors to suppress Tumbuka spirits. The anxiety this brought added to an already desperate situation caused by the Tumbuka conquest and loss of their political independence. Consequently, increased tension drove many Tumbuka to seek security in protective medicines.[155] We shall examine this point later.

---

[153] Rau has argued that the many years of Ngoni wandering in the wilderness molded their political and religious structures around the household. He writes, "The long period of migration (c. 1820-1870) had shaped and sharpened Ngoni military and political structures, and it also influenced their religious system which stressed only a minor ritual attachment to the land or to deities whose locations were geographically defined. Instead, religious life centred on the ancestors of the Paramount chief, notably upon Zwangendaba who had led the Ngoni out of South Africa". Rau, "Chewa Religion and the Ngoni Conquest", p. 31.

[154] For the defeat of Tumbuka-Nkhamanga see chapter two on the section dealing with "the Ngoni".

[155] A similar argument is given by McCracken. He states, "the eruption of the Ngoni and their attempts to assimilate Chewa and Tumbuka captives into their kingdoms, the perversion of the legal system by rulers anxious to sell their subjects, and the creating of stockaded villages, into which large numbers of desperate people were thrust - all had the effect of exacerbating witchcraft tensions". McCracken, *Politics and Christianity*, p. 14.

Administration of Mwavi, the poison cup ordeal
From King Kazembe by A.C.P. Gamitto

Unfamiliar with the spirits of the land and some religious practices of the Tumbuka, the Ngoni leadership sought the aid and advice of local priests and chiefs on a number of religious puzzles. One such puzzle mentioned by both Fraser and Elmslie was the use of *mwavi*, the poison ordeal whose use was prolific at the time the Ngoni entered Tumbukaland.[156] The use of *mwavi* so much attracted the Ngoni that they adopted it. *Mwavi* was the final judgement cup. It was administered to suspects. If a person was suspected of being a witch or to have breached a certain custom, to prove their innocence the person was made to drink *mwavi*. If the person died, they were regarded as guilty, and if they vomited and survived, as innocent. The power of *mwavi* was greatly increased by its adoption by the Ngoni and by its wider use than before.

---

[156] D. Fraser, *Livingstonia*, p. 144; also Elmslie, *Among the Wild Ngoni*, p. 61.

However, it may have been that not all religious leaders among the Tumbuka and the Ngoni adopted the use of *mwavi*. What is certain is that *mwavi* became one of the transformative forces used by the Ngoni, with assertions by the Tumbuka that it would reform and cleanse society from all ills. Elmslie later remarked on the effects of the use of *mwavi* as a "great evil": "Before the light of Christian truth came to them, and has, even where the doctrines are not wholly embraced, done away with this great evil, the number annually killed by drinking the *mwavi* cup cannot be estimated."[157] The use of *mwavi* only lessened with the advent of missionaries who taught against it. However, its use aroused further confusion as so many people died from its effect. Consequently spirit possession believed by both the Ngoni and the Tumbuka spread widely.

New forms of possession

Vimbuza

Dr A.B. Chilivumbo describes *vimbuza* possession among the Tumbuka as a form of a dance, an art and a religious ritual.[158] His approach to the subject is from a psychological point of view. He deals with both "patients" and *vimbuza* "doctors", showing how through the dance they are cured and rehabilitated in society.

As a religious ritual, *vimbuza* creates the spiritual linkage between the deity and individual human beings, however cryptic that link may be. A person possessed by *vimbuza* spirits communicates with spirits of the departed, regarded by the Tumbuka as now being near to God.[159] The meaning of the word *vimbuza*, from its derivations *vimbula*, to uncover or to reveal, *vumbuzi*, a revelation, carries the meaning of that which is revealed.[160] As such, *vimbuza* may be said to be connected with the revelation of spirits to the living, especially to those possessed. The nature of the possession, as we shall see later, may be for good or bad.

---

[157] Elmslie, *Among the Wild Ngoni*, p. 62.

[158] A.B. Chilivumbo, "Vimbuza or Mashawe: a Mystic Therapy", *African Music Society Journal* (1981), pp. 1-2.

[159] Personal interview with Mr Clement Chawura, a *vimbuza* doctor and former salesman at Sterling Products, at Chimara Vanthu, Chiwiniwa village, 17 February 1983.

[160] W.Y. Turner, *Tumbuka-Tonga English Dictionary*, Blantyre: Hetherwick Press, 1952, p. 273.

Vimbuza possession may have entered Malawi from the west, i.e. from Lwangwa valley in Zambia when the Tumbuka entered the country.[161] On the other hand, it may be that *vimbuza* was brought into Tumbukaland by the Nsenga and the Bemba from Marambo at a later date and that, when they intermarried with the Tumbuka, their spirit beliefs were adopted by the Tumbuka. What seems certain is that *vimbuza* entered into Tumbukaland from the direction that the Tumbuka came in entering their present home.

The large number of *vimbuza* spirits such as *mgoma, mphanda, kachekuru, fumu za pansi, mkakhachitutu basenga, magumbula, muharure,* and *luwemba*[162] is an indication of the variety of spirits involved. Thus *vimbuza,* as popularly used, is a generic term binding together different spirits. Their characteristics show through their medium. For example, a patient sees visions when possessed by *mgoma.* When possessed by *kachekuru,* the person suffers from stiff muscles; a *mkakhachitutu* patient goes dumb.[163]

Vimbuza is similar to *mashawe* spirit possession among the Lakeside Tonga. Elizabeth Colson shows that *mashawe* is also a spirit possession type among the Tonga of Zambia.[164] The Tumbuka use the two words *vimbuza* and *mashawe* interchangeably. This may reflect influence from the Lakeside Tonga, who use the same term, than from the Tonga of southern Zambia.[165] Both groups use the words *vimbuza* and *mashawe* interchangeably.

A prerequisite for becoming a *vimbuza* medium is illness or abnormal behaviour. Chilivumbo writes:

> A *vimbuza* patient experiences hallucinations, seeing terrible dreams, both in sleeping and in waking state. He groans frequently when in its acute stage, develops a taste of unorthodox foods, may lose his identity, may forget his name and call himself by one of the culturally accepted *vimbuza* names.[166]

A *vimbuza* patient may first suffer from headache, abnormal heart beat and so forth. These aspects of abnormality and illness prior to spirit possession are

---

[161] See chapter two on "The Origin of the Tumbuka".

[162] Personal interview with Mrs M. Nyirenda Mzimu, 49 year old *vimbuza* doctor, Mzimba, 16 February 1983.

[163] Ibid.

[164] Elizabeth Colson, *Spirit Possession Among the Tonga*, Beattie and Middleton (eds.), *Spirit Medium and Society*, pp. 69ff.

[165] M.L. Daneel says that among the Shona people of Zimbabwe *mashawe* are alien spirits which come from afar. For example, the *varungu* type of *mashawe* is a white man's spirit which possesses certain Shona mediums. In 1896, mediums possessed by this type of spirit played a significant role in influencing people to rebel against the white settlers. Daneel, *Old and New*, Vol. 1, pp. 91-96.

[166] Chilivumbo, "Vimbuza or Mashawe", pp. 6-7.

similar to those found among the Ndembu of Zambia. A further qualification for being a vimbuza *medium* is that:

> The novice must go through an experience which he interprets as evidence that a *vimbuza* spirit has chosen him as its vehicle. A test in the form of responsiveness to certain songs and drumming connected with the possession is given by a *vimbuza* medicine man. Once an appropriate song and drum beat is struck, the possessed responds in the normally accepted *vimbuza* fashion.[167]

This individual experience is well expressed and confirmed by a vimbuza medium when she says,

> I became a *vimbuza* medium when I was a young girl. At first I used to dream dancing wearing *madumbo* [Vimbuza costume]. In the dreams I saw different things some of which were terrifying. This continued even after I got married. Through the same dreams, I was, several times, compelled to go to a certain *vimbuza* doctor. I wanted to dance but my husband asked the doctor to give me medicine only. This could not cure me as the spirits had not expressed or identified themselves through dance.[168]

The reluctance to dance was because both husband and wife were Christians. The church discourages its members from dancing. However, the woman's wish was to dance in order to be made whole by going through the entire ceremony.

There is no age limit on *vimbuza* possession. Men and women, young people and little children may be possessed by *vimbuza*. However, more women than men tend to be possessed.[169] Some anthropologists have pointed to the status of marginal women as being a contributory factor to possession, i.e. childlessness and so forth. It also seems that women tend to be more sensitive and more responsive than men to religious experience of which spirit possession is one.

Vimbuza is both public and private in character. Where it is public, its medium is usually a healed *vimbuza* patient. He heals illness and through his

---

[167] Ibid., p. 8.

[168] Personal interview with Mrs M. Mhone, a Presbyterian minister's wife and former patient of *vimbuza*, Mzuzu, 24 February 1983.

[169] S.G. Lee ascribes Zulu women's proneness to possession to three factors viz.: stress is heaviest on married women in the patriarchal system with virilocal type of residence; - that once in a while, through spirit possession, women dominate the social order in their society; and that spirit possession is a therapeutic healing agent. S.G. Lee, "Spirit Possession among the Zulu", in Beattie and Middleton (eds.), *Spirit Mediumship and Society*, pp. 143-150. For more information on the differences between the sexes in regard to possession, see Schoffeleers, *Religion and the Dramatization of Life*, pp. 106-112.

utterances directs society to new order.[170] Where *vimbuza* is private, cases of hysterical dissociation occur frequently among the possessed. The affected person screams and squirms. If a medicine man is not brought in time, sometimes the novice runs away from home and wanders about.

Although there are other ways by which the doctor, *nganga*, tries to calm the possessed, the usual healing of *vimbuza* is by dance and medicine.

> *Vimbuza* dancing is a major therapy but he [the medicine man] also gives various medicines to exorcise and expel the evil spirits which are believed to cause hallucinations, to counteract the witchcraft and to remove other factors which are believed to be the root cause of the illness.[171]

The *vimbuza* dance is a public affair where all are welcome. It is often conducted at night in the patient's home, in the diviner's home or in the village court yard. The novice is the chief dancer although experienced *vimbuza* dancers take the floor in turns either to encourage the newly possessed to expend more energy or to keep the atmosphere alive when the novice is resting. In case of a small baby being possessed, the mother dances with the baby on her back. The dance lasts the whole night.[172]

The possession experience of *vimbuza* is personal. The possessed medium knows the name of the spirit possessing her/him. They alone know its nature and desires. A feast, a new dress or a partner may be some of the tangible requirements of the spirit. Immaterial things, such as longing to be in touch with the departed, healing of broken relationships, may also be wishes of a *vimbuza* medium as shown by Chilivumbo: "A co-wife may find in the vimbuza dance and songs a means of expressing her feelings ... a frustrated husband may equally use the *vimbuza* dance to his advantage."[173]

It is through the songs that the possessed express their feelings as evidenced in this song:

Fumu wane fumu wane	My lord [husband], my lord
Wayankhu?	Where have you gone?
Mwagarukirachi?	Why have you forsaken me?
Mwawona mwatola walero?	Have you seen you have taken a new wife?
Hayo ine, O lero![174]	Poor me, this day![175]

---

[170] The *nchimi* possessed by *vipili*, spirit snakes, incited the Tumbuka to revolt against the Ngoni in 1880. Their vision was of a new order in which the Tumbuka would be their own masters.

[171] Chilivumbo, "Vimbuza or Mashawe", p. 6.

[172] Ibid.

[173] Ibid., p. 8.

[174] Ibid.

While this is a song of protest by the first wife against her husband's abandonment of her, it is also a declaration of innocence and legitimization of the wife to the ancestral spirits and those in her community. The spectators accept the message contained in the songs in solidarity with the dancer. Their clapping hands, singing and tapping feet to the beat of the music testifies to this unity.

When the novice feels she has danced off her illness, she sings, "*malairano, malairano!*" meaning farewell, farewell![176] At this point everyone knows the patient is cured. However, the individual may suffer from the same "disease" at a later stage.

Meanwhile a sacrificial ceremony where the novice drinks fresh blood, *chilopa*, a sign of life takes place.[177] I observed that it was at dawn that the *vimbuza* doctor, who had been supervising the novice's dance the whole night, prepared her patient for discharge. First, she asked the patient what type of *chilopa* he wanted to drink: from a goat, a cow, a chicken, a dove, a duck or any other animal. This patient chose a goat. In naming the animal, the patient also indicated the colour. He chose a white spotted goat. The colour white symbolizing wholeness is the popular one, and the size of the animal signifies the magnitude of the spirit. This patient's spirit was a fairly strong one.

The administering of *chilopa* went like this: once the patient had made his choice of an animal, it was brought into the hut where the patient, the doctor, the drummers and the audience were. A song was sung and drums played to invigorate the patient. The patient danced and the onlookers clapped their hands. Women ululated while men blew their whistles. At the peak of the dance and drumming, the patient suddenly jumped up and seized the animal. Mouth to nose, he sucked the goat's blood until he dropped down from exhaustion and the animal was dead.[178]

In the third stage, the doctor prepared some medicine mixed with meat and plenty of soup. This was given to the patient who had to empty the bowl. Finally the patient received some medicine with which he shampooed his hair as he took a ritual bath. This is known as *kusinkha* (to seal or wash away the disease and protect the patient with medicine from evil witch spells). The meat left over from *chilopa* was shared among the people including the doctor, who had a generous helping.[179]

---

[175] Ibid.

[176] Ibid.

[177] Personal observation of a whole *chilopa* ceremony at the Tankhi in Mzimba township, with Mr J. Tumbwe, 27 February 1983.

[178] Ibid.

[179] Ibid.

The second stage of *vimbuza* possession leads a candidate to become a seer or a diviner. However, a *vimbuza* novice does not become a seer or diviner by virtue of being possessed. To qualify for this second stage, a person has to be specially chosen by the ancestral spirits and approved by society. First, through a dream or vision, the candidate gets appointed by one of his ancestors' spirits. (Usually the ancestor will have been a seer during his lifetime.) Still in the dream or vision, the candidate is shown different medicines and their uses. He also may receive a specific message to the community. Second comes the approval by the community. The community legitimizes the graduation of the candidate if the candidate has shown proof of his ability to cure diseases and upon his knowledge of characteristics of the ancestor who had chosen him. If the ancestor was one whom the community revered, the candidate is accepted, but if the ancestor is one the community did not favour, then the candidate is not approved. The community also approves the candidate if he shows the ability to communicate messages related to the community coming from the ancestral spirits. Finally the community expects the *diviner* or *nchimi* as the Tumbuka call him, to be in control of himself at all times including during possession periods. In this case the community controls who may take up the position of a seer and who may not.

In his or her practice, a *nchimi* may cure all diseases from minor headaches to complicated cases such as barrenness.[180] Prescriptions vary with diseases treated. Different root medicines are used in all cases. Even where possession cases are treated by the use of drums and music, medicine is also applied.

A *vimbuza nchimi* is also regarded by the Tumbuka as a prophet. When need arises in the community for reforms or a need for a return to old loyalties, the *nchimi* delivers a message to the community. His or her authority is through contact with ancestral spirits. The *nchimi* go through a symbolic death in which they get possessed by an ancestral spirit. By the spirit they are instructed for new reforms that are needed. If the *nchimi* says something which is not approved by the community, the people are free to reject the message and ridicule the prophet. On the other hand if the message is approved by the

---

[180] On the Malawi *sing'anga* association certificate, 1983 (chairman Mr Hoi Mkandawire, based in Rumphi), over twenty seven kinds are listed. All *nchimi* registered by the Malawi government are regarded by the Tumbuka as specialists in those areas. The association of *sing'angas* was initiated by the government in 1978. The aim of the association is to coordinate all the work of the *sing'angas* with the view to improving their skills and use of herbs. *Sing'anga* is an official role recognized by both the Malawi government and the traditional society; e.g. Mrs E. Mkandawire at Mzimba Boma is a *sing'anga* licensed by the government to heal diseases. This is approved by the community in which Mrs Mkandawire serves.

community and its leaders, the orders are carried out as pronounced. This indicates a possibility of the community rejecting something which the *nchimi* may genuinely believe came from the spirits. The possessed *nchimi's* message is thus controlled by the hearers. The activity of the *nchimi* as both a "doctor" and a "prophet" is dependent on the community. Their medicine is a mixture of meat and roots, and their message to the community depends on what is already there.[181]

To sum up, we have seen that to a *vimbuza* novice the significance of the ritual lies in the will of the individual. For the novice, it is a means for transcending the immediate physical environment into the world of spirits. In the possession experience, the novice mentally leaves this physical world and joins the spirits *(vizgezge)* of the ancestors. The transmission of the living to the land of the spirits is tangibly enacted through dance, dress, songs and sacrifice.

Chilopa, the communal meal at the end of the dance, fosters a sense of security, wholeness, belonging and newness of life. Admittedly, the outcome of *vimbuza* ritual may not always accomplish its explicit aim of liberating the individual and linking him or her to the divine. However, its revitalizing and reintegrative power in the life of the possessed in their community and in the world of spirits cannot be overlooked. Further, through the *vimbuza* ritual, the possessed gains religious fulfilment and medical treatment as well as psychological care which frees their consciousness.

Nchimi, the second stage in *vimbuza*, reveals maturity of an individual, his or her coming to terms with both the physical and the spirit world. It is also a stage where the individual accepts responsibility in the community. In their career, the *nchimi* associate themselves with the sufferers of their community because of their own experience. Because of their special calling, they also act as a bridge between the spirit world and the physical world.

Virombo spirit possession

Virombo, meaning "animals" or "creatures", denotes spirit-animal possession. Donald Fraser described *virombo* possession as follows: "Should you feel something biting you, or an itchiness in your body, don't scratch. That is the *chirombo* rising into activity."[182] The common use of the word *chirombo* (singular) or *virombo* (plural) refers to insects and animals. If a person was bitten by an insect, they were discouraged from scratching lest they spread the

---

[181] For my information on *vimbuza nchimi*, I have relied on notes sent to me by Mr Boston Soko, Department of Linguistics and French, University of Malawi.

[182] D. Fraser, *Livingstonia*, p. 191.

poison injected by the insect to unaffected parts of the body. On the other hand, the ritual use of the word *virombo* (always in the plural) is different from its everyday use, as one of my informants pointed out: "*Virombo* which possess people through disease are not ordinary snakes, hyenas or any other animal or creature which may be involved. They are *bazimu* [spirits or spirit animals]"[183] Fraser says "chirombos are spirits, and in all the shelves of the Mission dispensary there is no medicine which deals with evil spirits".[184]

Virombo in Tumbukaland are not to be equated with *nyau*, known as *virombo* among the Chewa people of central Malawi. *Nyau* is a secret society and its membership is selective.[185] Its similarity with *virombo* spirit possession in the northern region is that it is connected with ancestral spirits; drumming, hand clapping, and dancing, central to *virombo* healing ceremonies among the Tumbuka, are also prominent in Nyau practices.

The origin of *virombo* spirit possession is clearly given by a district commissioner resident at Kasungu in 1923:

> This kind of dancing was introduced among the Ngoni and Tumbuka long ago by the Awiza from the west. The women dance with their faces painted in white streaks and are believed by the people to have the power of turning themselves at will into wild beasts especially lions and leopards.[186]

This is in accord with historical events. Between 1830 and 1840 the Wiza, Bemba and Senga of eastern Zambia along Luangwa valley spilt into northern Malawi in considerable numbers. The Wiza and the Senga settled among the Tumbuka as refugees having fled their home for fear of the Ngoni, who, at this time, had crossed the Zambezi. The Ngoni presence north of the Zambezi stirred up much fear among villagers so that many found safety hiding in the thick woods. It may have been that the Tumbuka saw the newcomers as forsaken by their ancestral spirits and living like *virombo* which wander about without a proper home.

But the origin of *virombo* may not be as clear as this. Informants in Rumphi District, especially those in the Mzokoto area and those in Chiweta and Chitimba say that *Virombo* spirit possession came from the Tumbuka who seeped into Malawi from the north east. The Tumbuka of the Mzimba district, especially those from Njuyu, Euthini, extending to Mbalachanda on the

---

[183] Personal interview with Mr J. Chipeta, a village elder, Ekwendeni, 30 January 1983.

[184] D. Fraser, *Livingstonia*, p. 193.

[185] W.H.J. Rangeley, "Nyau in Nkhotakota District", *The Nyasaland Journal*, Vol. 3/2 (1949), pp. 35-49.

[186] J.A. Martin, A Note on Certain Local Dances and their Significance in Native Minds, Kasungu District Book, MNA, Government records Vol. 1, p. 1, 1927.

Malawi-Zambia border say that this *virombo* type of spirit possession came with the Tumbuka who entered Malawi from the Zambian direction. In this case, it may be that *virombo* spirit possession originated with the Tumbuka and entered Malawi at the same time by the same two routes the Tumbuka came, namely the north east and the west. Whatever its origin, *virombo* spirit possession has become part of Tumbuka religious practice and beliefs sanctioning behaviour. The Kasungu District Resident had observed its effects when he wrote: "Here these dances, I am sure, exercise an enormous influence on village life, especially in relation to crime and the concealment of it."[187] It may have been the popularity of such spirit dances that led the commissioner to regard them as sources of crime and perhaps other undesirable activities. But knowing the firm regimental Ngoni government under which the Tumbuka lived and with which Mwase of Kasungu aligned himself, it is doubtful if deliberate crime would have been condoned. However, what is clear here is that dances related to *virombo* attracted large congregations and affected their behaviour.

On all four borders of Tumbukaland, *virombo* practices may be observed, and they extend into neighbouring countries such as Mozambique, Tanzania and Zambia. Rather than this being an indication of where the spirit type came from, it is only a pointer to migration traits and the inter-territorial effects of the cult.

Virombo is similar to *mhondoro* spirit possession among the Zazuru people in Zimbabwe.[188] *Virombo* is a spirit animal possession. *Virombo* spirits are thought by the Tumbuka to have been men who have now become spirits and manifest themselves in both animals and humans. However, *virombo* is centred around the individual. It has no political function and does not have a religious function which extends beyond an individual medium and his ancestors.[189]

---

[187] Ibid.

[188] According to Daneel, a *mhondoro* medium was believed to be possessed by a spirit-lion, the lion being regarded as the king of all animals. The lineage of the *mhondoro* was vital to its influence and recognition. A *mhondoro* formed a political unity among those communities which recognized the *mhondoro's* concern and power extended beyond its immediate family and kin uniting the ethnic group as a whole. A *mhondoro* also mediated between *Mwari*, God, and the living humans. Its spiritual influence was more apparent in times of need such as drought. People appealed to the *mhondoro* for rain or any petition they wanted made on their behalf. Daneel, *Old and New*, Vol. 1, pp. 92-93.

[189] Personal interview with Mr A. M. Nyasulu, 16 February 1983, Mzokoto village, Rumphi.

All age groups of both sexes are susceptible to *virombo* possession. However, more women tend to be possessed by or be doctors of *virombo*.[190] When it is remembered that the Tumbuka were once a matrilineal society, i.e. tracing their descent through the mother's side, it is not surprising that women priestesses and doctors are a natural development.

A doctor of *virombo* described how a person gets possessed by *virombo* spirits:

> At the beginning of possession some novices portray symptoms of fatigue and sit down quietly, usually in solitude. Others start by falling sick, suffer from headache or stomach ache until they are brought to someone expert in *virombo*. If the condition persists without proper medical care, the patient may run mad and leave home to live in bush.[191]

The magnitude of the spirit is judged by the way the medium behaves. If the patient sits down quietly, this is taken as a sign that a gentle *chirombo* has seized the medium. On the other hand if the novice is restless and uncontrolled, the spirit animal in the medium is regarded by the experts as dangerous, and must be treated immediately.

Treatment of *virombo*, just like vimbuza, is by dancing and drinking a herb mixture administered by a specialist called *nganga* or *nchimi*. Donald Fraser's observation of healing *virombo* spirit possession by a *nchimi* he nicknames "Sir James" shows some of the practices:

> Cowering under the cloth, breathing smoke and steam, the girl sat rigid, while Sir James beat a drum behind her. Presently a shiver ran through her frame, and she began to tremble violently. 'The *chirombo* has risen', cried the doctor. Now three or four others begin to pound small ear-splitting drums. The people who fill the hut break into song and rhythmical clapping of hands, and the patient rises and essays a dance. [192]

The drum beat became wilder, the rhythm and the noise of song and hand clapping grew swifter and swifter invigorating the dancer. Jerking her arms forward and backwards, upwards and downwards in time with the music, the possessed expends enormous amounts of energy and utters sharp cries resembling the spirit-animal in the patient. The novice sinks utterly exhausted to the ground. This is regarded by the medicine man as a good sign that the patient is nearing full recovery. To ensure long health and protection from

---

[190] Ibid.

[191] Personal interview with Mr R. Nhlane, a *virombo* doctor, Embangweni, 31 January 1983.

[192] Donald Fraser, *African Idylls: Portraits and Impressions of Life on a Central African Mission Station*, London: Seeley, 1923, pp. 191.

further attack by the spirits and from witch spells, the *chilopa* is administered to the novice by the medicine man.

The similar practices in *virombo* and *vimbuza* may have been the result of intermarriage and agreement between Tumbuka, Senga and the Wiza.

For most mediums of *virombo*, possession is not a career, but an avenue through which they enter into harmony with the spirits. By being possessed, they are also inspired, thereby receiving "second sight". One of my informants related her experience:

> I was possessed once. Since then, I have been given power to see and know the evil people. Sometimes I see them in dreams and sometimes when I meet them during the day something tells me: "this is an evil person". I obey the wishes of the spirits. I do not eat fish, any fish without scales, and I do not go near dead bodies. Doing so would arouse the spirits' anger.[193]

Such mediums are looked upon by the public as *bamizimu*, of the spirits, or they can communicate with the spirits. This places spirit mediums in a privileged position. Their behaviour and talk may not be normal, but great attention is paid to what they say, as it is believed that spirits may speak to the community or to the next of kin through them. The possessed also enjoys the close association of all those who have gone through the same experience. Socially, the medium may obtain recognition for his or her prophetic and healing abilities and therefore may be accepted in circles closed to him or her formerly.

Few individuals rise to the position of *nchimi*, doctor - a level which is reached by spirit mediums whose possession condition is full of dreams and other signs pointing to that end. One *nchimi* informed me:

> I did not choose to be what I am. In fact I was happy working as a teacher in Zomba. My family had enough to eat every day and they were well dressed. But when I got ill I had to stop working. When I came here, my relations took me to several *nchimi* but my illness persisted. At last I was taken to Mzimu who told me that I was destined to be a *nchimi*. I stayed at Mzimu's home receiving treatment for six months. When I got well I could not go back to Zomba. My sleep was filled with dreams. I dreamt all kinds of medicines, where they could be found and what disease they were for. And I dreamt a stream of people being healed through my hand.[194]

Training to be a *nchimi* has no fixed time. Some candidates spend two months while others go on for two years. What the trainer looks for in his student is,

---

[193] Personal interview with M. Kondowe, a *vimbuza* medium, Embangweni, 31 January 1983.

[194] Personal interview with Mr C. Chavura, a *vimbuza nchimi*, Chimara Vanthu, Chiwiniwa village, Rumphi, 17 February 1983.

first, ability of the candidate to control himself and the spirits in the trance state; second, the candidate's power to discover potent medicine and diagnose disease. Under training, the candidate wears three strings of beads on the left arm.[195] Upon graduation, three or six strings of white and red beads are added on the same arm. I did not have a clear explanation of the meaning of the beads and why they are worn on the left arm. For me, it was a useful mark for picking out the doctors, *nchimi*.

Every *nchimi* operates independently of the others even where there are several *nchimi* in one village. Competition for clients may arise causing influential *nchimi* to move away to new areas.[196] The nature of *virombo* spirit possession is such that it has no central control, as did the Chikhangombe, Chisumphi and M'bona cults. Its religious teaching has never been systematized. Thus it has remained the *wanainchi's*, commoners', theology.

Vyanusi

Vyanusi, a corruption of the Ngoni *itshanusi*, is a new type of possession among the Tumbuka. It was brought there by the Ngoni in 1845. In the Ngoni language the word *hnusa* means to "smell out", to "detect". The *vyanusi* or "smeller", as the medium may be called, believed by the Ngoni to have supernatural powers to detect hidden danger, was a prophet.[197] One *such vyanusi* is said by Young to have prophesied a future meeting with white men, a prophecy which later influenced paramount Mbelwa's attitude towards Dr Laws when they met in 1879.[198]

A *vyanusi* was regarded with respect in both politics and religion. Young writes, "In addition to some rudimentary political authority held by a *vyanusi*, his primary position was a ritual one".[199] As a prophet behind the Ngoni military power, he was also concerned with the moral order and the relationship between the living and the dead. For example, before the *impi* engaged themselves in a raid, a *vyanusi* was consulted to "see" if there were any spirits angered by neglect or by some individual's misconduct which would be injurious to the army in battle. If the *vyanusi* detected any breach of

---

[195] I owe the information on the training of *nchimi* to Dr Boston Soko through personal correspondence. It should be noted that where *mzimu* is used in this work with capital M, it denotes a *nchimi* who assumes the name *Mzimu*. The example is in the quotation above.
[196] Ibid.
[197] Young, *Notes on the History of the Tumbuka-Nkhamanga Peoples*, p. 114; also Chibambo, *My Ngoni of Nyasaland*, p. 52.
[198] Young, *Notes on the History of the Tumbuka-Nkhamanga Peoples*, p. 116.
[199] Young, *Customs and Folklore*, p. 27.

relationship within the community, he suggested a remedy before the army could be allowed to go out to fight. The remedy depended on the magnitude of the offence. If a person was suspected of being a traitor, he was held prisoner until the war ended. If the results of the war were in favour of the Ngoni, the suspect gave a white fowl to the chief who declared him innocent. But if the Ngoni lost the war, the accused was guilty of treason and was sentenced to death.[200] In this sense, Young's words, "A vyanusi is safety doctor" hold true.[201]

After becoming part of the Tumbuka religious system, vyanusi possession went through a cultural change. Until the shrine of Chikhangombe had been destroyed, *vyanusi* played a very small part in the religious and social life of the Tumbuka. Its coming to surface after this period was characterized by people of mixed genealogies tracing their ancestors from both the Ngoni and the Tumbuka, as already noted. Consequently *vyanusi* was now more associated with the Tumbuka settled way of life than with the former Ngoni warlike lifestyle.[202] In this new social condition *vyanusi* found itself in, its role as an integrative factor was significant. Men and women who were now possessed by *vimbuza, vyanusi* etc. accommodated the various elements of possession derived from the contact. *Vyanusi's* high position in detecting danger and social enemies was absorbed by the more established *mwavi* ritual practised by Tumbuka medicine men. According to Vail, these medicine men were responsible for cleansing society from witchcraft.[203] It is observed that the former prophetic function of *vyanusi* gave way to *vimbuza* spirit possession through which individuals in Tumbuka society participated in decision making. Nevertheless, *vyanusi* continued to be practised among the Ngoni-Tumbuka without totally being submerged by Tumbuka spirit beliefs.

Mediums possessed by *vyanusi* spirits after 1870, when the Ngoni had imposed their language on the Tumbuka, spoke in foreign languages such as Ngoni and Karanga.[204] This is not surprising when it is remembered that *vyanusi* originated from the Ngoni, some of whom were assimilated from the Karanga stock. As stated earlier, later mediums were descendants from mixed marriages. For them, speaking Ngoni or Karanga in their trance state was as natural as speaking the Tumbuka language. What is interesting is that among

---

[200] Personal interview with Dada B. Silo, an Ngoni elder, about 104 years old, Ekwendeni, 13 February 1983.

[201] Young, *Customs and Folklore*, p. 27.

[202] Rau has advanced a similar argument in the case of Ngoni settlement among the Chewa of Central Malawi. Rau, "Chewa Religion and the Ngoni Conquest", p. 136.

[203] Vail, "Religion, Language and the Tribal Myth", p. 220.

[204] Personal interview with Mr Chaputa Chimaliro, *a vyanusi* doctor, Ekwendeni, 14 February 1983.

the Tumbuka, *vyanusi* possession became essentially centred on an agrarian community in fitting with the spirits of the land.

By 1890 the influence of *vyanusi* had begun to conform to the more settled life of the Tumbuka. A *vyanusi* became more of an interpreter of social events than a forecaster of battles, e.g. when there was drought the *vyanusi* interpreted this as a sign of displeasure among some ancestral spirits. Sacrifices of sheep, goat or cattle were made by the *vyanusi* who prayed for rain on behalf of the community. Also when an epidemic broke out, the *vyanusi* was consulted. The trust which both the Ngoni and the Tumbuka put upon the power of a *vyanusi* was commented on by Elmslie:

> From the deep religious feeling which the people have in regard to the presence and power of the ancestral spirits with whom the *itshanusi* is believed to be in communication, they are ready to acknowledge even that which may be to their hurt.[205]

The authority of a *vyanusi* was believed to derive from prophets, community leaders and *ng'anga* who were once men but were now spirits.[206]

Vyanusi spirit mediumship was acquired through inheritance. A potential candidate learnt about his or her calling in dreams.[207] In the dream, the novice communicated with an ancestor who was a medium when he was still alive. The novice was endowed with healing and prophetic power. Usually this dream experience was followed by abnormal behaviour. This was interpreted by experienced diviners as symptomatic of *vyanusi* possession. In some cases *vyanusi* possession was epitomized by illness which, like *vimbuza*, was ascribed to possession.

The new medium gained popularity through the success of his "seeing" and healing activities, with the public validating the *vyanusi's* message and authority by the events that followed his pronouncements. A *vyanusi* medium, like a *vimbuza* medium, was also a herbalist. They could cure diseases such as headaches, rheumatism and other pains.[208] In the Ngoni background, men were the chief mediums of *vyanusi* although women were also being possessed. Unlike the situation in *vimbuza*, little regard was accorded to children in *vyanusi*. They were expected to be silent before adults until they too became mature. The male dominance in *vyanusi* fitted with the paternal and militaristic social organization of the Ngoni, especially before they settled among the Tumbuka.

---

[205] Elmslie, *Among the Wild Ngoni*, p. 61; cf. Young, *Customs and Folklore*, p. 27.
[206] See section on "Ngoni Religion".
[207] Personal interview with Dada B. Silo, Ekwendeni, 29 February 1984.
[208] Chilivumbo, "Vimbuza or Mashawe", pp. 1-2.

There was no need for heavy drum beating and a prolonged dance to rid a *vyanusi* medium from his trance state. With their short spears and war shields which they beat in a rhythm, the people danced together with the *vyanusi* in the middle. After he delivered what message the spirits needed to communicate to the community, the *vyanusi* became normal without much help.[209] The agreement on spirit possession beliefs between Ngoni and Tumbuka both sustained *vyanusi* possession and encouraged *vimbuza* and *virombo* possession practices. At the same time, the impact of the contact of the two ethnic groups set *vyanusi* possession on a new course of development. However, this development did not go far before a new element, the Christian faith, was introduced in the 1880s by the missionaries. This drastically altered the spirit possession practices among the Tumbuka and their Ngoni neighbours. Possession was now coloured by Christian symbols and imagery. Conversely, when the local people accepted the Christian teaching, their response and faith were coloured by their history of possession beliefs and practices. The effect of this new contact will be dealt with in the following chapters.

---

[209] Personal interview with Mr Chaputa Chimaliro, a *vyanusi* doctor, Ekwendeni, 14 February 1983.

Chapter 4

The Mission and the Conversion: 1881-1910

The aim in this chapter is to examine the impact of the Christian Faith on spirit possession and to show to what extent spirit possession formed a substratum of Tumbuka religious beliefs from, and with which, they responded to the Christian faith.

To an outsider, spirit possession and its practice was not immediately noticeable in the way that polygamy was. First, its existence was embedded in social institutions such as marriage, worship, death, childbirth and initiation. Missionaries could easily miss the meaning of those rites, as Alexander Hetherwick later discovered: "The pioneer missionary is handicapped by a lack of full knowledge of the meaning and true character of the rites, customs, and religious practices of the people."[210] Hetherwick would also agree that the language barrier hindered missionaries' understanding of local beliefs and practices, in the area of our study - spirit possession. When the mission moved from Cape Maclear to Bandawe in 1881, missionaries spoke the Chewa language and soon learnt Chingoni, the language of the ruling Ngoni aristocrats. Later they also learnt Chitumbuka - the language spoken by the majority in the northern region. For this reason, and the shock one experiences in society different from one's own, missionaries' knowledge of spirit possession practices among the local people was inhibited, at least in the initial period. Again, according to James Jack, ritual ceremonies, possession included, were held away in the villages concealed from the Mission stations where missionaries lived.[211] Jack was writing about the Tumbuka ceremonies he presumably heard about from some missionaries and some early converts.

The first generation of Christians among the Tumbuka made a clear break between their old world-view and the new world-view instigated by the missionaries. J.B. Mhone, baptized in 1910, represents these early converts:

> From the beginning the church did not accept *mashawe* experiences [spirit possession and beliefs] in society. When I was baptized in 1910 I left everything behind. Church leaders had already shown that *mashawe* was not accepted as it is contrary to the teaching of the church. Up to date the church does not accept people who have not left their old life and beliefs behind.[212]

---

[210] Hetherwick, *The Gospel and the African*, pp. 156-157.

[211] J.W. Jack, *Daybreak in Livingstonia: the Story of Livingstonia Mission*, Edinburgh and London: Oliphant, Anderson and Ferrier, 1901, pp. 251-263.

[212] Personal interview with the Rev. J.B. Mhone, Mgodi village, 4 February 1983.

Yes, the break was necessary if a life's crisis brought about by the new religion had to be faced and if people had to make a choice. But this break was modified once converts settled down in the new faith. Their background influenced their understanding of the new faith. People saw their own prophets' prophecies fulfilled with their own eyes, as Yesaya Chibambo declares:

> Here in Ngoniland also, there were seers who were known as *Izanusi* or Dreamers. At that time when the Gospel was about to enter the land, before white men had been heard of, certain seers among the Ngoni were led to foretell of something great coming from the sea. Others were more explicit and said, the *balumbi* (Europeans) are coming, receiving them courteously.[213]

Such diviners prepared the way in the hearts of the local people to give heed to the white strangers when they came into the country. Indeed even at a later time, many of the people, when inclined to violence, may have remembered the words of their diviners and forebearers. The chiefs especially recalled what had been said, and extended their friendship to the newcomers. Thus the traditional priests had acted as prophets and forerunners of the missionary.

The years between 1881 and 1910 were planting years when the missionaries and the Tumbuka were sizing each other up. Each tried to attract the other with its best until the relationship had been firmly established. Magic lanterns and other western goods were baits of friendship, not just show pieces of western technology. Walter Elmslie's words point to this: "We gave Mombera a present of various articles, with which he expressed himself very much satisfied."[214] The local people, on the other hand, impressed missionaries with gifts of cattle, goats and chickens. For example, when the Ngoni overlords wanted missionaries to leave Tongaland and settle where they and the Tumbuka lived, they said: "Come and live with us and we will give you cattle. Can you milk fish that you remain at the lake?"[215]

Much bartering of beliefs and practices of the two groups happened during that period. The missionaries, who saw the Tumbuka as needing salvation of the body, mind and soul, gradually pushed their civilization and the Gospel forward. The Tumbuka, on the other hand, responded to the missionary contact from their own beliefs and experience. Consequently, friction over beliefs and practices was generated. However, it was much later that the problem of spirit possession crystallized in the church among the converts. Even then, each worker dealt with the issue locally as it arose.

---

[213] Chibambo, *My Ngoni of Nyasaland*, pp. 52f.
[214] Elmslie, *Among the Wild Ngoni*, p. 95.
[215] *Ibid.*

We have already examined some of the power structures which impinged upon the Tumbuka prior to the missionary advent and how those powers affected the spirit possession beliefs of the local people. Enlargement of traditional beliefs and re-ordering of it was the result of the missionaries' presence. Slaves who were formerly excluded from religious rites now worshipped God with dignity alongside everyone else. Through the door of education, everyone - the young, royalty, commoners and slaves - were all exposed to a new worldview. Thus missionaries not only stimulated the religious appetite of the people, but changed drastically the course of spirit possession and the social structure of the Tumbuka.

The mission task

Thomas Bowen, the old American missionary in West Africa, delineated the task of a mission as follows:

> Our designs and hopes in regard to Africa are not simply to bring as many individuals as possible to the knowledge of Christ. We desire to establish the Gospel in the hearts and minds and social life of the people, so that truth and righteousness may remain and flourish among them, without the instrumentality of foreign missionaries. This cannot be done without civilization. To establish the Gospel among any people, they must have Bibles and therefore must have art to make or the money to buy them. They must read the Bible and this implies instruction.[216]

A sense of obligation to take the Gospel to foreign lands was a clear missionary strategy. How far these schemes would be effected remained with messengers. Dr Robert Laws summarized the Mission task in these words:

> As a small missionary band, what do we want? The first and greatest desire of all our hearts can be summed up in simple words: the extension of Christ's cause and Kingdom; to evangelize is Christ's cause, the world, to evangelize the heathen around us. To evangelize is Christ's cause, and is the great cause for which we left our homes.[217]

---

[216] T.J. Bowen, *Missionary Labours and Adventures in Central Africa*, (reprint) London: Frank Cass, 1968, p. 321. Bowen was one of the earliest American missionaries in tropical Africa. In the 19th century he worked among the Yoruba people in Western Nigeria. His book provides valuable information on Yoruba life and society during the middle years of the 19th century. Bowen was an emissary of the Southern Baptist Convention. See also Alverson Luiz De Souza, "A Black Heart: The Work of Thomas Jefferson Bowen among Blacks in Africa and in Brazil between 1840 and 1875", MTh thesis, University of Natal, Pietermaritzburg, January 1998.

[217] Sermon preached by Dr Robert Laws, 1 January 1883, MNA L1 1/4/11.

Livingstonia missionaries believed that they were God's instruments to bring the gospel of salvation to the Tumbuka and give light to what they believed was a dark continent; and they regarded themselves as representatives of a civilization which was ideal for every "savage race". Emerging from a totally different society with a world-view of its own, the missionaries' work was to substitute the Tumbuka total world-view with that of the West. James Jack spoke for many when he said:

> It is no easy matter to be a Christian in such a land. Men who have been brought up in a savage state, accustomed to draw a spear at every insult, require a large amount of the grace of God before they can submit with meekness to the malice and taunts of their wicked neighbour.[218]

Faced with what was considered complete ignorance and darkness, some missionaries had seen their task as obliterating the present order so that a fresh start might be implemented.

Others saw their task as filling a religious vacuum believed to have existed among the Tumbuka and their neighbours. But as we noted earlier, missionaries did not have to start from a religious blank. Andrew Walls clearly shows that there is no such thing as a "religious blank":

> The fact then that 'if any man is in Christ he is a new creature' does not mean that he starts or continues his life in a vacuum or that his mind is a blank table. It has been formed by his own culture and history and, since God had accepted him as he is, his Christian mind will continue to be influenced by what was before. All churches are culture churches including our own.[219]

Other missionaries who cared to see this fact soon recognized it. Elmslie "saw many things which were admirable" in the local people's customs and beliefs when he remarked: "It is a mistake to suppose that even among barbarous tribes ... all their customs are bad. There were, before Christian teaching began to influence them, many things which were admirable."[220]

Words similar to Elmslie's were expressed by Clement Scott who championed the establishment of a truly African church in the Shire Highlands:

> Our purpose we lay down as the foundation of all our work, we are building the African Church-not Scotch nor English-but African. Rather we should say the African portion of the 'One Catholic and Apostolic Church'. The African has a part to play in the Church of Christ Universal. His character and his influence have still to be reckoned with. In the early days of Christianity, the African was a

---

[218] Jack, *Daybreak in Livingstonia*, p. 334.
[219] A.F. Walls, "The Gospel as the Prisoner and Liberator of Culture", *Faith and Thought*, Vol. 10/8(1-2) (1981), p. 44.
[220] Elmslie, *Among the Wild Ngoni*, p. 51.

leader in Christian life and thought, while the church of North Africa sent its representative to take part in great Church Councils. We Christian nations of Europe are the heirs to those ages and of the labours of those men. Our debt is consequently to be paid back to the new-born African races of today.[221]

Living by his word, Scott wanted to baptize a number of local customs and spirit beliefs. A typical illustration is when he attended an anniversary of a departed chief, Malemia, near Domasi. Impressed by what he saw, Scott wrote:

> An offering of beer was poured out. It is the anniversary of the old chief's death. The custom so far from being in our mind reprehensible, gave us beautiful illustrations of the chalice of the body filled with the wine of the blood of life, and of our Saviour's blood poured out without being broken.[222]

Scott's determination to build an African Church was seen in his keenness in understanding the local customs and religious beliefs. His construction of St Michael and All Angels Church in Blantyre (from 1888 to 1891) was an image of his desire to build the Church of Jesus Christ. It added to his building of an African church. This accomplishment of the first permanent and the most beautiful church anywhere between Transvaal and Sudan was the birth and symbol of unity and peace among the different peoples of Malawi. It was as if the ancestral spirits of various ethnic groups had agreed to leave behind all their differences and accept the Christian faith to guide the people's lives.[223]

Reflecting on missionary work between 1881 and 1925 at the Blantyre Missionary Conference, A.G. MacAlpine agreed with Scott, Laws and others on the need to build an African church. He described some missionary activities which tended to deride the local culture as "religious vandalism":

> Foreign preconception and prejudices as well as erroneous first impressions of local beliefs and practices have often done injustices to what is vaguely, and frequently ignorantly, called 'heathenism' or 'paganism' and set the missionary off on a smashing crusade, which on better informed reflection has appeared rather like a kind of religious vandalism. However much there may be to combat or correct in African life and habit, experience teaches the missionary to be more discriminating than he is wont to be, and to be as interested and eager to approve and develop the good as prompt and uncompromising to eradicate the evil.[224]

---

[221] C. Scott, *Life and Work in British Central Africa*, Vol. 16, Blantyre (May 1895), p. 4.

[222] LWBCA, 16 January 1895, p. 11.

[223] see Kenneth R. Ross, *The African Church and Eastern Orthodoxy: Reflections on the Centenary of St Michael and All Angels* in *Gospel Ferment in Malawi*, Kachere-Mambo, 1995

[224] A.G. MacAlpine, "Native Customs Which the Church Might Utilise in the Christian Life", *Federation Missions Report*, 1926, p. 30.

While MacAlpine's words cautioned his contemporaries and the newly arrived missionary, they were a critical reflection on the work of missionaries in those initial years and called for a modified approach to the task. With many cooks involved, the missionary task was bound to have many facets. J.W. Westgarth, a missionary in Nigeria in 1906, had sensed this problem when he said: "Forming a native church is no easy task. The church will be coloured by: (i) the kind of missionary commencing the work, (ii) native laws, customs, practices and beliefs."[225]

The success of the Livingstonia Mission task then depended on the Gospel as proclaimed by its messengers and interpreted by its receivers, and on the Scottish missionary-Tumbuka relationship.

The Gospel message

Gauging from a number of sermon collections I have examined, it appears that the primary objective of the early missionaries' preaching was twofold:

> to stir the natives to a greater knowledge of the reality and nearness of God, and of His Holiness, and to facilitate conversion experience leading to total commitment to Christ.[226]

First, Laws' vision of the Mission of the Church was the proclamation of the hope of the Tumbuka in the Gospel of Jesus Christ, the offering of worship to God through Jesus and the participation in the development of the local people through education, health, and acceptable trade. Laws' conviction that the gospel message embodied in a worshipping community was essential to fulfil the total needs of an individual and a whole society was evidenced by an industrial mission station he designed at Livingstonia.

Second, the missionary ideal of a native convert was personal commitment and baptism into the church as the missionaries themselves knew it. They pointed to the possibility for man's ultimate disaster and God's judgement as well as redemption and external life – but only if the Tumbuka forsook their evil ways.

Thus, initially, the missionaries thought that as long as the potential converts remained in their familiar environment, their abrogating traditional beliefs and totally committing themselves to Christ could not be achieved, as they would easily fall back. So side by side with the preaching of the Gospel, the church attracted people from their villages to settle on the Mission stations:

---

[225] J.W. Westgarth, Diary of J.W. Westgarth on his work in Nigeria, Qua Iboe Mission, 1906, University of Aberdeen, Centre of Non-Western Studies, Box M 12/2 W.

[226] Robert Laws, Miscellaneous Sermon Collection, MNA L1 1/3/12.

> The separation of the people from their tribal chiefs is, humanly, the only conceivable way in which they can be laid open to the reception of Christianity. For as long as they owe allegiance to the hereditary Chief of their tribe, they must use the tribal tattoo mark and be subjected to his will in all public ordeals, involving their nominal belief in witchcraft and a host of inferior spirits or demigods which cannot coexist with a belief in the Divine revelation.[227]

Usually these settlers were freed slaves or marginal people within their society where they were regarded as ostracized by their ancestral spirits. Thus, at first, Christianity was for the marginal people. Free Tumbuka may have regarded joining the church as "a form of delinquency".[228] However, experience soon taught the missionaries that uprooting people from their familiar surroundings was not the best way of winning converts, especially if they were expected to grow into a self-governing, self-propagating, self-supporting church. Fraser pointed out:

> I fear the evangel which de-nationalizes, which refuses to recognize the power of the Gospel to purify what is not essentially wrong, and which preaches first through prohibitions, rather than by the attraction of what is positive.[229]

The colony idea was abandoned and increasingly missionaries and their African agents took the Gospel to where the people lived. Emphasis in preaching was laid on an ever present all-powerful God who is creator, conqueror of all evil powers and father-protector of all people. Assurance was given that if the people put their trust in him they need not worry about witches or any evil power. This was a strong point of contact with the Tumbuka as it emphasized their belief in Chiuta, the great spirit God, Creator, Giver of rain and life. More than that, the Tumbuka learnt that this God was approachable and dynamically present among his people. As already noted, this idea of God in Tumbuka religion may have been eclipsed by the hierarchical spirit world and by the social organization which laid emphasis on gerontocracy.[230]

The direct object of worship was another aspect of the Gospel message the missionaries put forward. They raised high the God of the Bible, approachable through Jesus Christ, as the sole object of worship. The missionaries rejected the adoration of ancestral spirits practised by the Tumbuka because they saw it as a hindrance to the success of the Gospel: "the worship of the people of their forefathers' spirits (*vibanda*) was perhaps the greatest drawback to the progress

---

[227] Riddle to Dr Macrae, 8 January 1880, MNA L1 1/3/11.
[228] J.F.Ajayi, *Christian Missions in Nigeria 1841-1891*, London: Longmans, 1965, p. 72.
[229] Donald Fraser, "The Evangelistic Approach to the African", *International Reviews of Missions*, Vol. 15 (1926), p. 438.
[230] L. Mumba, "The Religion of my Fathers", *International Review Missions*, Vol. 17 (1927), p. 65.

of the Gospel."[231] The Tumbuka understood life as a continuous gamut embracing the whole creation - the physical and the spiritual. The dead were regarded as part of the living community. They took part in decision-making within their family, clan or ethnic group. Above all, they were the mediators between God and the living.[232] The Tumbuka aspect of worship contrasted with Christian thought. The missionaries taught that Jesus Christ was the only one able to solve man's problems, forgive sins and offer salvation to individuals. They assured the local people that God, known and approached through Jesus, was sufficient.

Eternal life was a further point of contact in the Gospel message. We have noted that in Tumbuka beliefs, life after death was regarded as a continuance of the present. The only difference between the two was in their mode; the present was lived in the body while the other was lived in the spirit.[233] It is enough to say that the Tumbuka believed that if the dead person was not given proper burial or was wronged during his lifetime, his spirit would return to take revenge. In this the missionaries perceived that the Tumbuka succumbed to fear of human enemies and evil forces they thought were the main causes of death. Thus in presenting the Gospel, the missionaries taught Jesus' triumph over death; that there is a resurrection of the body and judgement. The righteous, according to the missionary teaching, would be filled with the Spirit of God, inherit his Kingdom and live a sober life for ever. On the other hand, the unrighteous would be punished in hell fire for ever. The result of this teaching was that the Tumbuka were converted to the Christian faith, some from fear of fire, while others saw the new religion as an alternative spiritual power.[234]

Education: its effect on spirit possession

Robert Laws, crowned by the Ngoni as the "father" of all white men, saw education as the tool for transforming and bringing the Africans into God's household. To Murray of the Dutch Reformed Church at Livelezi, he wrote:

---

[231] Jack, *Day Break in Livingstonia*, p. 260.

[232] Young, *Contemporary Ancestors*, pp. 149-151.

[233] For detailed description of the Tumbuka beliefs about eternal life, see section on "Eschatology and Immortality".

[234] In his Ph.D thesis, Chiphangwi sufficiently dealt with "reasons why people join the Christian Church". One of the reasons he gives is that local worship of the spirits was less exclusive. His work is worth reading especially for those interested in pastoral care. Saindi D. Chiphangwi, "Why People Join the Christian Church: Trends in Church Growth in the Blantyre Synod of the Church of Central Africa Presbyterian 1960-1975", Ph.D, University of Aberdeen, 1978, p. 180.

My scheme is an earnest endeavour to bring all my past study, observation, experience, and travel to bear on the question how best to bring the Gospel of Christ to the people of Central Africa and their children.[235]

The education summary of Laws catered for both sexes and covered a wide range of subjects. It was as follows:[236]

Boys

Literary side		Technical side
I	Elementary or village school vernacular; and English std. I	I Native industries Basket and mat making
II	School or Junior Dept. Eng. stds. two, three and four (three year course)	II Junior Dept. or School of Manual Training Courses: carpentry, wood-turning, printing (alternative) Three years in all.
III	Normal Dept. or Literary course (three years)	III Senior Dept. or Apprenticeship traders: gardener or agriculturist, carpenter, builder, clerk or storeman, telegraphist. (four years)
IV	Theological Dept. (a) pastors (b) evangelists. (three year course)	

Girls

I	Elementary or village school	I	Native industries
II	Girls' school (same as II above)	II	Household work and baking
III	Bible school for married teachers' wives	III	The work of their cottage homes and gardens

W.P. Livingstone's comment on Laws' approach to education indicates the reason for the mission's engagement in it. "The Doctor regarded the schools as his greatest evangelizing agency."[237] Again the missionaries may have seen education as one way of casting away spirit beliefs and ancestral worship practised by the Tumbuka. To achieve their goal, boarding schools were set up where primary school pupils spent most of the year away from their parents

[235] Laws to Murray, 9 August 1906, MNA L1 1/3/7; cf. W.P. Livingstone, *Laws of Livingstonia*, London: Hodder and Stoughton, 1921, p. 256.
[236] The summary of Laws' education scheme is taken from W.P. Livingstone, *ibid.*, pp. 255-256.
[237] *Ibid.*, p. 257.

and traditional influences.[238] The boarding principle extended the "settlement" motif by creating a new environment for the "pliable" young generation. In strong figurative language Chiphangwi's comment clears any doubt with regard to the aim of mission education: "the aim was to hammer the iron into the required shape while it was hot and pliable and the ultimate hope was that, when these people returned home, they would be like light in darkness."[239]

It is clear that in Central Africa the church has grown out of the Christian school. The missionaries themselves would have been the first to admit that schools, indeed, served a dual purpose, i.e., as a nursery for converts and as an institution for secular education - in that order. Herd spoke for many missionaries of his time when he said:

> When we say 'school' it must be remembered that it is a place in which the gospel is taught day by day ... and from these schools at least ninety per cent of our own converts are drawn as a direct result of the religious teaching carried on in them. School is not used in the home sense of the word at all. For five days a week, the children are taught of God and his love, and on Sunday these schools are most convenient meeting places for worship.[240]

For the young people who went through the education system, it meant a clear break from the past and entry into a new world-view. At the same time, school sharpened the self-awareness of this young generation and prepared a way for enlightened African expression in the worshipping community. However, confusion lingered in the pupils' minds. Going to school was connected with the idea of becoming a Christian. This is demonstrated in a conversation between two young boys who attended a Roman Catholic primary school:

> Then we grew less afraid and one day, when we came out of school, we said, "Let's go on till we really know", and another said, "Let's go on till we wear the cross, for by now we knew that he who wore a cross was one who really knew his teaching and then we said, let us ask the teacher to teach us the cross", and he was very glad and he taught us and at the end of the month we went to Kongwe and we were made catechumens.[241]

In the Presbyterian Livingstonia Mission, Christians did not wear the cross, but the school was a symbol of change and an effective means for proselytism. It

---

[238] *Ibid*. Livingstone shows that primary schools at Bandawe, Khondowe, and Njuyu were boarding schools. This model of boarding schools at primary school level was not peculiar to Livingstonia Mission. Blantyre Mission, the Roman Catholic and other Missions in the country established boarding primary schools in their areas of influence. In fact it is as recently as 1963 that all boarding primary schools were abandoned.

[239] Chiphangwi, "Why People Join the Christian Church".

[240] Henry D. Herd, *Missionary Record*, September 1898, p. 300.

[241] P. Mabundo, *An African David and Jonathan*, Westminster, 1926, p. 14.

would not be too much to say that education was thought to be like an exorcist against spirit beliefs. These words illustrate the point:

> To those of us who believe that education will be at least a factor in reducing this bondage of evil spirits, if only by degrees, progress in educational facilities must be of great interest.[242]

It was with the best of intentions that these words were uttered. Education was looked upon as the most effective agent for liberating the Tumbuka from ignorance. Undoubtedly it was also a sure way for undermining their spirit beliefs.

By 1890, after only nine years of work among the Tumbuka, Tonga and Ngoni, the Livingstonia Mission had over 1,300 school boys and girls against 268 full communicant members. Being schooled was prerequisite to becoming Christian. Most of these children at school would eventually become Christians in spite of their parents. This trend of missionary influence upon the young continued into the twentieth century and the absence of adults was deplored by Robert Napier: "While lads and other young people abound in the churches and classes, persons of mature age are fewer, and aged converts are very few indeed."[243] While steps were taken to bring adults into the church, the school continued to be the strongest instrument for influencing the youth who became an ever-growing force challenging the existing order, and breaking away from traditional life and spirit beliefs.

There is no doubt that missionaries were intensely engaged in education not only because they saw it as an effective weapon against spirit beliefs, but they sincerely believed that a strong church must be well educated, as Alexander Hetherwick's words indicate: "An untrained mind can attain only a very feeble grasp of the truth."[244]

Elmslie and Rain Making 1886

> A few showers fell in the November of the previous year (1885), and the people had planted their maize. It sprang up for a fortnight, and then, as the rains ceased until the 18th January, the corn was burned up and people began to be greatly excited.[245]

---

[242] Frank Debenham, *Nyasaland: The Land of the Lake*, London: Her Majesty's Stationery Office, 1955, p. 171.

[243] R. Napier, *Foreign Missions Committee Report*, Edinburgh, 1913, p. 145.

[244] Alexander Hetherwick, *Church Service Annual*, Edinburgh: T. and T. Clark, 1924, p. 44.

[245] Elmslie, *Among the Wild Ngoni*, p. 168.

The excitement of the people, with looming famine, is not to be wondered at. If the drought persisted, many would die of starvation. To the Ngoni, Tonga and Tumbuka alike, nothing happens without cause. Someone had caused the drought. He had to be found and begged to release the rains.

In times of drought, diviners and spirit mediums reckoned to possess super-natural powers were usually consulted to find out the cause of the drought and to pray and offer sacrifices for rain. Thus when the rains failed in Mbelwa's chiefdom in 1886, diviners summoned could not agree on one cause:

> The doctors were divided in their opinion as to the cause of the drought. One party made the cause out to be the strife between Mombera and Mtwalo his brother, as the spirits were highly displeased therewith. Another party said that the spirits were at war among themselves, and the rain would come when they finished. The third party said it was true that the spirits were displeased, but not on account of Mombera's quarrel with Mtwalo, but because the tribe had given no heed to the message which we had brought to them.[246]

Amidst this anxiety, missionaries were also blamed for the drought.

> We were indeed blamed, and particularly as I had erected instruments in the garden to control the weather. These (meteorological instruments) I was known to consult morning and evening and to write in a book what I was doing.[247]

In the eyes of the people "the book" meant the Bible which they regarded together with new articles the missionaries brought as instruments of divi-nation. Thus when the people's offerings to appease the spirits failed them, several men:

> talked to us [Elmslie and his colleagues] in a quiet, suspicious way, as if insinuating that we had better send rain to save ourselves ... [They came to ask] us to pray to our God to send rain, as their own methods had entirely failed.[248]

The people came to Elmslie whom they saw as an alternative power medium. He seized this opportunity to preach the Word of God and explained:

> that the people themselves believed that when the spirits caused any calamity or, as they thought, withheld rain, they knew there was a reason for it. We believed it was for something in us that God withheld his blessings, and so it was needful for us to repent; and that this feeling of the necessity of repentance and of a sacrifice proved that we were all similarly constituted, and that for us God had provided the sacrifice in the person of his Son.[249]

---

[246] *Ibid.*, p. 170.
[247] *Ibid.*, p. 169.
[248] *Ibid.*, p. 171.
[249] *Ibid.*, p. 173.

Elmslie's preaching only increased the expectations of councillors and their people converging at the mission in large numbers to press upon the missionaries to pray for rain. Not wanting to be associated with rain makers or to present the Bible as a charm, Elmslie refused to take the Bible to the royal enclosure. Instead the elders came to the church. After a Sunday service in which he had prayed for rain and the rain fell the following day, Elmslie became labelled, to his embarrassment, as one of the rain specialists:

> The incident made a profound impression upon the minds of the natives, and no doubt indirectly, if not directly, advanced our work ... It aided greatly in the furtherance of our interests, as all believed that by our prayers we could give or withhold rain, and considered that we should have accorded to us equal rights with the witch-doctors whose incantations had so signally failed.[250]

Mbelwa's people had seen before their very eyes that "diviners" from afar with a new power and teaching were in their midst. Some rain callers and medicine men went in by the back door to buy Elmslie's rain power, but the majority were persuaded to seek this power by befriending Elmslie and through church adherence and membership. Chief Mbelwa himself, who had stubbornly resisted mission work in his area, now begged the white man and his colleagues to open a school in his village and later extend to other areas in his kingdom.

Incidents similar to Elmslie's praying for rain[251] occurred in other places too. William Murray, a Dutch Reformed missionary working in the south-east of Kongwe, was approached to pray for rain.[252] Unlike Elmslie's dramatic experience, Murray held an open-air service attended by chiefs and hundreds of villagers. When the rain fell after two days, the people's beliefs were strengthened and they named the place where the gathering took place Mvera, meaning "God has listened and answered his people".

Simple though the act of praying for rain may seem, it caused a theological headache to those early missionaries surrounded by beliefs unknown to them. Their understanding was that God was the giver and controller of rain. The Tumbuka believed that God was the giver of rain, but they also believed strongly that some people endowed with magical power could stop rain from falling in an area. The missionaries, like the Tumbuka and the Ngoni, knew about the power of prayer. How then were the missionaries to reconcile the two factors? An outright rejection of the opportunity of prayer should have betrayed God's revelation in His Son Jesus Christ who is the carrier,

---

[250] *Ibid.*, pp. 176-177.
[251] "W.A. Elmslie: Letter on the Rain Question, 1886", in Kenneth R. Ross (ed.), *Christianity in Malawi: A Source Book*, Gweru: Mambo, 1996, pp. 23-29.
[252] Bridglal Pachai, *Malawi: The History of the Nation*, London: Longman, 1972, p. 76.

pneumatophoros, of the Holy Spirit and the only archetype spiritual source of the church with its believing Christian community. On the other hand, a wholesale acceptance of the diviner's role would have meant identifying with the gods of the hills, rain controllers and diviners to the detriment of the Christian faith and worship. While by no means entirely satisfied with their acts of praying for rain lest their motives were misunderstood, Elmslie's and Murray's attitudes were sufficiently open to encourage local people to accept the Christian faith in the light of their culture, and to find a way which gave to that culture "a place to feel at home" in the Christian faith.

The period between 1885 and 1886 was marked by an increased interest in the church. MacAlpine described it as "revivalistic growth":

> The most striking feature in the past half year has been a most remarkable awakening of the people around to a deepened interest in the Gospel message ... We certainly are experiencing a revivalistic growth.[253]

Was this sudden outburst of a movement towards Christianity coincidental, the result of missionary enterprise, or was it that missionaries and their message had, in the eyes of people, gained a significant place among the spirit possessed mediums and prophets of the land? We are inclined to think that the latter was true. The councillors and chiefs may have thought that they had successfully adopted the Christian faith into local beliefs. Elmslie's success in praying for the much-needed rain may have won credibility for the missionaries before paramount Mbelwa and his councillors. Mbelwa, who had been privately sympathetic to the mission for a long time, now openly showed his friendship. He protected Dr Laws when some of the militant *nduna* wanted him and the mission expelled.[254] Further, schools previously resented were now permitted to operate. In 1882 William Koyi settled at Njuyu where he opened a mission station. He engaged in teaching and preaching. Many chiefs and their councillors gave him support and even attended church services. Thus their personal attendance at church services and approval of the establishment of schools, was taken by their people as an endorsement of the missionary presence and the Christian faith. Little did the local leaders think that the cultural transformation brought by the Christian faith would push them to the periphery of their own society. Educated young people were no longer submissive. They preferred to go to church and follow the teaching of the new religion when their elders wanted them to go to war. Interpretation of the signs of the times, and decision making traditionally in the hands of the elders, were now shared with the young elite.

---

[253] A.G. MacAlpine, Livingstonia Mission Report, January to July 1895, MNA L1 1/4/8.
[254] Free Church of Scotland, *Record*, Vol. 56 (18 August 1887), NLS.

William Koyi's influence

William Koyi was born in 1846 in the Cape Province in South Africa. He belonged to one of the ruling clans of the Xhosa. Through the influence of the Wesleyan Church, Koyi became a Christian and may have attended this Church's school for his elementary education. A change of jobs gave Koyi a wider scope. He first worked as a wagon-leader, then at one of the wool-washing factories at Uitenhage, and moved on to Port Elizabeth where he worked in the stores of Messrs A.C. Stewart and Company. However, desire for higher education led him to the famous Lovedale - institution of the Free Church of Scotland. It was there that in 1876 he responded to an appeal by Dr James Stewart to go to Malawi as a missionary.[255]

In Malawi, Koyi was to be the forerunner of the Livingstonia missionaries and a torch bearer to the Ngoni, the Tonga and the Tumbuka people in the Northern region. While it is proper that Koyi's story has remained intertwined with that of missionary endeavour (for he claimed no special position for himself as an individual in God's vineyard), it would not be an exaggeration to say that without Koyi, the success of the Livingstonia missionaries in penetrating the interior would have been impossible, or at best prolonged, hard and bloody.

From the inception of Livingstonia at Cape Maclear in 1875 to its move to old Bandawe in 1881, Koyi was not only a school teacher, he was actively involved in opening up new fields:

> In 1877 he accompanied Dr Stewart on his exploratory journey along the side of Lake Nyasa. In 1878 he accompanied Dr Laws and Mr James Stewart on their journey of further exploration of the west side of the Lake.[256]

Koyi's ability to communicate in Ngoni made him 'the mouthpiece' of the missionaries. His Xhosa background,[257] similar to that of the Ngoni, enabled him to communicate with them and understand their customs and beliefs. In return, the Ngoni, though not all of them, readily accepted Koyi and understood him well as their *umteteleli* (advocate).

---

[255] Elmslie, *Among the Wild Ngoni*, p. 91.

[256] *Ibid.*, p. 191. Apart from Elmslie's chapter in his book *Among the Wild Ngoni* dedicated to William Koyi, and George H. Campbell's recent book *Lonely Warrior* (1975), no one has succeeded in putting Koyi on a pedestal in the founding of the Church in Malawi.

[257] The Xhosa are the southernmost of the Nguni peoples of South Africa. See T. Jack Thompson, "Touching the Heart: Xhosa Missionaries to Malawi 1876 - 1888", Pretoria: UNISA Press, Blantyre: CLAIM, 1999.

At other times Koyi led the exploration party himself and managed to win the friendship of the Ngoni. "Tuesday, January 10th, 1882. Today William Koyi, with Albert and Jodi as carriers of goods, started for the hills to visit Mbelwa, going first to the village of Chipatula family."[258] Koyi carried in his hands both his life and the Gospel of Jesus Christ when he took the inter-mediary role between the missionaries and the local people, for some of the Ngoni were predisposed against white men.

Later in the same year (1882) when Koyi accompanied Dr Laws to meet Mbelwa with a view to establishing a school in his area, Koyi, in spite of Mbelwa's refusal of a mission school, pleaded to be left behind to be resident evangelist among the Ngoni and the Tumbuka. Writing home about this, Laws said:

> God's ways are best. We do not give up hope and we shall try again. Koyi wants to be left, as he will have more freedom of speech were I not here, and what he says will not implicate me. In all those delicate negotiations he has been my right hand. He is doing true pioneer work of an arduous kind and his heart thoroughly in it.[259]

Koyi's presence among the Ngoni achieved peace between the Ngoni and the Tonga. However, this peace was often broken by the hostile Ngoni. His presence also eased the relationship between missionaries and the Ngoni who had turned sour against the white men whom they saw as siding with the Tonga. The Ngoni demanded exclusive alliance with the white men - a move which would benefit the Ngoni only. The missionaries chose to remain neutral.

Although Koyi was left under paramount Mbelwa's protection, his life was constantly in danger from some who would have nothing to do with the white men and their church. Several times, Koyi escaped death by a hair's breadth. For instance, he and Sutherland were locked in a hut in the dark to await death because the chief's son had died after he had been patted on the head by Mrs Laws. The missionaries were accused of having bewitched the chief's son, and now the people were to have their pound of flesh. Outside the hut they administered the *mwavi* poison, to some unfortunate chickens to prove the guilt of Sutherland and Koyi. However, when the two chickens survived the ordeal, it was taken as proof that the two men were innocent, upon which they were released. As Koyi was familiar with *mwavi* practices from his past experiences, he was able to explain to his baffled colleague the ordeal they had just gone through.

---

[258] Bandawe Journal, 10 January 1882, MNA.
[259] Laws to Smith, November 1882, MNA L1 1/3/21.

The second time Koyi almost lost his life was the great ceremony when Ngoni youths were initiated into adulthood. Koyi was in the crowd when the cry instigated by Nawambi went up:

> [Kill Koyi! Kill Koyi!] With spear in hand he [Nawambi] began by walking with raised proud look round in front of his warriors. Then kicking the dust of the ground over those around, and pointing his spear in seeming indignation, said "submit". The assembled thousands of warriors, beating their shields with war clubs, cried "submit".[260]

Koyi was saved by the paramount who appeared on the scene just in time.

The effect of Koyi's patience drew large numbers of people to hear him preach the word of God. Commending Koyi's work to the Foreign Mission Committee in Scotland, Dr Laws wrote:

> August 30th, 1882. William Koyi is doing a noble work among the Ngoni which no European could have accomplished. The people are jealous and conservative in the extreme, and by no means ready to credit disinterested motives in others. William, by living among them, has already to great extent disarmed their suspicions. He is respected by all, and I think enjoys the confidence of Mombera, the head chief.[261]

Upon his arrival at Njuyu in 1884, Dr Elmslie also saw the lasting foundation for Christ's work that Koyi had lain. Agreeing with Dr Laws, he said, "William Koyi took possession of Ngoniland for Christ". By tapping the good will of the people, Koyi produced fertile soil for the planting of the gospel among the Ngoni.

When Elmslie arrived to take charge of the mission, he found Koyi and Sutherland with groups of Ngoni, Tonga and Tumbuka young men who frequented the mission by night to be taught and to pray. They came by night because the Ngoni protested:

> If we give you children to teach, your words will steal their hearts; they will grow up cowards, and refuse to fight for us when we are old; and knowing more than we do, they will despise us.[262]

One of the rebellious youths who attended the night classes, Mawelera Tembo, a diviner's son, approached Koyi with the view of "speaking to God" as he had seen his mentor do on many occasions. Although Koyi did not live to see the maturation of his labour, Mawelera was eventually baptized in 1890, becoming

---

[260] Elmslie, *Among the Wild Ngoni*, p. 198.
[261] Laws, *Foreign Missions Committee Report*, December, 1882; also Elmslie, *Among the Wild Ngoni*, p. 104.
[262] Elmslie, *ibid.*, p. 128.

the first Christian among the Ngoni.[263] Before long others joined, including his brother Makera, and a servant of the Tembo family, Mavuvu Tweya. Tembo, their father, did not seem to resent his children's apostasy. The question is, was Tembo really contented to see his sons join a new religion, or was he giving them an opening to what may have seemed to him an opportunity for untested divine energies? Could Koyi's trust in "the Book" have had a secret influence on Tembo's own life? Or could Elmslie's success with the rain and his western medical practice have attracted Tembo to wish Elmslie's "divine power" for his children? Tembo belonged to an open religion of the spirits able to accommodate new beliefs and practices. And undoubtedly he saw power in this new religion of the Book and chose his sons to tread in the path. However, if the reasons for the three boys' conversion were merely external and temporary, their Christian life would have been short-lived and without fruit. But Makera became a successful school teacher and elder of the Kirk; Mawelera became one of the most influential evangelists for forty years[264] while Tweya became the first of the ordained ministers from Ngoniland and served faithfully until his death in 1931.

That Tembo, the father, was *nganga* whose practices may have involved spirit possession as was usual with such people, did not create a gulf between Koyi and the Tembo family, and because Koyi did not condemn Tembo's old ways, Tembo could not fail to be drawn into the atmosphere of faith which was apparent in his sons, and the teachers of the new way.

Just before his death on 4th June 1886, Koyi, together with Elmslie, was directly involved in the question of praying for rain. His words to those present illustrate well how Koyi took the Gospel to fulfil in a new way the beliefs of the people:

> You believe the rain had been withheld because the spirits are not pleased about something and they need sacrifice. We too believe that the rain has been withheld by the Great Spirit who is not pleased with our sinful ways and who asks us to change our ways and accept the sacrifice which has already been made, that is, the sacrifice of Jesus Christ His son.[265]

Koyi's words, said out of his Christian conviction about the power of God to give rain, confirmed and expanded the Tumbuka belief in praying for rain. Further, when the rain did actually come, it was evident to the people that an

---

[263] Ekwendeni Minute Book, 1885-1890, MNA L1 1/3/12.

[264] Livingstonia Mission Minute Book, 1884-1895, MNA L1 1/3/14. A selection of his hymns can be found in *Christianity in Malawi: A Source Book*, Gweru: Mambo, 1996, pp. 50, 61 and 64.

[265] Elmslie, *Among the Wild Ngoni*, p. 172.

alternative view had emerged and life would never be the same. Being Black and distinguished in his Western clothes and education, Koyi was an accepted *umteteleli* advocate of his people and a living example of a clear break between the old world-view and the new.

Elliot K. Kamwana's campaign 1908-1909

A new type of African response to Mission contact was initiated by Elliot Kenan Kamwana.[266] When Kamwana, a protégé of Dr Laws, was refused admission to the church in 1901 because there were too many applicants for baptism, he went to the Shire Highlands where he came in contact with Joseph Booth at Thyolo.[267] At Plainfield Seventh Day Adventist Mission, he was baptized by Thomas Branch.[268] Though Kamwana was employed as a school teacher, his ambition was to be a preacher.

In 1903 or 1904 Kamwana moved on to South Africa where he worked as a hospital assistant in the Main Reef Mine, Johannesburg. During his spare time he organized prayer meetings and preached regularly. It was while Kamwana was in Johannesburg that he came in touch with the Watch Tower, again through Joseph Booth, and went to Cape Town to be instructed by him in Watchtower and Sabbath doctrine. With the support of Booth, he went back to Malawi to start the Watch Tower Society[269]

While still in South Africa, Kamwana's way of thinking had been further moulded by Ethiopianism - a movement whose slogan was 'Africa for the Africans'.[270]

Ethiopianism insisted that Ethiopia had the oldest church which was an ideal church for all Africa. The fact that Ethiopia was free from White domination was a novelty which added interest to the movement. Kamwana's experience in

---

[266] For his life story see J.C. Chakanza, *Voices of Preachers in Protest: The Ministry of Two Malawian Prophets: Elliot Kamwana and Wilfred Gudu*, Blantyre: CLAIM, 1998, pp. 12-54.

[267] Shepperson and Price, *Independent African*, pp. 153-154. For a somewhat different interpretation of this event and also for his stay in Cape Town see: Langworthy, *The Life of Joseph Booth, 201ff.*

[268] For this and for more about Kamwana's association with Joseph Booth see Harry Langworthy, 'Africa for the African'. The Life of Joseph Booth, Blantyre: CLAIM, 1996

[269] McCracken, *Politics and Christianity*, p. 189.

[270] B.G.M. Sundkler, *Bantu Prophets in South Africa*, 2nd ed., London: Oxford University Press, 1969, p. 216. A major exponent of this movement for Malawi was Joseph Booth, who published his ideas in: Joseph Booth, *Africa for the African*, Baltimore: Morgan College Press, 1897, reprinted as: (ed. Laura Perry), CLAIM: Blantyre, 1998.

South Africa exposed him to the realities of colonial power. The ugly side of the colonial system which Kamwana observed was the exploitation of African labour by whites.[271] This influenced his belief in the millennial solutions where the present African grievances of 'little wages, no liberty or franchise, overtax, injustice, no pension or allowance for children, wives or parents of the dead in the war'[272] would be corrected.

When Kamwana returned to Malawi in 1908 he started proselytizing in the West Nyasa District and within one year of its inception, the Watch Tower movement claimed 10,000 members.[273] Kamwana was a powerful preacher. His theme, the coming again of Jesus Christ in 1914 when Africans would be free of Whites,[274] sparked off a new mass religious movement.

Counter to the missionary church's three year apprenticeship, demand for literacy before baptism, and payment of school fees, conversion in the Watch Tower was instantaneous and immediately followed by baptism by total immersion; members of the movement were encouraged to take part in the propagation of the Watch Tower message and in running church affairs.[275]

How far Kamwana and his Watch Tower Movement drew upon traditional religious beliefs is not clear. Though Kamwana certainly never claimed to have possessed supernatural powers, he enjoyed the growth of his movement. It is tempting to suggest that Kamwana's followers may have ranked him high above the traditional priests and spirit mediums. This is indicated by the massive response to Kamwana's call for renewal through baptism: "Within six months of my work here, over five thousand people - men and women - have

---

[271] Joseph Booth expressed it in this way: "The closing decade of the nineteenth century witnesses the second magnificently unscrupulous proposal of the European to harness and exploit his African neighbour. The former clumsy proposal to annex and transplant the African's person was costly, cumbersome and infamous; the present proposal to purloin the land under his feet and adroitly to utilize the African as an instrument to disclose, develop and deposit its resources for the European's benefit, is the self-same in spirit, but more ingeniously dressed, further reaching in its effects, and far less likely to be challenged (Joseph Booth, *Africa for the African,* Baltimore: Morgan College Press, [2]1897, reprinted (ed. Laura Perry) by CLAIM: Blantyre, 1998.

[272] Kamwana's evidence on Chilembwe's rising, Kamwana's letters, 1915, Malawi Collection, University of Malawi.

[273] Kamwana to Russell, Kamwana's letters, 1909, Malawi Collection, University of Malawi.

[274] Livingstonia Presbytery Minutes 1908-1918, MNA L1 1/3/16; also Ian Linden, *Catholics, Peasants and Chewa Resistance in Nyasaland 1889-1939*, London: Longman, 1974, p. 77.

[275] Pachai, *Malawi: The Story of Domingo to Booth,* 10 April 1911, Domingo papers, Malawi Collection, University of Malawi.

been baptized and accepted to full church membership."[276] This indiscriminate baptism had traits similar to those of traditional religion which was inclusive. However, Kamwana's baptisms were revolutionary, rejecting the past and going beyond what the mission church was able to offer. These baptisms provided solace for the anxious, the message preached about a spiritual Kingdom satisfied the perplexed, and the community-oriented approach to the church gave hope and an answer to the apocalyptic climate of the time. Unconscious of it himself, Kamwana was an Africanizer who drew his teaching and preaching methods from the past. He borrowed Christian symbols to understand, live, and interpret the present and give hope for the future. While still able to reach the past, complete return to that past and its possession practices seemed unnecessary and undesirable. For Kamwana, the future lay in the merging of the old and the new.

As Kamwana's followers were largely drawn from the illiterates and from excommunicated members of the Livingstonia mission, the Watch Tower's life as a thriving alternative church was short-lived. Deprived of Kamwana's charismatic and dynamic leadership after his deportation to Chinde in 1909 and eventually to Mauritius,[277] the Watch Tower fervour subsided. However, Kamwana's impact on the missionary church and on the local people's religious affiliation was significant.

First, Livingstonia Mission was never again to be the only evangelizing church in northern Malawi, and its authority would not go unchallenged. Second, as a religious innovator, Kamwana had demonstrated, beyond any doubt, a possible religious independence hitherto unknown among the first generation Christians. Thus he began a new era in the religious sphere and brought to the surface African initiative. Kamwana regarded his own educated countrymen, such as Domingo, as being too prone to copy the white missionaries' ways and their emphasis on education. John Chilembwe was too politically-minded for Kamwana's other-worldly theology - though the two men were close friends. The Watch Tower Movement was well known among Malawians in the main line churches, but its stigma was that it was made in Malawi. In those early stages, white missionaries were regarded as good spirits who came to dwell physically among the people of the land. By not providing or promising any benefits found in the missionary church, such as work, education and material gains, the Watch Tower was unattractive as an agent for social change. The Watch Tower's label, given by the colonial government, of a

---

[276] Kamwana to Russell, Kamwana's Letters 1909, Malawi Collection, University of Malawi. See also Chakanza, *Voices of Preachers in Protest*, p. 21
[277] Chakanza, *Voices of Preachers in Protest*, p. 26

subversive organization, demoralized what able leadership was left in it, and its own lack of interest in education and politics was unpalatable to most Livingstonia graduates and ambitious young men.

Domingo's response

Charles Domingo was brought to northern Malawi as a small boy by William Koyi in 1881. Domingo came from Quelimane in Mozambique where his father worked as a cook for the African Lakes Company.[278]

Educated at Bandawe, Lovedale and Overtoun Institute, Domingo proved his intellectual capacity and ability and later played an important role in the religious life in the northern province. His integrity and influence as an able teacher won him favour as he became one of the first two theological graduates of Livingstonia Mission in 1900, though Domingo and Muwamba were never ordained.[279] For missionaries, the time was not yet ripe to ordain local people into the ministry even if educated. Fear of their relapsing to "heathenism" may have been one of the reason for the eight years' probation inflicted on Domingo, and, had he not died soon after completion of his course, would also have been imposed on Muwamba.[280] We are also tempted to suggest that missionaries, at that stage, were not decided in what position a local ordained pastor would stand in relation to his ordained missionary colleague.

Domingo could not wait indefinitely for an ordination whose date he never knew. Consequently he left Livingstonia Mission in 1908 and went south and joined the National Baptists of Providence Industrial Mission, where John Chilembwe baptized him.[281] Significant for Domingo's secession was the time at which he did it. Elliot Kamwana, who was bitterly opposed to Livingstonia Mission's slow pace of admitting people to full church membership and giving them responsible positions, returned to Malawi from South Africa in the same year, 1908. It is highly likely that Kamwana strengthened Domingo's decision to quit the mission church.

Equally important to Domingo's move at this time was John Chilembwe's church in Chiradzulu district, the Providence Industrial Mission associated with the (Black American) National Baptist Convention, Inc., whose missionary John Chilembwe was. His association with Chilembwe did not last very long, as Domingo took up missionary work in Chinde at the mouth of the Zambezi.[282]

---

[278] W.P. Livingstone, *Laws of Livingstonia*, pp. 194-195.
[279] Livingstonia Mission Council Minutes, 1900-1912, MNA L1 1/3/12.
[280] Ibid.
[281] Langworthy, *The Life of Joseph Booth*, p. 225.
[282] *Ibid.*

Through John Chilembwe, Domingo established contact with Joseph Booth in Cape Town, from whom he learnt both Watch Tower and Seventh Day Baptist doctrine, and with Booth he ultimately chose the Seventh Day Baptist Church,[283] and became its leader in the north.[284] Chilembwe and Kamwana were to Domingo a living demonstration of African initiative.

If these three men, Chilembwe, Kamwana and Domingo, were agreed on Africanization of churches, they were not agreed on what was to be done to achieve that goal. This was reflected in the churches they headed. Kamwana's apocalyptic and other-worldly theology was far removed from Chilembwe's free New Zion flavoured with nationalism.[285] If Kamwana's Watch Tower was a pointer to a spiritual era, Domingo's Seventh Day Baptists preached a secular kingdom based on intellectual and material advancement. The three men were not interested in spirit possession because they were preoccupied with the present, the Western intruders and the changes wrought in the local society.

Domingo's followers, like Kamwana's converts, were drawn from the marginal members of the community, and their participation in the church was limited by lack of education.[286] Church expansion methods did not draw anything from African religious experience. Domingo's upbringing, influenced by missionaries, may have blinded him to the value of anything African. He was typical of most educated people of his time in this. For him, possession was an element of backwardness which needed to be ironed out through proper western education. Domingo and his educated kind were a carbon copy of their mentors and as such the question about spirit possession in their churches did not arise.

Far from being uncritical of the west, Domingo was ready to point out the weakness of Livingstonia missionaries, business men and colonial government. He criticized them for their exploitation of Africans, their condescending attitude and failure to lead Christian-like lives.[287] Nevertheless, Domingo's full sympathy was with the missionaries and the Gospel they carried. He saw the future of Malawi in the adoption of western life style, the Christian faith and its

---

[283] *Ibid.*, p. 227-230.

[284] For Domingo's correspondence with Booth see: Charles Domingo, *Letters of Charles Domingo*, Harry Langworthy (ed.), University of Malawi, Sources for the Study of Religion in Malawi No. 9, 1983.

[285] Ian and Jane Linden, "John Chilembwe and the New Jerusalem", *Journal of African History*, Vol. 12/4 (1971), p. 21.

[286] George Shepperson, "The Politics of African Church Separatist Movements 1892-1916", *Africa*, Vol. 24 (1954), p. 240.

[287] Domingo to Booth, 20 September 1911, Domingo Papers, Malawi Collection, University of Malawi.

education system as introduced by Livingstonia Mission, and not in going back to former spirit beliefs. If by adopting the Christian faith Domingo legitimized Christianity among the Tumbuka, by his walking out from the missionary church he opened wide the gate in defiance of the church's limitative prohibitions.

In 1908 Charles Chinula, then a teacher, encouraged his students to hold African dances in a place unknown to missionaries.[288] Early in 1902 Domingo himself had delivered a paper at a conference in Blantyre supporting and praising some dances.[289] Now, after 1910, cases of Tumbuka Christian converts involved in Vimbuza possession dances began to appear in Kirk sessions.

The first case concerning traditional dances was that of Jane Nkata at Ekwendeni Kirk Session under Elmslie's moderatorship.[290] Jane was suspended for one year because she had been found dancing Virombo. The discussion that went on, and how the Kirk Session arrived at the one year verdict, are not given. However, it is clear that one of the local church elders in the Village brought the case to the notice of the Kirk Session. Most of the Tumbuka church elders were ready to condemn and denounce all traditional dances and ceremonies. This was not helped by the negative attitude with which some missionaries viewed African culture:

> In connection with this instruction there were special dances accompanied by a large amount of vice, performed amid drunken revelry. Both the ceremonies and dances connected with them were of mysterious nature. They were never thrust on the notice of the white man. In fact, they have seldom or never been witnessed by Europeans.[291]

A similar opinion was expressed by McMinn:

> They amused themselves chiefly by dancing - they danced often, danced all night. There were dances in great variety. But to an outsider they seemed much alike in that they were mostly somewhat wanting in decency, connected with the grossest sin, and accompanied by the exasperating di di di of a wooden drum which was an absolute necessity to village life and happiness.[292]

The insistence of the church on "no dancing" for Christian converts in the 1890s and early 1900s sent all cults underground. Dances formerly held during

---

[288] Life of Rev. Charles Chinula, n.d., MNA L1 1/3/18.

[289] LWBCA, 12 October 1901, p. 4. See also Ross (ed), *Christianity in Malawi*, p. 93.

[290] Ekwendeni Minutes Book, 1892-1912, MNA L1 1/3/12.

[291] Jack, *Daybreak in Livingstonia*, pp. 81, 312.

[292] R.D. McMinn, "Some Tumbuka Dances", *The Aurora*, Vol. 4/24 (1 December 1900), pp. 2-13

the day, or at night in full moonlight, were latterly conducted strictly at night.[293] This was also true of spirit possession practices as happened with the Nyau dance among the Chewa in the Central region. With the confidence engendered by rebel African Church leaders, the common Christians filled their religious gaps untouched by Christian faith by stretching back to the old religion through involvement in possession ceremonies.

The missionary church, formerly not interested in heathen practices such as possession but in what Dr Laws summed up as "the extension of Christ's cause and Kingdom",[294] could no longer ignore the issue after 1910. Missionaries met regularly, among themselves, to discuss their work and evaluate their method of approach to the local people. In one such meeting, Laws called his fellow missionaries to "be in close contact with them; to enable us [the missionaries] to understand their actions, ways of looking at things, prejudices, faults, their sins, cause of action and principles of action".[295] The tenor of Laws' address encouraged his colleagues to find what aspect of the Gospel would be most suited to the condition of the Tumbuka and their neighbours. The lack of pointed attack on spirit possession practices by the missionaries may have been due to what they saw from the beginning as a "multitude of evils standing like grim barriers before the missionaries ... and requiring to be overthrown".[296] Further, that people such as Domingo trained by missionaries remained orthodox even outside the missionary church, gave hope to the missionaries' efforts. On the other hand the confidence missionaries had in themselves had been shaken by Domingo's protest and they had to moderate their handling of local leaders and their attitude towards local customs and beliefs.

Domingo's response marked the end of a period of servitude when white leadership in the church would no longer be taken for granted. Indigenization or participatory leadership in the Church and a new perception of it had come. In future, African participation in the leadership of the church was to bring in new understanding. However, for leaders such as Domingo, the old world-view had been replaced by the new.

---

[293] Personal interview with Rev. S. Kauta, Mzokoto village, Rumphi, 14 February 1983. Today the Livingstonia Synod is calling people for a celebrating dance, dancing to celebrate the presence of Jesus Christ and his power over spirits which torment people.

[294] Sermons preached by Dr Robert Laws, 1 January 1883, MNA L1 1/4/11.

[295] Dr Laws' Addresses, n.d., MNA L1 1/4/11.

[296] Jack, *Daybreak in Livingstonia*, p. 251.

Fraser's conventions 1896-1910

Donald Fraser, a son of a minister in Glasgow, had already proved his worth when he was appointed a missionary to northern Malawi in 1896. While he was a student at Glasgow University, Fraser was actively involved in the Student Volunteer Missionary Movement, and his gift of public speaking gave him fame among the evangelicals.[297] Associated with the Keswick Convention,[298] Fraser participated in a number of missionary conferences in Europe and at home.[299] At Liverpool he demonstrated his competence as chairman.[300] Soon after, he left for Africa.[301]

---

[297] A. Fraser, *Donald Fraser*, pp. 12-24. By the qualifying adjective "evangelical", both Donald and Agnes Fraser would have agreed with Peter Toon that it is a tribute to one who holds true the theology contained in both the Old and New Testaments. Toon asserts that evangelical theology takes the Bible as the rule of faith. He says that evangelical theology is also the theology newly discovered and accepted by the Reformation of the 16th century. However, evangelical, according to Toon, refers primarily and decisively to the Bible. Peter Toon, *Evangelical Theology 1833-1856: A Response to Tractarianism*, London: Marshall, Morgan and Scott, 1979, pp. 114-116.

[298] The Keswick Convention was started by Canon Hardford-Battersby, vicar of Keswick, in 1875, succeeding the Brighton 1874 and Oxford 1875 Holiness Conventions with Hannah Withall Smith and Robert Pearsall Smith as the leading speakers. Keswick was an interdenominational convention with strong Anglican participation. The Theological emphasis of the Keswick Convention was on personal commitment to Christ, practical holiness and power for service. This was promoted by talks, prayer meetings, discussion and personal intercourse. Its members took a deep interest in foreign mission. J.C. Pollock, *The Keswick Story: The Authorized History of the Keswick Convention*, London: Hodder and Stoughton, 1964, pp. 74-75.

[299] A. Fraser, *Donald Fraser*, pp. 22-30.

[300] The Liverpool conference held in 1896 brought together eight hundred students of different nationalities from Asia, Africa, Europe and America. It was one of the largest international student missionary conferences organized by the World Student Christian Federation. The theme of the conference was: Make Jesus King. Among many topics discussed at the conference the involvement of students in missionary work was prominent. The results was that The Student Volunteer Missionary Union, formed not long before 1896, adopted the watchword "The evangelization of the world in this generation", as some church organizations had already done. From the generation of the students at the conference emerged outstanding church leaders and missionaries. Fraser, who had just retired as the movement's general secretary was the engineer and chairman of "Liverpool 1896". His impression upon the conference is described by Agnes de Sélincourt, an executive member at the conference, who later became Fraser's wife: "At this enthusiastic meeting a short speech from the chairman marked what some have described as one of the outstanding moments of the conference ... he described the place prayer had played in bringing the existing Movement into being, told how continual prayer had been made that it might spread to the Continental, reminded them of their mighty responsibility, and ended with an

Theologically, Fraser represented that evangelical section which rejected the conservative view of the Bible in which Scripture must interpret Scripture. Although his belief was based on the Bible, he did not take it literally. For Fraser, being a Christian did not mean following a set of rules or avoiding a series of prohibitions.[302] Instead he saw the Christian faith as providing freedom and dignity to every human being. This broad theological outlook later enabled Fraser to emphasize the need for the Church to identify as much as possible with the African environment and religious beliefs. Thus, Fraser wrote: "When we think of Christ the King, and the realm over which we would make Him King, we cannot isolate the souls of Africa from the soil of Africa nor from its social structures."[303] With this attitude, Fraser was to encourage Tumbuka - Ngoni music in church services.[304]

Before proceeding to Malawi, Fraser travelled for three months to schools and colleges in South Africa speaking on behalf of a missionary enterprise.[305] He held testimony meetings at which students were so moved that many confessed their sins. Thus Fraser's eloquence and power of preaching were made evident. Writing to Smith about his brief involvement with South African students, Fraser had this to say:

> At the close of my address, many a head was bending on the desks in great distress. I asked all who were anxious to follow me to the wood and talk it over. Very many came and for an hour they asked questions, candidly stating difficulties. Then we had prayer, but sometimes the prayer was almost drowned by the sobs of the anxious.[306]

Fraser had been appointed by the Mission Council to relieve Dr Elmslie at Ekwendeni whose furlough was due. The two men had met five years before in Britain, and Elmslie had left a lasting impression on the young student, Fraser. Now they were to be colleagues for many years that followed.[307]

Fraser's work was marked by a theological emphasis which stirred Livingstonia Mission into a new wave of spirituality flavoured by emotionalism. He held mass open air meetings where confession of sins was made publicly,

---

impassioned appeal to them to join hands in making a worldwide Christian brotherhood to make Jesus Christ King." *Ibid.*, p. 34.

[301] For a recent study of Fraser see: T. Jack Thompson, *Christianity in Northern Malawi. Donald Fraser's Missionary Methods and Ngoni Culture*, Leiden: Brill, 1995.

[302] Agnes Fraser, *Donald Fraser*, p. 16.

[303] *Ibid.*, p. 167.

[304] *Ibid.*, p. 169.

[305] D. Fraser, *Winning a Primitive People*, p. 38.

[306] Donald Fraser to Smith, 19 August 1896, MNA 4/7879.

[307] D. Fraser, *Winning a Primitive People*, p. 21.

providing a therapy to cleanse Tumbuka communities from witchcraft and other causes of misfortune.[308] In May 1898 a five day small Keswick convention attended by more three thousand people was held at Ekwendeni and "testimony after testimony of blessing received was given". Some people were hysterical and others were lifted into transcendental experience as Fraser later related:

> One morning two of the leading teachers came to me to relate strange experiences they were having. They had been out in the bush at night praying. They felt as if bodies had been lifted up from the earth, and bright angelic forms had come down to meet them, and they asked me to explain what these visions meant.[309]

Concerned about some of those heightened visionary experiences, Fraser resorted to pills from the dispensary to tranquilize his members.[310]

Nonetheless, Fraser's success in striking a deep note of response in his hearers created an atmosphere of mutual understanding in spiritual matters between missionaries and local people. In addition, Fraser's evangelical conventions and their emotionalism did much to awaken the religious consciousness of the Tumbuka-Ngoni and prepared them for full participation in the church's life in subsequent years. For the Tumbuka, Fraser's method and approach to the Gospel met with welcoming approval as it fulfilled, though partially, local thought forms and the pattern of spirit beliefs. What we mean here is that when the Tumbuka heard Fraser preach about the sacrificial death of Jesus Christ, his resurrection and his promise always to be with those who believe in him, they associated it with their beliefs in the continuous existence and influence of the "living dead". What was new in Fraser's teaching was Jesus Christ. First, the Cross symbol of Christ challenged the people's sense of power and justice. The power of Christ, Fraser taught, was to be expressed in love and willingness to suffer for the sake of others.[311] Forgiveness was to replace the Old Testament law of tit for tat[312] or the law of the jungle, "the survival of the fittest". Second, Fraser's teaching about Jesus Christ was that he was the final mediator and redeemer. For Fraser as a Christian, Christ's finality may have meant that God's intentions in soteriology are accomplished in Jesus Christ who brings about the eschaton. Therefore he was directing people to God through Jesus Christ. These new religious ideas together with the old ones

---

[308] *Ibid.*, p. 22.
[309] *Ibid.*, p. 89.
[310] *Ibid.*, pp. 205-207.
[311] 1 John 2:15.
[312] Exodus 20:1ff.

Fraser had confirmed, may have been palatable to the Tumbuka. Hence the overwhelming positive response, the zenith of which was in 1910 when Dr Charles Inwood visited Malawi as a guest speaker.

Inwood's Evangelistic Campaign 1910

An English Methodist minister and Deputy Secretary of the Keswick Convention, the Rev. Charles Inwood was world famous as an evangelical preacher in the 1900s. He had been a speaker at numerous evangelistic meetings not only in Britain but in various countries, including Australia, Canada, China, Germany, France, India, New Zealand and South Africa.[313] In 1909, Livingstonia Mission Council requested, through the Keswick Council, that Inwood go to Malawi to conduct a series of evangelistic meetings.[314] Inwood's favourite theme was "God's Holiness" and his preaching on previous occasions had emphasized Pentecostal experience, i.e. being "filled by the Spirit", as did the early church. Inwood took up this point again in Central Africa.[315]

When he arrived in Malawi, Inwood spent two weeks at Blantyre mission before proceeding to the Northern region. The first week he allotted to Europeans and the second week to Africans.[316] Every day Inwood first met with the mission staff (fifteen in number) for a quiet time, prayer and reflection. These meetings knitted the missionaries together:

> From the very first, these "Quiet Hours" were marked in a special degree as seasons of grace and power. Each missionary came with a hungry and receptive spirit, and the Lord met us every day. I was conscious of His presence and help in each message, and that consciousness grew tender day and day.[317]

Evening meetings with the general European community were not as successful as the ones with missionaries. In spite of a large European population in Blantyre at the time, few attended:

> The night meetings were a sharp test. Of course, all the missionaries were with us, and their eagerness for blessing was a continual cheer. But the other Europeans, many of them nominal Church members, left us severely alone. I don't think more than half a dozen came near us; their indifference to religion is

---

[313] M.A. Hay, *Charles Inwood: His Ministry and his Secret*, London: Marshall, Morgan and Scott, 1929, p. 157.

[314] Livingstonia Mission Council Minutes, 9 September 1909, MNA L1 1/3/17; also Inwood, *An African Pentecost*, Edinburgh and London: Longman, 1962, p. 70.

[315] Hay, *Charles Inwood*, pp. 44, 134-138.

[316] Inwood, *An African Pentecost*, p. 17.

[317] *Ibid.*, pp. 17-18.

> the hardest thing to bear out here. The average Sunday morning European congregation is not more than thirty, and this includes missionaries and their families.[318]

Inwood's presence and meetings left little impression on the white settlers. This may have been because the whites saw Christianity as a civilizing agent which they were not in need of. Further, they may have been indifferent to religion because of the secularization process Europe was going through during that period. But Inwood seems to have wanted his race to have set a good example to the "heathens" around. He was disappointed, but would not refer to them as pagans as he readily did to the Africans who crowded in churches to hear him.

In his second week, Inwood turned to the local people. All the meetings he conducted were crowded with people eager to learn about the new faith:

> At these meetings we must have had fully 300 present daily, and at the night meetings the large church was crowded - never less than 700. In all these services one was speaking to hungry souls, and the power which rested upon these gatherings was truly wonderful. Many a conscience was searched, many a heart cleansed, and, many for the first time were set on fire with a passion for souls. Without any suggestion from the missionaries these dear souls arranged for a daily united prayer-meeting amongst themselves; indeed, many of them entered upon a new prayer life.[319]

The receptiveness of Africans in Blantyre and Zomba to the Gospel during Inwood's conventions was to be repeated in the northern region.

Well before Inwood arrived in Malawi, especially in the northern region, Donald Fraser had been preparing the Tumbuka and their Ngoni neighbours, raising their expectations on spiritual matters:

> For months before he [Inwood] came we did our best to rouse the expectations of the people, and spoke much on the great good that might come to them were they athirst for truth, and obedient.[320]

Inwood's first meeting was held at Loudon on 17 August 1910.[321] The meeting was attended by over 2500 people during the week and by over 7000 on the closing Sunday.[322]

---

[318] *Ibid.*, p. 18.

[319] *Ibid.*, pp. 18-19.

[320] *United Free Church of Scotland Mission Report*, 1910, p. 544.

[321] For a detailed report on the convention, taken from D. Fraser, *Winning a Primitive People*, pp. 282-286, see Kenneth R. Ross (ed.), *Christianity in Malawi. A Source Book*, Gweru: Mambo, 1996, pp. 30-33.

[322] Inwood, *An African Pentecost*, p. 46.

A day's programme consisted of: morning prayer meeting, and two addresses - one in the morning and one in the afternoon - by Inwood, interpreted by Fraser.[323] Not much seemed to happen until Saturday when, after preaching for one hour about the Holy Spirit, Inwood asked for "a time of silent prayer":

> Suddenly there came the sound of a 'rushing mighty wind'. It was the thrilling sound of two thousand five hundred people praying audibly, no man apparently conscious of no better image to describe the noise than the rushing of wind through the trees.[324]

Inwood described the same scene in some detail:

> Slowly one after another rose, and some sad confessions of sin were made. Then two prayed together, then three, then suddenly, as if a Divine breath passed over us, everyone began to pray. The sound rose like a murmur of the sea, deep, solemn, sacred, beyond description. I buried my face in my hands, and, with joy unspeakable, adored and praised the Lord.[325]

Missionaries present at these meetings were ambivalent about the religious experience and response of the people. First, when nothing seemed to be gripping the meeting in the week, they were not sure if Inwood's campaign would make any significant impression. Second, when the whole assembly was immersed in and by the Spirit, Europeans accepted it as an authentic religious experience. Yet they were, at the same time, uneasy about the emotionalism displayed. Even Donald Fraser, who seemed enthusiastic about the event and subsequent meetings, was not too sure about the strong response and was opposed to "unwholesome physical excitement".[326]

At subsequent meetings, Fraser, the leading figure in the campaign, instructed his evangelists "to discourage any physical manifestations". However, basically, Fraser was favourable to the evangelistic gatherings which included an emotional element. In reflecting on Inwood's campaigns and the people's responses, Fraser was more favourable than otherwise:

> 'What an emotional story' some will say. But why would we be so suspicious of the free expression of deep feeling? We do not want to superimpose on those sons of Africa our expressionless Scottish character.[327]

Fraser had colleagues such as Young, Kirkwood and Henderson who supported him. He also knew that other missionaries such as Laws and Elmslie did

---

[323] Hay, *Charles Inwood*, p. 172.
[324] D. Fraser, *Winning a Primitive People*, p. 283.
[325] Inwood, *An African Pentecost*, p. 44.
[326] D. Fraser, *Winning a Primitive People*, pp. 283, 285.
[327] *Ibid.*, p. 287.

not share his views or appreciate Inwood's campaign, especially its emotional tendencies.[328]

After Loudon, Charles Inwood and Donald Fraser held two days' conventions at most main mission stations, including Chinde, Ekwendeni, Bandawe and Khondowe. In all these places, people were blessed with the gifts of the Spirit. At Khondowe some people were so hysterical that they had to be carried out of the church. Shutting out any accusation that Inwood intentionally stirred people's emotions, Fraser wrote:

> The addresses were given in English, and sentence by sentence I interpreted into Tumbuka language. Friends who had heard of our purpose, wrote to me greatly doubting the possibility of making any impression on our people by interpretation. But while one recognizes that this method of address has great disadvantages, the history of religious movements gives many an instance where it has been supremely effective. One great advantage attends it. You cannot get a purely physical emotion by interpretation, the constant interruption of the address arrests the emotional spell which the speaker might cast upon his audience.[329]

Inwood and Fraser were convinced that the people's response was from deep conviction impressed upon them by the Word preached to them. It may also have been that the people were encouraged to respond as they did from their spirit belief background - in this case, spirit possession. At every place Inwood preached, his close touch with his audience enabled him to reach deep down to the people's hearts and feelings. In the traditional setting, spirit possession accompanied by dancing and witch eradication ceremonies provided a religious ritual, community renewal and wholeness, but this had been stifled. Now this direct emotional approach, appeal for confession of sins, assurance and promise of forgiveness, Inwood's message and his method of communication, encouraged the people to find answers to their problems, and fulfilment and release in the new religion. I agree with Jack Thompson's conclusion that:

> Opportunities for spiritual cleansing and community renewal, traditionally found in witchcraft movements, were by 1910, limited ... The Livingstonia appeal was almost always to the individual, and while strictly speaking, Inwood's theological approach was similar, in practice its emotional and immediate nature gave opportunity for what amounted to a communal response. While he may have not been aware of the fact, his own concern with personal holiness became for his listeners a unique opportunity for community wholeness.[330]

---

[328] McCracken, *Politics and Christianity*, p. 121.

[329] D. Fraser, *Winning a Primitive People*, pp. 281-282.

[330] T. Jack Thompson, *Christianity in Northern Malawi: Donald Fraser's Missionary Methods and Ngoni Culture*, Leiden: E.J. Brill, 1995, p. 145.

Thompson asserts that the local people were not passive recipients, but with their theological background founded on the power derived from ancestral spirits, they were actively involved in adopting and translating the Gospel message into their own experience.

The authenticity of the people's emotional response in Inwood's campaign stemming from Christian religious conviction as they understood it, was doubted by many missionaries. Even Donald Fraser, who was keen to see that the congregation did not go away "empty handed", was uncertain about the abundance of Spirit experience by the people: "but Fraser was already down among them, passing from one to the other, laying a calming hand upon them and getting them to sit down quietly". Later he had a talk about it with the church leaders, and pressed on them that outward expression of the Spirit be minimized.[331] This raises the question - could it have been that the missionaries suspected that people already saturated with spirit beliefs found Inwood's message and method related to their spirit beliefs and practices? Could they have considered the people's response totally new and unnatural? Or did they just not like emotion? The missionary opinion was divided on this point. Old missionaries such as Robert Laws and Walter Elmslie favoured a conscientious spiritual steady growth guided by knowledgeable teaching, while people like James Jack regarded the people's responses as influenced by spirit beliefs and practices undesirable in the Christian faith; Fraser and others accepted it when it could be controlled.

As far as it went, Inwood's preaching about the need to be filled with the Holy Spirit was clear. The Spirit preached was that which emanated from God the Father, and from Jesus Christ who was born, lived, and died a sacrificial death and was resurrected, and is alive in his glorified nature. It was natural for the Tumbuka to accommodate such a teaching, as they strongly believed in a spiritual world-view; the spiritual world was constantly interacting with the physical, and therefore Jesus was seen by the people as fulfilling the mediatory role played by ancestral spirits.

When Inwood asked those who wanted to receive the Holy Spirit to stand up, at first there was confusion as what was meant. But once understood in their own terms, i.e. being possessed by an all powerful Spirit, almost the whole congregation of 7000 stood up.

Charles Inwood sums up the response in the following words:

> Pentecost had come. Then the deep emotion overpowered some of the women. They sprang to their feet, weeping, praying, and waving their hands. Then a number rose and ran towards the door, and Mr Fraser feared a panic. We learned

---

[331] A. Fraser, *Donald Fraser*, pp. 209-210.

afterwards that they were running not from panic, but to fetch other women, that they might share the blessing which all felt was descending so copiously upon us. In a few moments quiet was restored, and the silence was sacred beyond description during the closing prayer.[332]

The response became a community response rather than the individual commitment Inwood was asking for. This communal experience enabled the Ngoni-Tumbuka to accept the Christian faith in their own terms. Each congregation Inwood preached to received the Holy Spirit collectively, as at Loudon:

As I entered the vestry, Mr Fraser came out of the church, weeping for joy. He had asked all who knew they had received the fullness of the Spirit to stand and raise their hand. Every hand was raised, and all they could do was to sing the Doxology.[333]

Inwood's itineration throughout Livingstonia Mission was assessed by the Mission Council as a great success:

Mr Inwood has been mightily used to stir up the native church to a greater knowledge of the reality and nearness of God, of His Holiness, and His moral demands upon His Children.[334]

Inwood's conventions in 1910 marked a religious watershed in Livingstonia Mission. The missionary enterprise appeared firmly established among the Tumbuka-Ngoni people. A new Christian community, led by missionaries and encouraged by the emerging educated elite, was a torchlight in what had been considered "total darkness". On the other hand, 1910 and the years immediately following were of vital growth in the area of independent religious response. That is to say, if spirit possession had not been a recognizable phenomenon in the period 1881-1910, or was deliberately ignored by the missionaries, it had now become an integral part of the people's response to the new faith. The church could no longer ignore African initiative coloured by their own traditional beliefs.

In summary, it has been observed that the missionaries made a significant impact upon the Tumbuka in the years 1881-1910. The slow beginning experienced by the missionaries did not remain long. The church grew steadily and by 1910 it had grown significantly. This is clear from the following figures.[335]

---

[332] Inwood, *An African Pentecost*, p. 45.

[333] *Ibid.*

[334] Livingstonia Mission Council Minutes, September 1910, MNA L1 1/316; also Inwood, *ibid.*, p. 70.

[335] The figures are extracted from the report of the Fifth General Mission Conference of the

Date	Livingstonia Mission	Blantyre Mission
1890	48	23
1900	1315	364
1911	6898	2800
1921	13877	8000
1929	19730	17021
1931	22726	21418
1943	28854	32916
1950	32121	45634
1955	35481	50247
1957	39291	51806

This increase in converts meant that many people were incorporated into the church's religious mode of thought and behaviour. They received the Gospel message through mission education, giving them a new consciousness. For this reason, people reordered their world-view using both old and new elements. This brought confusion in the minds of some converts. Perhaps they may have viewed the new religion as an alternative belief system with new demands, or they may have seen a possibility of a mixture of the old and the new. Whatever the case may have been, the Christian Faith posed a challenged to the Tumbuka and their religion. People who converted to Christianity had broken away from their old religion and were pilgrims in the new. Possession did not come to surface, at least in the initial period. When it did, it was so interwoven with the new beliefs that it was strange to both the missionaries and the converts.

In the independent churches founded by African leaders, Kamwana, Domingo, Mwasi and others, possession did not arise. If it had arisen at any point, they would have noticed it, they being more familiar with the customs and practices of the Tumbuka than the missionaries. However, this is not to suggest that possession was absent in these new churches.[336] Perhaps possession occurred in the independent churches but the leaders neglected it, regarding the phenomenon as only a natural religious expression. If this is true, it may have minimized the pathological features of persons so inclined, and maximized instead the religious experience and social process coherent with the Tumbuka tradition. This means that people found release and satisfaction, unofficially, within the church.

Federated Missions held in Blantyre, Nyasaland, in 1926, p. 45, MNA L1 1/3/27; and also from Reports to the General Assembly of the Church of Scotland 1930-1957, NLS.

[336] John Parratt has argued that in Malawi, African leaders who broke away from mission churches to form their own were more concerned with the question of leadership than with doctrine or liturgy. (John K. Parratt, "Mwasi and the Origins of the Blackman's Church", *Journal of Religion in Africa*, Vol. 9/3 (1978), p. 205.)

The wider responses which occurred in the years 1900-1910 were an assertion of the new religion. The religious beliefs of the Tumbuka had been changed by the missionary activities in the twenty-two years of their work among the Tumbuka. The Bible had become the most valuable religious symbol in Tumbukaland. The Keswick conventions of 1908-1910 opened up new possibilities for power, healing and a religious message relevant to the lives of the Tumbuka. The dynamic for renewal and growth in the new religion came from the power of the Spirit made visible during that period. Thereafter, the Tumbuka were ever to move forward in the new religion in their increasing numbers, adapting it and recognizing its power.

Attending a revival meeting between 1908 and 1910
From 'The Future of Africa' by Donald Fraser

Chapter 5

Livingstonia Mission's Attitude to Possession

The missionaries' position with regard to possession

The position of Livingstonia Mission with regard to possession was influenced by the missionaries' cultural background and their experience of the Christian Faith. For many centuries Westerners had believed in nature spirits, dwarfs, fairies, trolls and kobolds. When the church could not admit the existence of spiritual entities other than God, angels and the devil, the belief lost its hold on society.[1] The church equated the nature spirits with demons and therefore condemned the beliefs as pagan and demonic. The origin of the familiars in folklore may not have been in demonology but in traditional beliefs. However, by rejecting it, the church set the Westerners in a new world-view. Therefore they came to regard possession as the work of the devil.[2]

It is not surprising, then, that when the missionaries met with a spirit oriented Tumbuka people, their attitude to the manifestation of possession was, on the whole, negative. Some regarded it as a psychopathological disease and others regarded it as superstitious and associated with evil spirits.[3] The missionaries were in a strange cultural setting to plant a faith which did not tolerate synthesis or syncretism. Therefore, they could not allow possession tendencies in the missionary church.

To prevent doubtful practices such as possession from slipping into the church, the missionaries drew up a question which read,

Kasi mukukana Satana na ntchito zake zose pamoza na uzaghali wose; kasi mukukana ntchito zake zapano pasi izo zikwendezgana chara na mazgo gha Chiuta kuti muzileke nakuziluwa?[4]	Do you renounce Satan and all his works together with all [his] craftiness; do you renounce all his practices here on earth which are in conflict with the Word of God so that you abandon and forget them all?

[1]   Lynn Thorndike, *A History of Magic and Experimental Science during the First Thirteen Centuries of our Era*, London: Macmillan, 1923, pp. 30f.
[2]   Cf. Bruce S. Bennett, "Slow Cooking: Some European Historical Parallels for the Adaptation of Christianity in Africa", in *Theology Cooked in an African Pot*, ATISCA Bulletin no. 5/6 (1996/1997), pp. 122-124.
[3]   D. Fraser, *African Idylls*, pp. 191-194.
[4]   *Katekesimu*, Livingstonia: Mission Press, n.d., p. 7. The question was put to candidates for adult baptism by the minister just before they were baptized. In the Church of Scotland *Book of Common Order* the question did not appear, maybe because adult baptism was rare. The question was something new put up by Livingstonia Mission to meet a new situation.

What this meant in missionary terms was that their converts experienced a complete conversion where an individual renounced his old life and pledged to walk in the way of Christ alone. This conversion or change of heart was expected to show a difference in the life of the individual.

For the Tumbuka converts, the first part of the question would be simple for them to answer with a superficial "yes". Satana was a foreign idea in Tumbuka religion. Perhaps witchcraft would have been closest to the Tumbuka conception of Satana; and yet Satan in Christian teaching is more than a witch. There was no easy solution to the problem.

The second part of the question posed more difficulty to the Tumbuka. Which practices of their land were contrary to the Word of God? Who was to say which practices were contrary to the Word of God and by what norm would the judgement be passed?[5]

The meeting of the old and the new

In 1908, a young convert, Chitezi, fell ill. In accordance with Tumbuka tradition, his father sought advice from a *nganga*. He was informed that his son was possessed by *virombo* spirits and needed a *virombo* expert to arrange a dance for Chitezi to be healed.[6] Chitezi's loyalty was now divided between his father's tradition and the new religion. He chose a middle way. He submitted to his father's treatment and at the same time showed his new belief when he asked for a Bible to be brought to him. It may be that for Chitezi, the dance and the Bible were complementary methods for healing disease, and both assisted in his quick recovery. Of course, the fact that Chitezi called for a Bible may have been a hopeful sign to the missionaries that the old spirits were losing ground, as Elmslie's words suggest:

> In the midst of his divining instruments, and in a circle around him and his son, who sat reading the Bible, the drummers and dancers performed. It was a strange sight. Such dances and performances were common enough in the country, but never before where the subject of them sat reading the Word of God.[7]

---

[5]   A personal note may serve as an illustration here. During my field-work, I was introduced as a minister of religion to a Tonga Member of Parliament. In response to my greeting this man said, "I am glad to meet you, Sir. So you are one of those people who have left everything." Though said as a joke, the honourable M.P. was referring to this vow. The MP's response is a typical reflection of most people's understanding of that vow. Perhaps the Tumbuka read into the vow what it does not say. Personal interview with Mr X., M.P., at Mzuzu on 12 February 1983.

[6]   Elmslie, *Among the Wild Ngoni*, p. 224.

[7]   *Ibid.*, p. 225.

In practice this means that the old and the new met. Consequently, the Tumbuka were breaking away from their tradition. They allowed Chitezi to read the Bible, accepting a new power. At the same time they were making an effort to indigenize the Bible and the Christian faith.

Manifestations of *vimbuza, virombo* and *vyanusi* formerly associated with traditional spirits, now took the form of possession by the Holy Spirit. For instance, at Livingstonia congregation,

> the session heard from Messrs Lameck M. Aphili, Robert Nyirenda and Esa Tumkani of Chiweta who had come under the influence of the Holy Spirit and now sought guidance and advice. This was as a result of consecration meetings.[8]

Though nothing further was said about these men's spiritual experience in the meeting, the Kirk session's response was favourable as it encouraged consecration meetings to be held in various places. The religious expression by these men, no doubt, was strange to them as well as to the missionaries. It was a successful blending of Tumbuka traditional beliefs and the Christian faith. Whereas in the past these men would have attributed their experience to ancestral spirits, now they saw it as the power wrought in the new religion.

The intense fervour of Charles Inwood and Donald Fraser's convention of 1908-1910, opened a new element. Converts were allowed to express their religious emotions within the parameters of Christian worship. This led to physical manifestation of the spirit which spread like wildfire. Later Fraser had to discourage any manifestations of the spirit, "lest the people should attend to those rather than the spiritual".[9] Fraser went further and promoted systematic instruction in the Bible to lead the converts and adherents "into deeper truths and to an expression in conduct of their devotion to Christ".[10] According to Fraser, the result was that those people were moved to their depth with a sense that God was among them. Perhaps the glowing presence of the power of the Spirit set in motion by the Keswick convention continued to convince people.

Undoubtedly, 1910 was the end of the planting years of missionary work and the beginning of church growth and meaningful religious exchange.

> Throughout the whole mission there are 8 central stations [mission stations from which missionary outreach work was conducted], 43 European missionaries, 9 native congregations and 3 licentiates; 4,500 communicants [in 1904 the Presbytery of Livingstonia had a total of 790 communicants], 30,000 under instruction. 500 schools, 1,000 qualified teachers and 53,000 scholars.[11]

---

8   Livingstonia congregation minutes book, 1900-1927, MNA L1 1/3/16.
9   D. Fraser, *African Idylls*, p. 287.
10   *Ibid.*, p. 288.
11   Livingstonia Mission annual statistics, 1898-1912, MNA L1 1/9/1.

At this period the basis of admission changed, as already noted. This allowed more people in the church than the missionaries could effectively train, even with the assistance of a large staff of local people. Hence the situation was open to individual experimentation within the new religion. Perhaps it was a deliberate attempt by the Tumbuka converts to fit their old beliefs within the Christian faith. However, while the Tumbuka were attempting to understand the new religion in the context of their spirit beliefs, *vimbuza, vyanusi* and *virombo*, the mission church put up a barrier of discipline.

Discipline cases for possession

Cases of possession among Tumbuka converts began to appear in 1910 more frequently than before. Converts were possessed by *virombo, vimbuza* and *vyanusi*. This possession appeared in its traditional forms, compelling the church to expel those involved in it. For example, at Ekwendeni congregation "Jessie Chiunga and Maggie Nyirenda confessed having been dancing *virombo*. The Kirk session agreed that they be suspended for one year".[12] Similar cases in the same congregation and in the same year involved the suspension of Jane Nkhata, Maranyao Wasya, Yotamu Gondwe, and Chitoya Ngoma.[13]

Loudon congregation, in 1913, suspended Marion Mpata, Nehemia Phiri and Elizabeth Mpando for taking part in possession ceremonies.[14] The appearance of *vimbuza, virombo* and *vyanusi* forms of possession was experienced throughout Livingstonia Mission. Perhaps church members had not found spiritual satisfaction and release from their fears within the new religion and were tempted to return to familiar ground. Or it may be that the masses who flocked into the church were too many to have received adequate instruction. Therefore their former beliefs which barely had been affected soon showed up.

A Livingstonia Mission record book, 'Expelled members 1910-1919', covering a distance of well over three hundred km, is revealing. It shows that in addition to the many cases of polygamy, beer drinking, marriages outside the church etc. brought before Kirk sessions between 1901 and 1919, possession cases constituted a new problem the church had to deal with. Major congregations where converts were expelled included Khondowe, Ekwendeni, Ruarwe, Enkondhleni and Ehinyeni. Minor places of worship where possession cases were brought before Kirk sessions included: Kazuni, Emcisweni, Luzi, Katowo, Lubazi, Chiweta and Bwengu. The latter had no resident minister whereas most of the former had either a minister or an evangelist.

---

[12] Ekwendeni congregation minutes book, 1910-1938, MNA L1 1/3/5.
[13] *Ibid.*
[14] Loudon congregation minutes book, 1910-1916, MNA L1 1/3/39.

other reports of this committee subsequent to its first meeting, it is possible that the committee never had another one.

In the 1920s Fraser studied the beliefs of the Tumbuka. He included possession in that study. Fraser discovered that possession was not just a psychological disease as the Charms and Superstitions Committee had reported earlier on. He found that possession was entrenched in Tumbuka religion. He writes, *"chirombos* are spirits, and they are divided into four or five classes, each requiring special treatment, and in all the shelves of the mission dispensary there is no medicine which deals with evil spirits".[19] Fraser points out that possession was connected with spirits and therefore was part of Tumbuka religion. Perhaps it is this quality of possession which formed a good reason for the missionaries' objection to it and the drum-beating. They saw it as the manifestation of heathenism, the very thing which they were fighting against.

We have seen that many missionaries approached the problem of possession from a scientific viewpoint. They needed to investigate and verify the nature of *virombo*, *vyanusi* and *vimbuza*. For them, possession was a disease which could be cured scientifically with drugs. Its connection with spirits was a misguided faith which had to be checked. The dancing and drum-beating which accompanied possession was simply "idle". It encouraged superstitions and therefore had to be stopped.

Positive attempts to Christianize the possession method

Between 1920 and 1930 a strong wave of possession within the church and outside it was accentuated by a movement of miracle workers. First, was Lameck Chirongo. Formerly a convert at Buyombe congregation in Karonga district, Chirongo claimed to have been possessed by the Holy Spirit.[20] From God, he said he had received power to heal the sick, power to perform miracles and to know effective herbs. Chirongo moved from village to village treating the sick and administering herbs to protect people from disease and from witchcraft. Chirongo's activities appealed to non-Christians and Christians alike. George Nyasulu, an evangelist at Buyombe, was so convinced by Chirongo's healing power that he recommended him to his congregation.[21] No sooner was this done than Chirongo was held responsible by the Presbytery for leading many Christians astray. Nyasulu, the evangelist, was reported to the Presbytery for collaborating with Chirongo. Though much discussion on the

---

[19] D. Fraser, *African Idylls*, p. 193.
[20] Livingstonia Presbytery minutes book, 1920-1932, MNA L1 1/3/25.
[21] Ibid.

case took place in the Presbytery, a motion that the case be referred back to Karonga was carried.[22] It is worth noting the influence the local church leaders had in that Presbytery meeting. There were sixty African church elders and pastors, and thirteen missionaries. Compared to the 1910 situation where there were forty-three missionaries and twenty-seven local elders, the present situation was the reverse of the old order. Perhaps the missionaries present at this Presbytery meeting would rather have seen Nyasulu dismissed for reverting to "heathenism" lest he led people astray, but those local leaders put pressure upon the Presbytery to vote the way it did. This was the first time a case had been referred back to a congregational session from Presbytery without directives. Previously, the mission council would have given its verdict.

Zerenji Mwasi's complaint in 1915 that missionaries decided Presbytery matters in their exclusive mission council may have been effective.[23] Back in Buyombe, Nyasulu was reprimanded by the session, but retained his position as evangelist. When the mission council heard about the decision to keep Nyasulu, it withheld his salary for three months. But the decision was ratified. Chirongo, the miracle worker, was ostracized and discouraged from working near church buildings and among Christians.

Chirongo had attempted to bring the possession method of healing within the church perimeter. Perhaps he had read in the Bible about how Jesus went about healing the sick, and how his disciples did the same after they received the Holy Spirit. He may have seen himself standing in the same tradition as these early disciples and therefore went to test the power of the new religion. At the same time, Chirongo drew from traditional religion where possessed individuals were regarded as endowed with healing power. Chirongo's activities among both Christians and non-Christians were in accordance with the Tumbuka community approach to religion instead of the individualistic and exclusive method of the church.[24] However, his method was a radical departure from church tradition and it was rejected.

The time for active local participation in the church came in the difficult period. The 1914-18 war took most able African teachers and evangelists as interpreters, teachers and chaplains. Out of the 1,000 trained teachers in Livingstonia Mission, only a handful remained. Among the sixteen male missionaries, only six did not serve in the war in the then German East Africa (now Tanzania).[25] The acute shortage of workers in the mission resulted in

[22] Ibid.

[23] Livingstonia Presbytery minutes book, 1899-1920, MNA L1 1/3/21.

[24] In Tumbuka religion, every person within the community is also a member of that community's religion.

[25] Livingstonia Mission Council minutes book, June 1916, MNA L1 1/3/17.

more Malawians being left at home taking responsible positions in the church. For instance, Yoram Mphande was posted Fife while Patrick Mwamlima was put in charge of Karonga mission station; Levi Mumba was appointed secretary for the Livingstonia Mission.[26] No doubt these men were capable. When they filled the posts which had been held by missionaries, the church membership increased.[27] The work which missionaries had left was carried on, removing the anxiety which missionaries had about a possible withering of the mission in their absence. However, no innovations seem to have taken place during this period. Perhaps the local personnel regarded themselves as only acting temporarily. They would hand back the responsibilities as soon as the missionaries returned.

When the war ended, the dark cloud of uncertainty cast on the local leaders and their people was lifted. The white men, who had until then been, in the eyes of the Tumbuka and their neighbours, peacemakers and possessors of supernatural powers, had now lost their authority. The local people, toughened by wartime experiences, were ready to express themselves. Stephen Kundecha of Blantyre Presbytery saw a bright cloud of hope when more African leadership and African expression in the church would be realized:

> In those past years, the native converts have taken little part in the service of Christ. They have always depended upon the missionaries as those who had the responsibility. They did all things in servile manner, and put the *mzungu* (white man) always in front as if he were the owner of the Gospel. Yes, that was right, because it was not their time. But now that time has come they should not be as people bound hand and foot. The native church ought to have her qualities too.[28]

As if to prove part of Kundecha's vision, in 1924 when Livingstonia Presbytery and Blantyre Presbytery joined to form the Church of Central Africa Presbyterian (CCAP), all the ministers of the two Presbyteries met for the first time.[29] These included Hezekia Tweya, Harry Matecheta, Edward Boti Manda, James Kandulu, Yafeti Mkandawire, Thomas Maseya; Patrick Mwamlima, Jonathan Chirwa, Stephen Kundecha, Andrew Mitochi, Harry Mtuwa, Yesaya Zerenje Mwase, and Joseph Kaunde. The meeting of these men and the formation of the CCAP was a significant event. It signified a break from a Church of Scotland mission in Central Africa to an indigenous church. The CCAP became an autonomous body. The qualities of the "native church", as dreamt

---

[26] *Ibid.*
[27] Livingstonia Mission statistics, 1904-1920, MNA L1 1/3/18.
[28] Stephen Kundecha, in Foreign Mission Conference Report, 1924, p. 65.
[29] Livingstonia Mission Council minutes book, November 1924, MNA L1 1/3/17.

by Kundecha, were to ripen or fail depending on the initiative of these and other local leaders.

One of the most significant innovations made by these leaders in the church was the adaptation and development of local tunes for use in services. As both a pastor and a teacher, Charles Chinula developed an interest in Tumbuka music.[366] He composed hymns and taught them to school children on week days. On Sunday, Chinula practised his hymns with his congregation before and after the service. The popularity of his hymns drew many people to his service. One of Chinula's well known hymns sung to this day is:[367]

Lero ndi nyengo	Now 'tis time
Yakuwukira mu tulo twithu,	For all of us to rise from sleep
Chifukwa Yesu wawara	For the light of Christ has shone
Ku mitima ya chisi.	In the darkened hearts.

Chorus

Kwacha ngwe	Dawn has come,
Ku mtima tihenere	In our hearts let us rejoice.
Ndi Yesu wawara	Jesus Christ gives us light,
Ku mitima yithu.	To our hearts.
Inya chisi chikwenera	Yes, indeed this heavy darkness
Kufumamo mu mtima,	Must be driven from our hearts.
Chifukwa ndi mpanji	Otherwise we will be engulfed
Ya urwani wa mkati mwithu.	By hostile forces from within
Mu chisi mulije kaweme	In this darkness there can never
Na kanthini kose,	Be a single good at all,
Muli mabuwu na visinga	There are pitfalls, snares and death -
Na nyifwa ndipera.[368]	Traps into which we're bound to fall.

Such hymns sung in the familiar vibrant rhythm of the people expressed the deep feelings of the worshippers.

With the encouragement and assistance of Donald Fraser, Chinula had many of his hymns put in writing and included in the Tumbuka hymn book.[369]

---

[366] Papers on the life of Rev. Charles Chinula, MNA L1 1/3/27.
[367] Kenneth R. Ross, *Christianity in Malawi: A Source Book*, Gweru: Mambo, 1996, p. 65.
[368] Charles Chinula, *Lero ndi nyengo yakuwukira, in Sumu za Ukristu*, (reprint) Blantyre: Hetherwick Press, 1960, p. 117; see also Kenneth R. Ross (ed.), *Christianity in Malawi*, Gweru: Mambo, 1996, p. 65.

Consequently, Chinula's hymns together with those of other composers were used far and wide.[34] Among other best known hymn writers were Peter Z. Thole, and Amoni Mwakasungula. Undoubtedly, the Tumbuka hymn book, with limited translated hymns from the Scottish Church Hymnary included in it displays the richness of Tumbuka and Ngoni tradition. Above all, it is a monument of the attempt made by the early converts to christianize their beliefs.

Some of the attempts were essentially adjustment movements within the old religion. One such attempt was made by Tomo Nyirenda. He was a former Christian at Khondowe and a graduate of Overtoun Institute at Livingstonia. Nyirenda adopted Christian symbols in his healing movement of 1924 to 1927.[35] He assumed the title of Mwana Lesa, the son of God, and claimed to have been commissioned by God to heal and deliver societies from all pain and evils. To fulfil his mission, Nyirenda operated between the northern parts of Malawi and the eastern parts of Zambia. He cleansed people from witchcraft and reassured them through baptism by immersion. Both Christians and non-Christians flocked to Nyirenda's mass meetings to be healed and cleansed.[36] If a person died during or after Nyirenda's baptism it was, according to him, a witch or evil spirit that was killed. Nyirenda's career did not last long as he was found guilty of manslaughter. He was sentenced to death by the government in Zambia, then Northern Rhodesia.[37]

Nyirenda's activities were outside the church though he had many Christians attending his meetings. He certainly moved away from Tumbuka religion by adopting baptism, a practice unknown in the old religion. But in his activities, he did not hold Christ at the centre of his movement. Instead, he replaced Christ, living his scheme apparently without Christian manifestations.

From the showing of the Livingstonia records and literature, the 1930s and subsequent years were quiet with regard to possession manifestation. Insignificant and isolated cases were reported in various Kirk sessions.[38] A number of reasons may account for this low ebb, e.g.

---

[33] Ten hymns composed by Chinula are included in the Tumbuka hymn book.

[34] Bwalya Chuba says that among canonized indigenous hymns used in the United Church of Zambia, "most of them are of Tumbuka origin". Bwalya, S. Chuba, "African Culture and Christian Worship in Zambian Protestant Churches", M.Th., University of Aberdeen, 1983, p. 57.

[35] Livingstonia Presbytery minutes book, 1922-1935, MNA L1 1/3/12.

[36] *Ibid.*

[37] *Ibid.*

[38] Livingstonia Presbytery minutes book, 1925-1940, May 1931, MNA L1 1/3/7.

all pioneer missionaries were retiring and new ones were coming in, causing more laxity in the place of the rigidity engaged in former years.

the church had gained more ground in local society than before and therefore felt comfortable to co-exist with the diminishing practices,

converts had so broken away from the old religion and matured in the new that possession was no longer by vimbuza, vyanusi and virombo.

They now interpreted their experience in terms of being possessed with the Holy Spirit in accordance with the Bible teaching.

The last point seems true to the situation. The converts, together with their increasing local pastors,[39] were in a process of spiritual growth. They had broken free from the old religion and now conceived their experience in a new way. For instance dreams, a very important medium for communicating with ancestral spirits in the traditional setting, became a vehicle through which individuals experienced their Christian life.[40]

It has been noted that the post-1920 period was characterized by definite positive attempts to christianize African life. Tumbuka converts began to assume responsible positions in the church. At the same time, the church experienced numerical growth as well as Christian maturity among its converts. Christianization of possession method became a remarkable feature of the age. Nevertheless, it appears that liturgically and theologically, the past still to a great or lesser extent controlled the present.

The decline of possession

By the end of 1949, cases of spirit possession had subsided within church circles. This is evidenced by Ekwendeni Kirk Session report to the District Church Council in 1950 during the moderatorship of Rev. P.C. Mzembe. The report reads:

> Mpara ya Kirk Session ya Ekwendeni pakukhumba kupereka makani gha umoyo
> na milimo ya mpingo yikuona kuti mpingo uli makora chifukwa tumaluso twene

---

[39] A full up to date list of ordained ministers of Livingstonia Synod is given in the appendix.

[40] Rev. F. Chunga explained how he received a call to the ministry through a dream. He tried to resist the dream, but to his surprise the experience recurred several times. In the end, in a vision he experienced at night, he surrendered to what he described as "a dazzling light". Chunga knew that it was Jesus calling him in his service. Personal interview with Rev. F. Chunga, chairman of the Zomba Theological Board, Blantyre Mission, 12 March 1983. Such experiences in dreams are common among the ministers of the Church of Central Africa Presbyterian.

utu tukisananga mpingo nga ndi bagule ma dance virombo na vyanusi kuti tukuchitika vivi naba kristu chara, tukuchepa, ndipo chigaba na chigaba milimo yose yikwenda makora.[41]

A free translation of this reads:

> In submitting its report on the life and work of the congregation, Ekwendeni Kirk Session is happy to report that evil practices which used to taint the church are now disappearing. Dances connected with *virombo* and *vyanusi* no more attract Christians. Work in all areas of the congregation is progressing well.

This report spoke for most congregations at that time. Viewed in the light of Ekwendeni session report, the Christian faith had been firmly established and taken a significant place in the life of the Tumbuka. The divine purpose to transform his people through the power of the Gospel as preached by the missionaries and by the conviction of the Holy Spirit had been realized. Many people joined the church and served as teachers, evangelists, medical orderlies and ordained ministers.[42]

The rise of nationalism throughout Africa in the 1940s also took place in Malawi and reached its peak in the 1950s. Traditional rites and customs now appeared as respectable to many. Perhaps possession in its traditional forms became secularized, taken simply as a mode of healing. On the other hand, it may be that the old spirits had taken flight having been confronted by a superior power, the Spirit of Jesus.[43] It is not surprising, therefore, that from that period up to 1983, church records do not show any cases or discussion of possession. However the official position of the church with regard to possession is that when its manifestation is in the traditional form, Christians may seek the help of a traditional herbalist.[44] The church still discourages its members from the part of the cure by the herbalist involving dancing lest this

---

[41] Ekwendeni congregation minutes book, 20 May 1950, MNA L1 1/13/27.

[42] The minute book of Livingstonia Presbytery records 12,000 communicants in 1948 as opposed to 3,000 members in 1910 - the first 35 years of missionary work. Livingstonia Presbytery minutes book, 1944-August 1948, MNA L1 1/13/27.

[43] O. Kalu has argued that when Christianity came into contact with traditional religions in Africa, the local spirit deities retreated, giving way to the new power. Kalu, "Gods in Retreat: Models of Religious Change in Africa", *Journal of Humanities* (Lagos), Vol. 1/1 (1977), p. 43.

[44] Personal interview with the Rev. H. Mhone, Deputy General Secretary, Livingstonia Synod, at Mzuzu, 23 February 1983. This became a policy in 1965 after Chikanga, a medicine man who claimed to cleanse society from witchcraft and other ills, had caused much trouble in the region. The Livingstonia Synod preferred that its ill members be treated in the hospitals, and to a lesser extent, by *riganga*, traditional herbalist.

implies a return to the old ways. But it does not penalize those who dance to be cured.

While it is recognized that the church has come a long way from expelling converts for participating in possession ceremonies, to its present stance on the subject, the church has yet to take a radical step. It has to bring into its liturgy the whole healing process which possession provides in the traditional setting. Such a deliberate and daring action requires a theological and pastoral perspective which stems from the worshipping community. The church may take its example from the Independent Churches which have pioneered this method, though not perfectly.

A recent survey by this writer shows the proportion of the decline of possession in its traditional forms. The survey was carried out in a semi-rural area outside Mzuzu, a major town in the northern region of Malawi. Both Christians and non-Christians were interviewed. They were of different ages and degrees of literacy, and of both sexes. 757 people were interviewed. It is evident from the diagram given below that while there is still a strong belief in traditional possession among non-Christians, there is a considerable drop in the belief among Christians. An interesting point to note, however, is that among the Christian interviewees were ministers of religion and their wives. We discovered that five percent of the ministers had a personal experience of possession and twelve percent of the ministers' wives had at one time or other been *vimbuza*, *vyanusi* or *virombo* patients. This strengthens the suggestion that the whole process of possession healing be brought into the church and christianized.

Conclusion

We have seen that missionaries were in Tumbukaland to present a pure Gospel as they understood it in the West. They made no concession for spirit beliefs and other cultural traits of the Tumbuka to colour the Christianity. The Christian faith had to be taken by the Tumbuka as it was prescribed by the missionaries. To ensure that no heathen spirits encroached into the church, a penalty of nine to twelve months' suspension was imposed. Nevertheless, the Tumbuka came to Christianity in their increasing numbers.

In their response to the missionaries' preaching about God and the power of the Holy Spirit, the Tumbuka converts wanted to experience that power of the Spirit in a more concrete way than had been demonstrated by the missionaries. For the Tumbuka, the power of the spirit was especially felt in healing and in ritual; the physical and the spiritual were indivisible. As such, bodily cures needed both herbal medicine and a spiritual antidote. Therefore possession was an essential method for satisfying this need.

Today the mission church, formerly in the hands of missionaries, is an indigenous church in the hands of indigenous people. Its immediate challenge is to 'unfreeze' its rigidity and christianize African life. A.F. Walls has remarked, "African life is ordered, has a sense of the appropriate time, place and person; but it is also spontaneous, improvisatory and responsive".[381] When these qualities of African life have been utilized,

> in the end, the history of African Christianity will be a single story, in which the missionary period is only an episode. The judgement of the churches of Africa will not be whether one can dominate them "older" or "independent" - that distinction, I believe, will in time, and perhaps soon, become meaningless. Their judgement, like that of all the churches, will be by Lord of the church on the basis of his Word.[382]

---

[381] A.F. Walls, "The Anabaptists of Africa? The Challenge of the African Independent Churches", *Occasional Bulletin of Missionary Research*, Vol. 3/2 (April 1979), p. 51.
[382] *Ibid.*

Existence of Vimbuza, Vyanusi and Virombo

Existence of vimbuza, vyanusi and virombo	Christians M & F	Non-Christians M & F
All three exist at present	152	644
Vimbuza, *Virombo* and *Vyanusi* non-existent	25	6
Vimbuza existent, not *vyanusi* and *virombo*	5	1
Vyanusi existent, not *vimbuza* and *virombo*		
Virombo existent, not *vimbuza* and *vyanusi*		
Don't know or uncertain	12	7
Total	**194**	**658**

Vimbuza activities
Vimbuza's prophetic powers

	Christians M & F	Non-Christians M & F
Vimbuza spirits empower persons to prophesy	96	520
Vimbuza cannot empower persons to prophesy	67	45
Vimbuza can empower persons to prophesy dependent on God's will	35	106
Don't know uncertain	10	2
Total	**208**	**673**

Vyanusi activities
Vyanusi's healing powers

	Christians M & F	Non-Christians M & F
Vyanusi spirits heal	125	549
Vyanusi spirits cannot heal	87	124
Vyanusi spirits can heal dependent on God's will	25	42
Don't know or uncertain	15	8
Total	**252**	**723**

Virombo activities
Virombo's ability to kill

	Christians M & F	Non-Christians M & F
Virombo spirits kill	25	105
Virombo spirits cannot kill	53	34
Virombo kills dependent on God's will		2
Don't know or uncertain	2	
Total	**80**	**141**

Chapter 6

The Church's Ministry to the Possessed: A Modern Pastoral Concern among Tumbuka Christians

What is pastoral concern for the possessed?

Christian pastoral concern for the possessed is a relatively new area of interest within the established churches. Yet possession is a recurring theme in the religious story of humanity and of the Tumbuka in particular. When we consider pastoral concern for the possessed, we are faced with different approaches and practices and therefore are "sailing at the edge of a heavy storm". By pastoral concern for the possessed we mean the form of healing, in the broad sense of the term *healing*, which is offered in a Christian setting or is the expression of a particular form of ministry. Healing in this situation is what Francis MacNutt has defined as that which touches the human experience; this includes inner healing of emotional problems, deliverance from evil spirits, physical healing and forgiveness of sin.[1] MacNutt takes the view that such healing is a gift from God and can be effected within the church by the individuals who have faith in the healing power of Jesus. The aim of such comprehensive healing is total deliverance of man or woman from all that impinges on his/her life.

In the Tumbuka context, such healing is related to possession in that the spirit world has a bearing on the welfare of the people. We have already noted that an ill person was regarded as being in that condition because of some disharmony between the spirit world and the physical world, or because the individual had neglected his or her duty to some spirits. For the person to be healed, the two worlds met symbolically in the healing dance, or the spirits were placated through gifts of food. We also noted that the healing was performed by one endowed with power to heal and who had himself at one time been possessed by some spirit and was now healed.[2] In its traditional form, this method no longer applies to the Tumbuka Christians due to their religion and therefore of their world view. The method needs to be transformed in order to give meaningful pastoral care to the Tumbuka who convert to Christianity.

---

[1]   Francis MacNutt, *The Power of Healing*, London: Bantam, 1979, pp. 33f.
[2]   See chapter three on the relationship between the spirit world and the physical world.

This requires that the church takes up the religious concept of possession among the Tumbuka and let it be judged by the Bible standard.

The Bible as the norm for judging possession

In turning to the Bible as the norm for understanding pastoral concern for the possessed among the Tumbuka, I am not proposing that we maintain the phraseology of the apostolic age, neither that we should retain the meaning of possession held in that age. Rather, to be biblical is to be engaged in a hermeneutical process which results in the application of the Bible message to a given situation today, that of the Tumbuka in our case. This is what W.D. Davies means, in a Canadian setting, when he says that Christianity assumed characteristics of local places when it spread in various places.[3] Therefore the questions dealt with in each place ought to reflect the characteristics of that area. What would Jesus or Paul, for example, say to the Tumbuka of today who claim to be possessed by the Spirit of Christ or by an ancestral spirit? The adaptation of the Bible message to particular situations is the method Jesus or Paul used. For example, when Jesus healed a woman possessed by a spirit he laid his hands on her.[4] Faced with a possession case in a different situation, Jesus ordered the evil spirits to come out of "Legion", the Gerasine who had been possessed and troubled by evil spirits.[5]

However, in taking the Bible as the norm for judging the possession method, it must be noted that the history of the Tumbuka also counts; for surely God revealed himself in that history prior to the introduction of the Bible. Further, the history of Tumbuka is important in our understanding of their response to the Bible message. It forms their background. But this history takes a secondary role to the Bible in which God has specially revealed himself.

Before we proceed, we shall outline what we mean by the term "possession method". Among the Tumbuka, there is no division between secular and sacred.[6] The two are so interwoven that one exists in the other. Therefore possession practices in that religion include social, physical, emotional and spiritual dimensions. By employing the possession method within the Christian church, we are saying that Christianity is a religious system which recognizes *Chiuta* as the supreme spirit and makes him a central point of reference. This method allows the Spirit of God to intervene in human life and to up lift every

---

[3] W.D. Davies, "The Apostolic Age the Life of Paul", in *Peakes' Commentary on the Bible*, Toronto: Thomas Nelson and Sons, 1962, p. 871.

[4] Luke 13:10-13.

[5] Luke 8:26 30.

[6] See chapter three.

individual to his wholeness, i.e. to being an integrated human being. Further, the possession method means a religious system which recognizes the existence of various spirits. While these spirits, especially the evil ones, may cause illness, disharmony, jealousy, apostasy etc., human beings have the Spirit of God at their disposal by which to overcome them. Therefore, by possession method we mean a healing process which embraces the whole of life, religious and secular, and which takes place within a religious setting. For us, this religious setting is the church. As we shall now see, in the New Testament Jesus and his disciples believed that they were possessed[7] with the spirit of God in order to overcome evil spirits and liberate humanity.

Pastoral concern for the possessed in the Bible

Luke makes use of the spirit theme throughout his Gospel. He consistently refers to the Spirit which was in Jesus, and how this Spirit enabled Jesus to heal disease and to exorcise evil spirits. In doing so, he enunciates different aspects of the story at different points. At one time he emphasizes the impact of Jesus' pastoral concern for the possessed. He presents an encounter of Jesus with unbelievers. When Jesus was driving out an evil spirit from a dumb man, his opponents accused Jesus of driving out evil spirits by the power of Beelzebub. Jesus asked them if their people drove out demons by Beelzebub. His opponents did not answer. However, their silence meant that their own people did not exorcise evil spirits by the power of the Beelzebub. Jesus, being a Jew, therefore could not have been using the power of Beelzebub. Then Jesus challenged his opponents that if he was driving out evil spirits by "the finger of God", then they were to accept that the kingdom of God was among them.[8] Immediately following this incident, Luke makes explicit use of the spirit theme as a pastoral concern for the church.

> When an unclean spirit comes out of a man it wanders over the deserts seeking a resting place; and if it finds none, it says, 'I will go back to the home I left'. So it returns and finds the house swept clean, and tidy. Off it goes and collects seven other spirits more wicked than itself, and they all come in and settle down; and in the end the man's plight is worse than before.[9]

In Luke's view, driving out evil spirits must be followed by filling the empty space with the Spirit of God lest the evil spirits return and re-inhabit the space. Just as Jesus had demonstrated the displacement of evil spirits with the Spirit

---

[7]   Instead of "possessed", most Bible translations use words such as "filled with the spirit", "inspired by the Holy Spirit", "full of the Spirit" etc.

[8]   Luke 11:14-20.

[9]   Luke 11:24-26.

of God, so were the disciples and the church to do the same. At another point Luke shows that individuals who had been healed by Jesus became whole, gaining physical and mental health. For instance, when Jesus healed a woman who had been possessed by a spirit for eighteen years and was a cripple, she was released of all her troubles.[10] Throughout his usage of the word 'Spirit', Luke continually maintains the tension which was present between the Kingdom of God and the evil spirits. Jesus' activities were concerned with ushering in the Kingdom in which individuals would be liberated from all ills. By the same token, Jesus' activity was a sure way of bringing the Spirit of God into human life. This Spirit would fill people's lives and guide them to all truth and peace.

The authority with which Jesus Christ exercised his pastoral concern was delivered from the Spirit. This is evidenced by Jesus' profound sense of the presence of the Spirit. We have already noted how the Spirit was present at Jesus' birth, his baptism and at the beginning of his ministry. Mark records different occasions when the authority of Jesus surfaced. When Jesus was teaching in a synagogue in Capernaum, a man possessed by an evil spirit recognized the authority of Jesus and began to shout, "Jesus of Nazareth, have you come to destroy us? I know you are the Holy One of God".[11] When Jesus healed the possessed individual, those who witnessed the healing and heard Jesus' teaching testified to his authority. On another occasion a woman came to Jesus begging him to heal her daughter who was at home possessed with an evil spirit. Impressed by the faith of the woman, Jesus ordered her to go home content that her daughter had been healed.[12] With the same authority, Jesus fed a huge crowd of people with just seven loaves of bread and a few fishes;[13] he blessed the little children,[14] and entered into Jerusalem where he challenged the religious authorities.[15] In his pastoral activities, Jesus' authority was expressed, as we have seen, in touching the needs of individuals. He taught about the Kingdom of God to those who needed to hear the good news; he drove out demons from those who were possessed, healed the lame and challenged the powers which were in opposition to the Kingdom of God. In all this, Jesus was healing the ills which rob men and women of the integrated life intended them by God.

---

[10] Luke 12:10-15.
[11] Mark 1:21-24.
[12] Mark 7:24-30.
[13] Mark 8:1-10.
[14] Mark 10:13.
[15] Mark 11-12.

Jesus' method of healing varied from one case to the other. He treated each individually, giving the whole of himself to the individual. For instance, a woman who had suffered from haemorrhages for twelve years came and touched Jesus' cloak in order to be healed. Although she touched Jesus secretly, and when he was busy with the crowd which was pressing upon him, Jesus turned to the woman, blessing her because of her faith.[16] She went home whole again. The most profound communication is demonstrated here where in eloquent silence between Jesus and the woman, healing took place. It must be admitted that the healing purpose of God, in Jesus, is here portrayed as independent of what humans call "normal". Another instance is when Jesus' disciples were unable to heal a boy possessed by a spirit which made him speechless. The disciples had failed to heal the boy when Jesus arrived from the mountain where he had to pray. Jesus told his disciples that that sort of possession could be healed through prayer.[17] From these examples, it is evident that Jesus' method of pastoral concern took each individual and his problem seriously. The unity of his purpose in his method was in the healing, liberation and reintegration of individuals.

Paul's pastoral approach to possession is revealed in his Epistles. He shared the belief of the Jews about the existence of evil spirits and their ruinous effect upon human life. In Thessalonica there emerged a group of Christians who were expecting the world to end immediately. These Christians regarded themselves as Spirit-filled people endowed with the divine power. Consequently, they left their jobs, awaiting the return of Jesus. Their concern was more with the manifestation of the Spirit and personal commune with the divine than with the immediate life.[18]

Paul's pastoral approach to these people was not to condemn them as unchristian, nor did he order their excommunication. He reasoned with them, pointing out that prophetism and the power of the Spirit were indeed elements to be found among Christians. But he also pointed out to them that these elements should be carefully examined by the Christian community lest there should be confusion. To illustrate the Spirit of Jesus which should fill or possess Christians, Paul pointed to his own life. He said that it was the Spirit of Jesus in his life which influenced him to preach the Gospel which transforms people's lives.[19] He recognized the need to be filled with the Spirit of God in order to fight against evil spirits. He also emphasized the need to be careful in

---

[16]   Mark 5:25-34.
[17]   Mark 9:14-29.
[18]   2 Thessalonians 2:2.
[19]   1 Thessalonians 1:5-6.

accepting the manifestation of the Spirit as there were other spirits which could be confused with the right spirit.

A similar problem emerged at Corinth. G.T. Montague notes that the Christians were carried away by the experience of the Spirit. So many Christians were inclined to speaking in tongues that confusion arose.[20] He says that Paul's pastoral approach shows his wide understanding of the work of the Spirit. He appreciated that these Christians had a gift that witnessed to the presence of the Spirit. However, he showed them that there were other gifts of the Spirit that better enriched the life of the community than speaking in tongues.[21] Montague says that Paul shows his pastoral strategy by guiding Christians to value the work of the Spirit which benefits the whole community.[22] Paul says, "To each person, the manifestation of the Spirit is given for the common good." [23] In a sense, Paul's pastoral concern for the possessed was a continuation of the war begun by Jesus against evil forces. It may be said that Paul entered into the depth of human existence, enabling him to empathize with the spiritual enthusiasts and those more reserved Christians. More importantly, he showed that the Spirit was given to each individual for the welfare of the community. Therefore his pastoral strategy was based on the creativity and love of the Spirit, on Paul's own human understanding and helpfulness.

The examples cited above show that pastoral concern for the possessed is an activity treated in the Bible with a considerable amount of importance and urgency. It may be noted that although the term possession is used in the New Testament to denote evil spirits and also disease, the Bible writers agree that God's Spirit or Jesus' Spirit filled believers. The Spirit enabled them to exorcise evil spirits, heal disease and prophesy. [24] This filling of individuals with the Spirit of God is a kind of possession. The presence of the Spirit of God, or of Jesus, in the life of a believer in the early church, had a great control over the role played by the individual in the community. As already noted, Paul and the other disciples of Jesus felt this tremendous power in their lives. The difference between this sort of possession and the other possession is the quality of Spirit. Those possessed with the Spirit of Jesus are enhanced by the Spirit, enabling them to love, serve and care for others. This compassion for humankind stems from the Spirit of Jesus which manifests itself in the lives and activities of individuals. On the other hand, individuals possessed by evil spirits lose their

---

[20] 1 Corinthians 12:22.

[21] 1 Corinthians 14:1ff.

[22] G.T. Montague, *The Holy Spirit: Growth of a Biblical Tradition*, New York: Paulist Press, 1976, pp. 156-159.

[23] 1 Corinthians 12:7.

Churches in Malawi, the congregation sings and dances to the decorous clapping and drumming rhythm. This takes place following a baptism ceremony, a marriage or an ordinary Sunday worship. Certain individuals get possessed and begin to shake. Others are contented with loud shouts of 'Hallelujah'.[31] Practices of this nature are reported by many writers on African Independent churches. Perhaps these elements, especially dancing, are what further differentiates African Independent churches from Christian worship as known in the West. E.W. Smith long ago said, "We cannot imagine an Anglo-Saxon dancing as a religious exercise but I can readily conceive of an African doing so. And why not ?"[32]

Dance and song in African Independent churches may seem to some observers to be wild gestures. But to the participants, these elements provide an opportunity for emotional release and "a way of witnessing the arrival of the Holy Spirit".[33] The rather noisy atmosphere can be reduced to dead silence and solemn worship by one pronouncement of 'Hallelujah' by the leader. Singing and dancing may take the form of happy or sad gestures in Christian worship. The mood of the occasion, e. g. at a funeral, a calamitous time, wedding, baptism, Holy Communion etc. dictates the kind of music and dance used. The use of singing and dancing in African Independent churches relates to the Tumbuka tradition. The Tumbuka expressed their feelings in the songs and in the steps they danced. When this practice is utilized by African Independent churches, it catches the whole being of the indigenous people enabling them to enter wholly into God's house of prayer.

H.W. Turner observed that the songs to which the Church of the Lord (Aladura) sing and dance cater for the people's natural desire to commune with their departed and therefore provide a much needed pastoral need.[34] He says that the songs have a heavy rhythm and are often accompanied by clapping of hands and drum-beat. When members of this independent church sing and dance before the Lord, and sometimes get possessed, they get healed from that desire to have communion with those in the spirit world. At the same time they realize that they are in the presence of the greatest Spirit, God himself. Many African Independent churches would identify with the Church of the Lord (Aladura) in this respect. Turner describes the Church of the Lord's pattern of worship embraced by most African Independent churches. He sums it up thus:

---

[31] Personal interview with John Nyirenda, a prophet of the Full Gospel of God. International Church, Bangala Village, Rumphi, 15 February 1983.
[32] E.W. Smith, *The Golden Stool* (3rd edition), London: Cargate Press, 1927, p.275
[33] B. Jules-Rossette, "Song and Spirit: The Use of Songs in the Management of Ritual Context", *Africa*, Vol. 45/23 (1975), p. 152.
[34] Turner, *African Independent Churches*, p. 120.

> Avoiding the deprecatory term emotionalism, we may regard this type of worship [i.e. worship which employs joyful singing and dance] as calling forth personal participation physical as well as mental, emotional as well as intellectual, corporate as well as individual.[35]

While we observe here that Christianity linked to the African notions and rhythm throbs with the spirit and genius of Africa, we also note that it provides the African worshipper with a deep sense of togetherness. It links ancient people's notion of communion with the departed with the present generation in the light of the Spirit and communion with the Saints made clear in the Bible. This is a pastoral need which cannot be over-emphasized among the Tumbuka. In Tumbuka tradition, we have already seen that the spirit world is a reality and that the bond between the living and the departed is strong. It is for this reason that a pastoral approach emphasizing this aspect of life would find support in Tumbuka.[36]

We have seen that the pastoral approach to the possessed as practised by African Independent churches aims at healing and integrating people within the framework of the church. Whereas in Tumbuka tradition, the sick and the possessed were taken to spirit mediums to be healed, in African Independent churches that function is taken over. The African Independent churches encourage their members to bring their sick and possessed to ministers within the church. There the people are set free from all illnesses and fears. Laying on of hands and exorcism are done in the Christian context. In the process, the

---

[35] *Ibid.*

[36] In a Presbyterian hymn, Tom Colvin has presented a way to meeting the need for communion with those in the spirit world:

God sends us his spirit to befriend and help us,
Recreate and guide us, spirit-friend.
Spirit who enlivens, sanctifies, enlightens,
Sets us free, is now our spirit-friend.

Chorus:
Spirit of our Father-friend,
Spirit of our Jesus, spirit friend,
Spirit of God's people, spirit-friend.

Now we are God's people, bonded by his presence,
Agents of his purpose, spirit-friend,
Lead us forward ever, slipping backward never,
To your re-made world, our spirit-friend.

The song is from Tamale in Ghana and is also popular among Presbyterians in Malawi. Tom S. Colvin, *Free to Serve: Hymns from Africa*, Glasgow: Iona Community. n.d. [1978], p. 19.

people are helped to trust in the supreme Spirit of God. At the same time, the people are helped to understand the power contained in the Christian faith. African Independent churches' approach to the problem of possession is certainly in the right direction. It attempts to meet the African people in their own culture and let that culture be transformed and judged by the power of the word.

Today the Livingstonia Synod among the Tumbuka is faced with the same pastoral problem, as African Independent churches have attempted to resolve, possession. Its members come from a background where possession is institutionalized. In their new religion, Tumbuka Christians are influenced by their past history. Their traditional understanding of spirit and its function makes them more receptive to the churches' teaching about the Spirit. The fundamental question is, how can the Livingstonia Mission accommodate the possession method and provide pastoral care which will assist its members to grow and express their faith in the local idiom? To do this, the church must use the Bible as its norm. The church will also need thorough self-examination and readjustment. It will have to change in many aspects, including liturgy, organization and theology.

Possession and Tumbuka Christians

Vimbuza spirit in Tumbuka tradition versus the Spirit of Jesus

We have noted earlier that possession in Tumbuka tradition was a sure way of authenticating religious experience. The Tumbuka regarded an individual priest as genuine and as having effective communication with a deity if he was possessed; in the state of possession, family members communicate with their lineage spirits. A healer was regarded as able to diagnose disease and to prescribe herbal medicine if he was possessed.

We also noted that possession in Tumbuka tradition provided a means for explaining disease. Physical illness of one kind or the other was explained in terms of spiritual forces made to bear upon the life of an individual. Disease was taken as a sign of disharmony between the physical world and the spirit world. Healing in this case was through a ritual involving possession.

In this section our interest is to discuss the pastoral problem of possession among Tumbuka Christians and suggest a possible solution. Within the Christian tradition, especially in the Bible, the radical and essential manifestation of the Spirit has been pointed out as freedom, effective communication, responsibility, love, etc. In the Bible we have also noted the manifestation of evil spirits and their suppressive power over human personality. The tension created by these two opposing forces upon humanity has been made evident and the pastoral approach to the problem given in the Bible has direct application for Tumbuka Christians.

One might ask, what is a Tumbuka Christian liberated from? To be a Tumbuka Christian is to be free from all other spirits and it is to be possessed with the Spirit of Jesus. This is what many Christians who have committed themselves to Jesus have experienced and still continue to experience. For example, Rev. Y. Kaunda confessed to having at one time been a patient of *vimbuza* . He stated that when he became a Christian, *vimbuza* spirits no longer had control over his life. Instead, the Spirit of Jesus possessed him, enabling him to live a Christian life and preach the good news of salvation to his people.[37]

A second example is that of Emeli Gwirangula at Mbalachanda. This lady became a Christian in 1960 after a serious illness. She was believed by her family to have been possessed by *virombo* and therefore was taken to a *virombo* doctor. When she recovered, Gwirangula became a Christian of the Livingstonia Synod. She said that while she was ill, she had felt specially called by God through dreams. Gwirangula claims that she is gifted with a gift of the Spirit. When there are certain events in the community or within the church which are about to happen, Gwirangula may see the events in her dreams before they actually happen. She told this writer and his colleagues that she didn't make the trip she had planned for the day we called on her because she had dreamed of receiving visitors from afar. Gwirangula does not make a business out of her gift. She is a faithful member of the church and, as a Christian, is involved in women's work within the church and in the community.[38] Certainly in the Tumbuka tradition, individuals possessed with *virombo* were known to be dreamers. Their dreams were connected with medicines and sometimes with social events. Some of their dreams were taken seriously by their family members and community. In the case of Gwirangula, her dreams do not direct her to herbal medicines. She is only happy to know that her gift is from God and enables her to understand her environment and live a Christian life in fellowship with other people.

If the cases of Kaunda and Gwirangula seem to separate them from the rest of the Christian community, it is because the theology in which they were formed has not made categories which express their cases. The categorizing of

---

[37] Personal interview with Rev. Y. Kaunda, Mzuzu congregation, 23 February 1983. Mr Kaunda is a prominent minister of religion within the Livingstonia Synod of the CCAP.

[38] Personal interview with Emeli Gwirangula, Mbalachanda, 7 March 1983.

possession among Tumbuka Christians should seek to respond creatively to the demands of the Gospel and of the people oppressed by spiritual forces. We saw in Luke 11:24-26 that Jesus recommended that when an individual has been freed from demonic spirits, he must not remain empty, but that the Spirit of God must occupy the empty space. Tumbuka Christians need to experience this presence of the Spirit of Jesus.

It is not enough to have theological categories which express the demands of the Gospel in the context of the Tumbuka. What is needed is a spirituality which embraces every detail of human life. Rowan Williams has defined spirituality as the dominion of the Spirit which touches "every area of human experience, the public and the social, the painful, negative, even pathological byways of the mind, the moral and rational world".[39]

This view of spirituality relates to Tumbuka Christians in that it opens up interpretation of their history, change and growth in terms of the salvific activity of God. This means that the Spirit of Jesus becomes the guiding agent in Tumbuka self-consciousness and interpretation of their history. It follows then that where the Spirit of Jesus is, there is liberation.[40] Such understanding of spirituality goes beyond the African Independent churches' pastoral approach in that the Spirit of Jesus permeates the whole life of a believer - his/her community and the cosmos. This Spirit of Jesus becomes the basis on which a Tumbuka Christian finds his freedom and unity with other people.

In Luke 4:1ff we noted how Jesus' spirituality was lived in possession of the Spirit. It was a spirituality inspired by the Spirit of God and lived in oneness with Him. It was also lived in love and service to humanity. It was a spirituality which arose from an intense spiritual experience. Tumbuka Christians ought to have, or rather, should share, this experience of the Spirit. They can share this experience of the Spirit if the pastoral strategy of the Livingstonia Synod accepts the possession method into the church. This would assist Tumbuka Christians to commit themselves to Jesus so that they become possessed with his Spirit and live in solidarity with all people.

Undoubtedly, a spirituality which lays emphasis on possession of the Spirit has its own problems. For some people it may mean giving up unprofitable speculations about the end of the world, or personal satisfaction resulting from a "holier than thou" attitude. We have already noted how this attitude led astray the Christians at Thessalonica. Being possessed with the Spirit of Jesus should enable a Tumbuka Christian to nourish his or her own spiritual life and to be

---

[39] Rowan Williams, *Christian Spirituality: a Theological History from the New Testament to Luther and St John of the Cross*, Atlanta: John Knox Press, 1979, p. 2.
[40] John 16:13.

creative, to love and serve the community. Such life for a Christian was comm-
ended by Paul when he said, "the harvest of the Spirit is love, joy, peace,
patience, kindness, goodness, fidelity, gentleness, and self-control"[41]

The second issue is celebration of life. Adrian Hastings has argued that
mission churches in Africa tended to be more concerned with the preservation
of their doctrines than developing a liturgy pattern which met African needs.[42]
Celebration of life is one such aspect of religion which should be built in the
liturgy of the church among the Tumbuka. This celebration denotes harmon-
ization and healing of life gained through the presence of the Spirit of Jesus
who liberates people from possession by evil spirits and other forces. The
celebration can be fostered in hymn singing, drum-beat, dance, hearing of the
Bible message, etc. This writer attended a service of worship at Ekwendeni in
which the celebration of life was a reality. When the collection was being
received, the whole congregation burst into hymn singing, clapping of hands
and drum-beat. About forty members of the congregation stood up and began
to dance to the rhythm. Soon they were joined by their minister who was
wearing his Calvinistic preaching gown. He too danced. The singing and
clapping increased and ululation decorated the joyful movement of the dancers.
Indeed, the atmosphere was that of celebration. The celebration was a natural
cultivation of the characteristics of Tumbuka personality and of local entities. It
was not just an emotional expression, but a celebration which expressed the
presence of Jesus and a deep sense of liberation. The whole congregation was
united in praising God through their offering, hymn singing, dance and their
whole being. They were uplifted and made to trust in the Spirit and power of
Jesus. This celebration has a healing effect. It makes the inexhaustible riches of
Jesus become a tangible reality.

The healing wrought in a liturgy of celebration of life allows spontaneity and
participation. Congregational members choose hymns at one point of worship,
or Bible verses which touch them and relate to their situation. The whole
congregation joins the individual in singing or in hearing a Bible verse being
read. Those who are moved to stand up and dance or shout 'Hallelujah', do so
without feeling out of place, because the structure of worship allows self-exp-
ression in that form. Harvey Sindima has pointed out that the significance of
celebration in African Christian worship should not scare mission churches
because it is a form tied to rigorous African tradition. Just as Jesus had power
to speak to Europe through the organ played in the church, so too Jesus has

---

[41] Galatians 5:72
[42] Adrian Hastings, *African Christianity: an Essay in Interpretation,* London: Geoffrey
Chapman, 1976, p. 9.

power to turn the drums of Africa into drums of salvation.[43] Without doubt, the celebration of life in worship among Tumbuka Christians has a healing effect. It unites individuals with the whole church, giving the assurance and hope in the power of Jesus. The whole church celebrates the Lordship of Jesus affirming his power over all other forces. In the process of celebration, the church finds its identity and stands together with individuals oppressed by evil spirits.

The method of exorcism is a pastoral strategy used by Jesus and later by his disciples. This is made apparent in our section on pastoral concern for the possessed in the Bible, as delineated above. For instance, we noted in Mark 1:21-27 how Jesus exorcised evil spirits in a man who was among worshippers in a synagogue. Jesus exorcised evil spirits both in places of worship and in public places. In the exorcisms, Jesus took seriously the belief held by the Jews about the existence of evil spirits. Therefore, by his action against these spirits, he constantly demonstrated his compassion and will for humanity. He wanted individuals who were oppressed by evil spirits to have abundant life, i.e. a life of freedom, peace, love, dignity, unity and service. The source of Jesus' power over evil spirits was his special relationship with God. He was aware of God's Spirit and through that Spirit, Jesus exorcised evil spirits.

Exorcism is therefore one pastoral strategy which should be applied in the Tumbuka situation. It is a radical substitution of past Tumbuka elements with something very important that has a Biblical basis. First, what is needed on the part of the church is an openness to the healing power of the Spirit of Jesus. This means that church leaders who are concerned with the possessed should be people who have themselves experienced this healing power of Jesus. Martin Israel alludes to this when he says, "for a pastor to be able to distinguish between false spirits and the Spirit of God, he must be a man who has himself drunk deeply of the Spirit of God".[44] It is for this reason that the church must examine itself and take seriously the healing power endowed upon it by Jesus.

Second, the existence of spirits and their effect on individuals must be taken seriously by the church. Recently David Alexander and Bill Rau have reported spirit possession at Chalumbe primary school in Zambia. Thirty-eight pupils were possessed and fell into trance - rubbing and scratching their bodies. Possession cases at the school grew so much that the school had to be closed down.[45] Alexander and Rau suggest that the children who got possessed were

---

[43] Harvey Sindima, paper presented at a seminar on Church and Society, Princeton University, 1983, p. 12.

[44] Martin Israel, *The Spirit of Counsel: Spiritual Perspectives in the Counselling Process*, London: Hodder and Stoughton, 1983, p.9.

[45] David Alexander and Bill Rau, "Spirit Possession at Chalumbe Primary School", paper

victims of social problems in the villages they came from. These social problems include extreme poverty, malnutrition, lack of recognition or status for the children in their community.

In the case of the Tumbuka situation, as already noted, possession was interpreted in religious terms. An individual was possessed by a spirit in order to enable him to perform a religious function on behalf of the community or family. On the other hand, possession came as an invasion by foreign spirits which made the possessed individual sick. In this sense, spirits in Tumbuka tradition are real. It is for this reason that the Livingstonia Synod cannot afford to push aside the idea of spirits among the Tumbuka as unreal.

By accepting the existence of spirits and their effect upon individuals, and relying on the healing power of Jesus, the Livingstonia Synod can then preach Christ as an alternative power able to exorcise those evil spirits. This makes it possible for the church to exercise faith healing within its circles and to offer meaningful pastoral help to individuals. In a situation like this, there will be no need for individuals to seek healing from diviners. In the atmosphere of a more powerful healer, Jesus Christ, the church will be in a position to cure diseases and exorcise evil spirits. Bishop Emmanuel Milingo in Zambia saw how members of his diocese were being possessed by evil spirits and needed help. He believed himself to have been possessed by a more powerful spirit, the Spirit of Jesus. Consequently, he exorcised evil spirits whenever the need arose.[46] Only a church which is in touch with the deeper religious aspects of human needs can appeal to the depths of the people's personality. This is what the church among the Tumbuka is called to.

Another aspect in pastoral concern for the possessed is the support of the community to the individual. In the Gospel of Mark 1:25ff we saw that wherever Jesus exorcised evil spirits and healed the sick, he did it in the presence of a group of people. And when he healed, he usually asked the individual to return to his own community. Jesus seems to have regarded the community as the root for pastoral care. He saw the community as having a direct relationship with the restoration of individuality and one's identity. In Jesus' view, the community also provided the healed individual with a base for service, participation and growth. Applied in the Tumbuka tradition, possession cure was a community affair. The possessed individual was cured in public and there in public, the healed individual was reintegrated into the

presented at a conference on the history of Central Africa religious systems, Lusaka, Zambia, n.d., pp. 1-2.

[46] Emmanuel Milingo is a Zambian Roman Catholic Archbishop whose work in exorcism has received wide publicity both in Africa and Europe. See Milingo, *The World in Between: Christian Healing and the Struggle for Spiritual Survival*, Maryknoll: Orbis, 1984.

community. By adapting this approach, the church would be basing its activity on the biblical teaching, as seen above. The churches, which form the community of believers, would give support to the healed individual by accepting that individual as a brother or sister. It would also be the church community which would share its liberated life with the individual so that he or she begins to taste the Spirit of Jesus. For example, M. Singleton cites a case of a girl who was cured of possession when she received assurance from both a Roman Catholic priest [Singleton himself] and her family.[47] The girl had fallen into possession, according to Singleton, due to an arranged marriage forced upon her by her father. This caused bitterness between the girl and her father. Consequently, she was possessed. When she received support from the priest and her family, she had in this group of people a sort of community which reconciled her with her father and resolved the problem which existed between them. Therefore, it is clear that a community of believers plays a significant role in the healing process of a possessed individual.

Ancestral spirits versus the Spirit of Jesus

How should the Livingstonia Synod deal pastorally with the question of ancestors in worship among Tumbuka Christians? In an earlier chapter, we noted that ancestors had great authority over their lineage in Tumbuka tradition. They made their presence felt by possessing their lineage. They possessed them to participate in decision making of their family, to warn them of serious disasters such as epidemics, illness, etc. They also possessed their lineage to remind them of their duty to the ancestors, i.e. offering of sacrifice and remembering them. Generally, ancestors were benevolent. When they punished people by sending illness or other misfortune, it was only to remind them of neglected duties or breach of some customs. Consequently, the authority exercised by ancestors over the living members of their family gave them a central position in worship. The Tumbuka regarded them as *vibanda* or *mizimu*, spirits, who were closer to *Chiuta*, God who was himself the Spirit. As the ancestors had lived an earthly life and shared their joys and sorrows with their kin, they were now in the best position to represent those of their kind to God. For this reason, possession by an ancestral spirit in Tumbuka tradition carried significant value.

When the Tumbuka convert to Christianity, the centrality of Jesus takes precedence over all spirits. The Bible teaching affirms that Jesus is the centre of

---

[47] M. Singleton, "Spirits and Spiritual Direction: the Pastoral Counseling of the Possessed", in E. Fashole-Luke (ed.), *Christianity in Independent Africa*, London: Rex Collings, 1979, pp. 472-473.

God's family and it is to this family that he draws all people, saving them from the power of Satan. Ancestors are not evil, neither are they saving powers, but they are loved departed lineages. Thus Jesus adopts people of different lineages into the one family of God. He himself becomes a brother to all.[48] Since liberation in the Tumbuka world-view means freedom from spiritual forces which impinge upon both the physical and spiritual life of the people, the brotherhood of Jesus must relate to such a world view. The Tumbuka is concerned with his or her ancestors or "spirit fathers", as Kwame Bediako calls them.[49] He or she wants to know whether the unique position of Jesus in the family of God fulfils the position of ancestors.

In Luke 4ff we noted how Jesus was aware of the Spirit of God. It was this awareness of the Spirit which made Jesus occupy the unique position in God's family. Jesus' relationship with God was a perfect relationship between Father and Son. In that relationship is demonstrated the notion of filial piety. When Jesus comes into the Tumbuka situation, he not only fulfils the position of ancestors but also transforms it. He fulfils the role of ancestors in that he assumes all power including the power of the ancestors. John Pobee has suggested that we regard Jesus as "the Great and Greatest Ancestor because of his final authority and power to provide good life.[50] In the Tumbuka situation, this approach fits in with the traditional thought forms. It is obvious that if Jesus becomes a brother to the Tumbuka, he also becomes an ancestor to them. His vicarious life and salvific death become meaningful to all human lineages, including the Tumbuka. When Jesus' Spirit influences a Tumbuka Christian, that Spirit is not regarded as coming from a foreigner. It is the Spirit of Jesus, their brother and ancestor. When Jesus comes into the Tumbuka situation, he transforms the role of ancestor. The unique position of Jesus in the Family of God puts him far above ancestors. The Bible teaching says that Jesus is the Saviour of humanity and the whole of creation. His life, death and resurrection affirm his Lordship. Consequently, when the Spirit of Jesus fills or possesses Tumbuka Christians, they become members of the family of God. Their blood ancestors who also need to be liberated by the Spirit of Jesus become mere earthly parents without divine power to protect or to threaten their lineage.

The pastoral viewpoint presented above emphasizes the Lordship of Jesus over the position of ancestors in Tumbuka tradition. Jesus comes into

---

[48]   Hebrews 2:10-13.

[49]   Kwame Bediako, *Biblical Christologies in the Context of African Traditional Religions*, V. Samuel and C. Sugden (eds.), Sharing *Jesus in the Two Thirds World*, Bangalore: Partnership in Mission-Asia, 1983, p. 140.

[50]   John S. Pobee, *Toward an African Theology*, Nashville: Abingdon, 1979.

Tumbuka tradition and affirms the important fatherly role played by the ancestors. At the same time, Jesus assumes all power and enables Tumbuka Christians to join the household of God and therefore live under the influence of the Spirit of Jesus. The Spirit becomes a living and meaningful personality whose power and influence upon the living is stronger than the numerous ancestral spirits. The Spirit of Jesus becomes a bridge between lineages who formerly looked to their particular ancestors. In this suggested pastoral approach, the solidarity which the Spirit of Jesus creates among Tumbuka Christians and their neighbours should be allowed to manifest itself in love, peace, joy, self-control and fidelity.

What we have said relates to ancestor spirit possession in that in our Tumbuka setting, Christians will view their ancestors in a new way. They will see their ancestors as individuals worth every respect due to a parent from a child. But the ancestors cease to be the influencing spirits on the living because Jesus Christ has assumed this responsibility. He has even gone further than ancestor spirit possession because his spirit renews, influences and unites various lineages and peoples. The Apostle Paul wrote to the Galatians:

> During our minority we were slaves to the elemental spirits of the universe, but when the term was completed, God sent his Son, to purchase freedom for the subjects of the law, in order that we might attain the status of sons.[51]

Paul recognized the unity between the Galatians and the Jews. This was wrought in by the Spirit of Jesus. As the Tumbuka convert to Christianity they too come under the influence of Jesus' Spirit and therefore unite with various Christians in Malawi and in the world.

We have seen that pastoral concern for the possessed among Tumbuka Christians begins with the assumption of conflict between the spirits in the Tumbuka world-view and the Spirit of Jesus. The goal of this pastoral concern is to heal and liberate individuals from suppressive spirits. The healing and liberating process has been seen to be concerned with physical, spiritual and emotional needs of the Tumbuka. In short, it is the healing and liberation of the whole person.

The healing process is made possible by the Spirit of Jesus who "fills" or "possesses" the Christian community, giving them power to commune with God and to serve their neighbours. The Spirit of Jesus, the ultimate source of power made available to the Christian community, is the instrument by which the Livingstonia Synod can provide the needed pastoral care to those oppressed by demonic spirits.

---

[51] Galatians 4:4-5.

The Livingstonia Synod can provide an effective pastoral care to the possessed by Christianizing the possession method. African Independent churches have attempted this, though not perfectly. The nature of healing sessions in African Independent churches does not differ from healing ceremonies in African traditional setting. The old order is transferred from the traditional setting into the church without alteration. For example, Felicity Edward's describes exorcism in a Zionist congregation in Grahamstown in South Africa. He says:

> After being put down, the patient was bound with a prayed-for card and was to whirl around on the spot faster and faster, while the drum was beaten and the congregation sang with increasing intensity ... and after the typical 'dancing in circle'(*ukugida*) which symbolizes wholeness, the patient collapsed to the floor.[52]

The dancing of the patient encouraged by loud singing and drum beat is a major part of the healing process in African Independent churches. This is not different from healing of *vimbuza* among the Tumbuka. It is only a reordering of the old religion in the new situation. Emphasis ought to be placed on the healing power and those who heal should always heal in the name of Jesus Christ. The disciples of Jesus healed various diseases including demon possession in Jesus' name. Prayer and laying on of hands, as practised by African Independent churches, should certainly be encouraged. The apostle Paul used prayer and laying on of hands on several occasions.[53] The dancing and singing practised by African Independent churches may come in the healing service as a way of praising God and celebrating the new life given to the healed individual. Another point which needs to be considered is spiritual experience. African Independent Churches' liturgy revolves around the idea of Spiritual experiences. Their practices of healing, prophesying and spirit possession are linked with the idea of spiritual experience.[54] Spiritual experience ought to be balanced by intellectual understanding so that Christians in the pew may be able to articulate their faith. But the Livingstonia Synod can improve upon the method by anchoring its theological understanding and biblical insights.

Tumbuka Christians are susceptible to a Christianity which emphasizes spiritual experiences and the manifestation of the Spirit. This is because in their tradition, the spirit world is regarded as having influence in everyday life, and possession by spirits was common. Now in their new religion, Tumbuka

---

[52] Felicity S. Edward's, "Amafufunyana Spirit Possession: A Report on some Recent Developments", *Religion in South Africa*, Vol. 5/2 (July 1984).

[53] Acts 11-19.

[54] Dillon-Mallone, *The Korsten Basketmakers*, p. 80ff.

Christians need a pastoral approach which will direct them to value the experience of the Spirit of Jesus and his creativity. Such an approach will require the liberation of the Tumbuka from *vimbuza*, *virombo* and *vyanusi* types of spirits. These spirits would be replaced by the Spirit of Jesus who will lead Tumbuka Christians to maturity in their new faith. The Apostle Paul refers to the Spirit of Jesus which inhabits a Christian when he says, "But you are not in the flesh, you in the Spirit, if the Spirit of God really dwells in you. Anyone who does not have the Spirit of Christ does not belong to him".[55]

We propose that the Livingstonia Synod, and indeed, the "mission churches" throughout, must take the beliefs of the indigenous people seriously. First, it must emphasize the existence of evil spirits, their power to influence people to do evil things and to cause illness. MacNutt says, "it is important to recognize them [evil spirits] rather than deny them".[56] By recognizing evil spirits, the church will then be able to deal with them effectively. In our study of spirit possession in the New Testament we saw that Jesus and later his disciples, took evil spirits seriously and through the Spirit of God they were able to conquer them. The church in Tumbukaland needs to be possessed with the Spirit of Jesus in order to confront evil spirits. It is in demonstrating its confidence in the power of Jesus over evil spirits that the church will meet the needs of those who feel enslaved by evil spirits.

Second, worship must be viewed as a healing process entailing interaction of individuals, the community and the intervention of God in human life. Worship of this nature will imply the restoration of broken relationship between one human and another, environment and God. This type of worship embraces the physical, emotional, social and spiritual dimension of life. We have already seen that in his healing ministry and preaching about the Kingdom of God, Jesus dealt with the total person. He went into the deep causes of disorder in an individual's life and put the individual in touch with the spirit world.

Third, the Livingstonia Synod ought to emphasize the Christian teaching of communion of saints. Most Tumbuka Christians have come to believe that saints are people like Saint Andrew and Saint Columba of Britain. This is because the Livingstonia Synod has neglected local saintly ancestors. The church is made up of the local saints and the distant saints. This is made possible by the spirit of Jesus which unites and frees all people.[57]

---

[55] Romans 8:9-10.
[56] MacNutt, *The Power of Healing*, p. 74.
[57] John 14-17.

We have noted several pastoral concerns among Tumbuka Christians in relation to possession and how these concerns can be met. It has become clear that the Spirit of Jesus is the power individuals can find liberation and regain their integrity. The church in Tumbukaland is called to make religious innovations and create relevant symbols to meet the needs of the present generation.

General Conclusion

1. The significance of possession and change in Tumbuka tradition

Given the understanding of possession in Tumbuka tradition as delineated in previous chapters, it can be said that this phenomenon had both religious and social implications. In both areas, it is a means by which society transforms itself.

In the religious sphere

Until 1845 when the Ngoni invaded Tumbukaland and destroyed Mlowoka's dynasty, possession in Tumbuka religion was a means for communicating with a deity and a means for healing disease.[58] Individuals who ascended to the summit of Chikhangombe hill to pray on behalf of the community, were regarded as susceptible to the spirit Chikhangombe. More often than not, priests and priestesses would be possessed by the spirit of Chikhangombe while they were on the summit. After the invasion by the Ngoni, possession by the spirit of Chikhangombe subsided and was replaced by vipiri, spirit snakes. As already noted in chapter three, vipiri were unlike the spirit of Chikhangombe. The old spirit Chikhangombe worked for the good of society. The individual possessed by it had, together with his community, full claim of the protective power of that spirit. Consequently, an individual possessed by Chikhangombe brought happiness, feasting and celebration into the community. The new spirits, vipiri, were dangerous and rebellious. Individuals did not need to go up Chikhangombe hill in order to be possessed by vipiri. And those possessed by vipiri became like snakes to the Ngoni. Therefore, the Tumbuka staged a rebellion in 1888 believing that vipiri would deliver them.[59] Vipiri failed to protect the Tumbuka leaving them humiliated by the Ngoni army.

---

[58] See chapter three on priests and priestesses of Chikhangombe.
[59] See chapter three on the Tumbuka rebellion.

After the rebellion, Tumbuka spirits of the land, i.e. *vimbuza* and *virombo* took from the old priests, providing the Tumbuka with a new religious power through which they could cope with the changing world. As the Ngoni married Tumbuka girls, the offspring from such marriages were susceptible to both Tumbuka and Ngoni spirits.[60] In such circumstances, possession by *vimbuza* or by Ngoni spirits, *vyanusi*, provided a common religious ground accepted by both the conquerors and the vanquished. However, Tumbuka spirits dominated the new religious scene. When certain issues threatened the welfare of the community, Tumbuka priests and diviners were better equipped to deal with the problem as they were more familiar with the environment than the Ngoni. For example, when the drought of 1896 threatened human and animal life, it was the Tumbuka diviners who were consulted.[61] Perhaps some of the Tumbuka diviners went up Chikhangombe hill to pray for the rain as had been done in Mlowoka's time. Although the rains did not come through their effort, Tumbuka diviners and their religion were a recognized force, at least before the advent of the missionaries.

The first major test of possession as a religious factor among the Tumbuka was the advent of missionaries in 1881. The missionaries brought a new religion whose power was radically different from of the Tumbuka religion. The missionaries, in a departure from the Tumbuka experience of spirits, brought the Bible and its teaching about Jesus, the only one Saviour able to deliver people from evil spirits.[62] The Tumbuka came to realize that they could not carry on with their spirit possession beliefs as they had done when they were under the Ngoni or Mlowoka. Christian religion was certainly the new religion and an alternative power. Therefore, converts to the new religion opted out of their old religion. Possession by *vimbuza*, *virombo* and *vyanusi* became a thing of the past.

In the social sphere

I have touched on the social significance of possession in Tumbuka tradition in our discussion about the religious sphere of the phenomenon. One point needs further clarification. Possession is a means for release from collective frustrations. Sheila Walker asserts that in possession ceremonies, the possessed individual, and his or her dance and acts, provide the community with a mirror

---

[60] See chapter three.
[61] See chapter four on Elmslie and the drought.
[62] We have discussed at length the question of Tumbuka conversion to Christianity in chapter four.

to see itself and some of its absurdities.[63] In the case of the Tumbuka, they were constantly under foreign domination and this must have been frustrating. In the 1740s Mlowoka established himself over a wide area of Tumbukaland. Studies on his movement have shown that his relationship with the Tumbuka was amicable. While he put his own viceroys to administer Tumbuka territories where there were no chiefs, or where weak chiefs existed, he promoted indigenous chiefs within his jurisdiction. He also strengthened his position by marrying daughters of the Tumbuka chiefs. Further, Mlowoka, a shrewd trader, exploited the ignorance of Tumbuka in such valuables as animal skins, ivory, iron ore and so forth. His trade with the Arabs on the east coast made him powerful in both the political and social life of the Tumbuka. Perhaps the Tumbuka felt the pressure brought to bear upon their lives by Mlowoka. The natural way open to the Tumbuka to dispel their emotions was through possession. It is not surprising that Vail argues that possession cases increased in Tumbukaland during Chikulamayembe's reign,[64] as Mlowoka's dynasty was later known. In the possession ceremonies, the Tumbuka exerted themselves establishing their identity. We have noted that the Tumbuka managed to hold on together through their possession ceremonies when they were defeated by the Ngoni in 1845.

2. Identifying possession practices among the Tumbuka by the missionaries

The main areas of interaction between Livingstonia missionaries and the Tumbuka in the 1881-1902 period were in issues related to particular interests of the two groups. Missionaries regarded their role as one of penetrating the various ethnic groups, challenging their beliefs, and changing the whole local way of life through education and evangelism. In this regard, Livingstonia missionaries had an economic advantage. This was wrought by the African Lakes Company which shuttled between Lake Malawi and Beira bringing in supplies to support the missionaries. While the missionaries engaged in Church work, they at the same time were a reliable source for the much needed calico, salt and other goods produced in the West.[65] The Tumbuka saw the missionaries as providing access to Western products, and as useful neutralizers of the political quarrels between the Ngoni on the one hand and the Tonga and

---

[63] Sheila Walker, *Ceremonial Spirit Possession in Africa and Afro-America:* Leiden: Brill, 1972.

[64] Vail, "Religion, Language and the Tribal Myth", pp. 221-213.

[65] McCracken, *Politics and Christianity*, p. 43.

the Tumbuka on the other. The Tumbuka change of religion was a gradual process which left their possession practices and deep spiritual experiences to surface at a much later period.

Missionaries, at least in the initial period, restricted their penetration into the heart of Tumbuka spirit beliefs when they built "mission station colonies". In these colonies, insulated from Tumbuka tradition, the missionaries invited their converts to settle.[66] While this idea of mission colonies provided the missionaries with an opportunity to study Tumbuka language and concentrate their evangelization work on a specific group of people, it sheltered them from studying the customs and beliefs of the people at close range. Possession practices and ceremonies went on freely in the traditional villages where missionaries had no control. Further, the weakness of the colonies was that people who were attracted to them were often marginal people who had no influence on possession practices and the whole religious life of the Tumbuka. It is therefore not surprising that the missionaries learned little about possession cults among the Tumbuka, at least in the initial period. However, the idea of colonies was soon abandoned.

It needs to be added that the missionaries were sheltered from identifying possession tendencies among the Tumbuka because the first Christians broke away from their traditional world-view. Personalities like Domingo and Mwase had grown up on mission stations, being educated under missionary influence. Later they were able to influence many Tumbuka because of their style of life and manners of worship which were closer to that of the admired missionaries than that known in Tumbukaland. Tumbuka Christians of that early period were new converts and imitators of the white men's religion and style of life. Thus they did not see the value of possession and their own ways of worship in facing the emerging new world. However, there were always missionaries like Fraser who saw value in certain religious beliefs and customs of the Tumbuka and wanted them Christianized. The opinion and work of such individuals tended to capture the responsiveness of the indigenous people in religious matters.[67]

Fraser's significance for the identification of possession practices derived mainly from his sympathy with the beliefs and customs of the Tumbuka. He had the task of bridging the religious gap between the missionaries and the indigenous people. In chapters four and five, we noted that Fraser was the one who studied possession practices among the Tumbuka. He informed the

---

[66] See chapter four for a detailed discussion on mission colonies and conversion of the Tumbuka.
[67] See chapter four for the contributions of Donald Fraser.

mission that the phenomenon was interwoven with the religion of the land and was not just a psycho-pathological disease as other missionaries had believed. Without Fraser, it is doubtful if the fiery evangelistic convention of 1908-1910 could have taken place in Tumbukaland. Without him, it is likely that Charles Inwood's campaign of 1910 which awakened the Tumbuka religious consciousness may not have received the publicity it did both within Malawi and abroad. However, Fraser's religious enthusiasm was not shared by many of the older missionaries. He had to cool down the religious zeal and manifestations of the spirit which had caught up Tumbuka Christians in the 1908-1910 period.

It was during and immediately after the 1908-1910 evangelistic campaign that the missionaries identified possession tendencies among Tumbuka Christians. The simple theme, "The power of the Holy Spirit", preached during the campaign as an important aspect of Christian life triggered off religious experiences never seen before among the Tumbuka Christians. Some people were blessed with visions and dreams, others shook during meetings while others were hysterical.[68] Perhaps possession beliefs in Tumbuka religion had become mixed with the Christian teaching about being filled with the Holy Spirit. This mixing of the old and the new produced a religious experience similar to that of Pentecostals. It became important for the missionaries to check this rather strange religious experience. Mission agents, who were the eyes of the missionaries in remote villages, brought to the notice of the missionaries individual Christians who were involved in possession activities. By 1915 the whole mission was aware of the extent to which Christians were involved in possession practices. This is made evident by the "superstitions and charms committee" formed in that year.

The first, and perhaps only Livingstonia Mission meeting called to discuss the issue of possession was in 1915. It was attended by all Tumbuka elders and licentiates. Only two missionary doctors were at the meeting, Turner and McIne. The former was the secretary of the meeting while the latter was the chairman. The meeting's conclusions were that *vimbuza, virombo* and *vyanusi* were a pathological disease which could be cured medically. The presence of the two physicians in the meeting and the absence of missionary pastors suggested strongly that the missionaries saw the phenomenon as purely medical. It is not surprising that the Presbytery received the report of the meeting without any debate.[69] The view adopted by the missionaries on the issue was different from that of missionaries elsewhere in Africa. In Kenya

---

[68] See chapter four on Fraser and Inwood's campaigns.
[69] See chapter five on the study of possession by the missionaries.

possession was viewed by missionaries as the work of the devil, and therefore antagonistic to Christianity.[70] What was common among Livingstonia missionaries and those elsewhere on the issue was that converts involved in possession ceremonies were excluded from church membership. In Malawi converts found guilty were suspended for a period of nine to twelve months. [71]

The conviction that Christianity is the only way to salvation also played its role as a motivating factor among the missionaries. In a New Year's service of worship attended by missionaries only in 1916, Dr Laws explained that the mission's task, among other things, was to liberate the indigenous people from superstitions by preaching Jesus Christ as Saviour.[72] According to Laws, Tumbuka spirit beliefs could not coexist with the Christians faith. Therefore, with the best of intentions, the missionaries insisted that those Tumbuka who became Christians were to abandon their traditional beliefs and join the family of God through Jesus Christ. It is for this reason that the mission continued to reject possession whenever it occurred among its members.

3. Tumbuka point of entry into the Christian Faith

The point of entry in Tumbuka Christianity is certainly not sin, but evil spirits. The Tumbuka world-view has been shown to be divided into two, but inseparable components: the physical world where man lives and acts his life, and the spirit world. There are power structures in both the physical and the spirit worlds. The latter includes *Chiuta*, the Almighty Creator, who is beyond man and exerts authority over man and the whole physical world. In the spirit world there are two sections comprised of spirits from below and spirits from above. The spirits from below include witches and various enemies of society, *fumu za pasi*. These spirits from below are generally evil. On the other side there are spirits from above which include ancestors, spirits which are independent of man, and *Chiuta*, the Greatest Spirit. If these spirits from above punish man, it is only a corrective measure.

The two sections of the spirit world, the spirits from below and from above meet in the physical world where man lives. The Tumbuka find themselves under the influence of both sections. Therefore, in their whole life, the Tumbuka attempt, through ritual, to find freedom from these 'spirit forces'.

---

[70] F.B. Welbourn, "Spirit Initiation in Ankole and a Christian Spirit Movement in Kenya", in Beattie and Middleton, *Spirit Mediumship and Society*, p. 302.
[71] See chapter five.
[72] Robert Laws, Miscellaneous sermons by Dr Robert Laws, archival material of the Livingstonia Mission, MNA L1 1/3/12.

They try to appease the spirits above so that they can receive their blessings and protection. When they appease spirits from below, it is to ward off their evil intentions. Therefore, in such a situation, possession is a way or a means by which the Tumbuka attains his or her salvation, i.e. peace and harmony between the spirit world and the physical world. This peace and harmony is epitomized by good relationships in the community and in individual families.

When the Tumbuka convert to Christianity, the major attraction is an existential one. They want the protecting power of the Spirit of Jesus to shield them from malevolent spirits and other fears. To be sure that the Spirit of Jesus is adequate, they need to experience this Spirit. To the Tumbuka Christian, this experience comes through possession with that Spirit of Jesus. This attitude of converts is not peculiar to them. M.J. Field alludes to it among the Ga of Southern Ghana when she says, "They claim that their worship is in the manner of the Christian communities described in the Acts of the Apostles and that they are possessed and moved by the same spirit in the same way and in same numbers".[73] Field explains this attitude as resulting from a blending of the 'old' and the 'new'. In some converts, the blending may be a mere reordering of the old in a new situation. In others the blending may be a genuine shift from the old to the new. Rather, the old forms reduce their importance while the new take over. Therefore, the 'old' may, to a certain degree and at some later point, influence the individual's response to the new. This point is summed up by Adrian Hastings when he says,

> At the conversion, one almost inevitably stresses the degree of rupture rather than continuity involved in the process. At a later date the dimension of continuity will reassert itself: Once one is surely established in the new fellowship, one will bit by bit realize better the deep congruity of much that went before with one's present understanding.[74]

Therefore, among Tumbuka Christians, possession continues as a religious imagery. The difference between the old and the new is that in the new, possession becomes a means for experiencing the Spirit of Jesus. The old *vimbuza*, *virombo*, and *vyanusi* no longer have power to influence them. The Apostle Paul speaks for the Tumbuka Christians when he says,

> During our minority we were slaves to the elemental spirits of the universe, but when the term was completed, God sent his own Son ... to purchase freedom for the subjects of law, in order that we might attain the status of sons.[75]

---

[73] M.J. Field, "Spirit Possession in Ghana", in Beattie and Middleton (eds.), *Spirit Mediumship and Society*, p. 10

[74] Hastings, *African Christianity*, p. 44.

[75] Galatians 4:3-5.

What should rule Tumbuka Christians' lives is the Spirit of Jesus that gives them freedom and hope for a glorious future in the family of God.

The apparent ambivalence in the Tumbuka converts is due to unsatisfactory redefinition of the possessing spirit. While new Tumbuka Christians embrace Christianity because of the power of the Spirit of Jesus which liberates and gives hope, some of them continue to be possessed by *vimbuza* etc. Perhaps, such people are not challenged enough to experience the power of the Spirit of Jesus and to make the necessary adjustments in their new religion. Or it may be that some of them want to have the advantage of both worlds at the same time. This state of affairs continues to be a problem for many Tumbuka Christians today, and among many Christians throughout Africa.

An option open to the mission church among the Tumbuka to solve the problem is a pastoral strategy which utilizes the possession method. This method, based on biblical teaching and deep theological reflection, should offer healing for both the physical and spiritual needs of the Tumbuka. It will also respond to the questions which Tumbuka Christians ask relating to possession and the people's fears. With the alternative power the church offers, Tumbuka Christian life should be expressed more in celebration of life rather than doctrine, and more in local imagery than in Western formulations.

Finally, spirit possession among Tumbuka Christians has not yet been studied in the church, but Livingstonia Synod has recently been less vocal about this subject than it was during the missionary period. However, Livingstonia Synod is aware of the subject and has at certain times spoken out on the issue. It has publicly warned its members against false prophets like Chikanga who claim to be possessed with the Spirit of God by which they are empowered to heal disease and cleanse society of every evil.[76] One important step the church ought to take is to convince its members and those outside it that possession with the Spirit of Jesus is biblical and final. Through this spirit, both individuals and society are made free from fear of evil spirits and disease. Those possessed with the spirit of Jesus become agents of God's Spirit and his liberating power.

---

[76] Livingstonia Synod minute book, 1965. For eye witness accounts see Boston Soko Nchimi Chikanga, *The Battle against Witchcraft in Malawi*, Blantyre: CLAIM-Kachere, 2002.

Oral sources

Interviews

Laiton Banda: A preacher of the Gospel of God International Church. Interviewed at Katoto village, Mzuzu, 7 February 1983.

Clement Chawura: A *vimbuza nchimi*, interviewed at Chimara banthu, Chiwiniwa village, Rumphi, 17 February 1983.

Chaputa Chimaliro: A *vyanusi* doctor, interviewed at Ekwendeni, 14 February 1983.

Elizabeth Chirwa: A former *vimbuza* patient, interviewed at Rumphi Secondary School, 17 February 1983.

Rev. F. Chunga: Chairman of the Zomba Theological Board, interviewed at Blantyre mission, 12 March 1983.

Laiton C. Gondwe: A grandchild of Mlowoka, interviewed at Bangalala village, Rumphi, 15 February 1983.

Rev. S. Kamanga: Moderator of Livingstonia Synod, formerly pastor of Henga Valley, interviewed at Ekwendeni, 14 February 1983.

Rev. Y.C. Kaunda: Pastor at Mzuzu congregation and an Ngoni historian, interviewed, 7 February, 1983.

M. Kondowe: A *vimbuza nchimi*, interviewed at Embangweni, 31 January 1983.

Rev. W. Manda: Pastor of Bandawe congregation, interviewed at Bandawe, 25 January 1983.

Rev. H. Mhone: Deputy General Secretary for Livingstonia Synod, interviewed at Mzuzu 23 February 1983.

Rev. J.B. Mhone: Retired pastor and the first Malawian General Secretary of Livingstonia Synod, interviewed at Mgodi village, 4 February 1983.

M. Mhone: Wife of a Presbyterian minister, interviewed at Mzuzu, February 1983.

C. Mkandawire: A Tumbuka *msofi*, priest, interviewed at Ngonga village, Rumphi, 17 January 1983.

Moyo: A Tumbuka elder, interviewed at Bangala village, Rumphi, 15 February 1983.

R. Nhlane: A *virombo nchimi*, interviewed at Embangweni, 31 January 1983.

A.M. Nyasulu: Former Cabinet Minister of the Malawi Government, interviewed at Mzokoto village, 16 February 1983.

M. Nyirenda Mzimu: A *vimbuza nchimi*, interviewed at Mzimba, 16 February 1983.

B. Silo: An Ngoni elder, interviewed at Ekwendeni, 13 and 29 February 1983.

Solomon Vitendwe: A village elder, interviewed at Luvili village, Bolera, 15 February 1983.

Personal correspondence

Rev. Evans Jere: Youth director at Ekwendeni Lay Training Centre.

Rev. Hastings Mhone: Deputy General Secretary for the Synod of Livingstonia, Mzuzu.

Mr P. Ndovi: A Tumbuka Christian and elder at St Michael and All Angels, Blantyre.

Dr Kings Phiri: Head of the department of History, Chancellor College, University of Malawi.

Mr Boston Soko: Lecturer in Linguistics and French, Chancellor College, University of Malawi, then on study leave in France.

Manuscripts

Department of Religious Studies, University of Aberdeen

Law Papers

National Library of Scotland

Letterbooks of the secretaries of the Foreign Missions Committee of the Free Church of Scotland, 1875-1920.
Letters from the missionaries at Livingstonia to the Secretaries in Scotland, 1881-1925.
Letters from the Foreign Missions Committee to Dr Robert Laws, 1875-1907.

Malawi National Archives

Letter from Dr Robert Laws to Secretaries of the Foreign Missions Committee of the Free Church of Scotland, 1885-1916.
Letters from Dr Robert Laws to Dr Hetherwick, Blantyre Mission, 1908-1912.
Life of Rev. Charles Chinula, n.d.
A note of certain local dances and their significance in native minds, by J. Martin, 1927. Government records, Kasungu district (1).
Miscellaneous sermon collection and addresses by Dr Laws, 1883-1907.

National Bible Society of Scotland

Letters from W. Turner to W.M. Knight, 1918-1930.
Tumbuka Bible Translation, 1929.

Malawi collection, Library of the University of Malawi.

Domingo papers
Kamwana papers

Magazines

Aurora 1897-1902
Bandawe Journals 1881-1890
Church of Scotland Foreign Mission Reports 1908-1936.
Church of Scotland year book 1874-1920.
Livingstonia Mission annual reports 1890-1925.
Livingstonia Mission Council minutes 1895-1924, 1965
Livingstonia Presbytery minutes 1899-1983.
Livingstonia Mission statistics 1890-1936.
Life and Work in British Central Africa 1888-1916.
Minutes of congregations of the Livingstonia Mission 1890-1950.
Minutes of the Foreign Missions Committee of the Free Church of Scotland 1874-1926.

Unpublished thesis and papers

Alexander, D. and B. Rau, "Spirit Possession in Cholumbe Primary School", paper presented at a conference on the history of Central African religious systems, Lusaka, Zambia, n.d.

Chakanza, J.C., "A General Survey of Independent Churches in Malawi", M. Litt., University of Aberdeen, 1979.

Chiphangwi, S.D., "Why People Join the Christian Church: Trends in Church Growth in the Blantyre Synod of the Church of Central Africa Presbyterian, 1960-1975", Ph.D., University of Aberdeen, 1978.

Chuba, B.S., "African Culture and Christian Worship in Zambian Protestant Churches", M.Th., University of Aberdeen, 1983.

Dillon-Mallone, C.M., "The Korsten Basketmakers: A Study of the Masowe Apostles, an Indigenous African Religious Movement", Ph.D., University of Manchester, 1976.

Dudley, G., "Mircea Eliade and the Recovery of Archaic Religions", Ph.D. University of Pennsylvania, 1972.

Houser, T., "The Extent of Karonga Spirit Possession among the Hlengwe in Rhodesia", seminar paper presented at a conference on African Religion held in Harare, n.d.

Komba, J.J., "God and Man", Ph.D., Pontifical Urbanian University, Rome, 1956.

Okorocha, C.C., "Salvation in Igbo Religious Experience: Its Influence on Igbo Christianity", Ph.D., University of Aberdeen, 1982.

Osume, C.E., "A Study of Okpe Theophanies and their Correspondences in the Old Testament", Ph.D., University of Aberdeen, 1984.

Ross, A.C., "The Origin and Development of the Church of Scotland Mission, Blantyre, Nyasaland 1875-1926", Ph.D., University of Edinburgh, 1968; published as *Blantyre Mission and the Making of Modern Malawi*, Blantyre: CLAIM, 1996.

Sindima, H., "The Drums of Africa", paper presented at a seminar on Church and Society at Princeton University, 1983.

Soko, B., "*Vimbuza* Spirit Possession", a cyclostyled book, University of Malawi, 1978.

Souza, Alverson L. de, "A Black Heart: The Work of Thomas Jefferson Bowen among Blacks in Africa and in Brazil between 1840 and 1875", M.Th., University of Natal, 1998.

Thompson, J., "Fraser and the Ngoni", Ph.D., University of Edinburgh, 1978.

I obtained some helpful information on spirit possession through Dr John Parratt, head of the department of Religious Studies at Chancellor College, University of Malawi. He gave me access to relevant seminar papers of his third year undergraduate students, 1977-1980.

Books and articles

Abdallah, Y.B., The Yaos: *Chikala cha waYao*, Zomba: Government Press, 1919, 2nd ed., ed. and trans. M. Sanderson, London: Frank Cass, 1973.

Abraham, DP., "The Roles of Chaminuka and the Mhondoro Cults in Shona Political History", in E. Stokes and R. Brown (eds), *The Zambesian Past: Studies in Central African History*, Manchester: University of Manchester Press, 1966.

Ajayi, J.F.A., *Christian Missions in Nigeria 1841-1891*, London: Longman, 1965.

Alden, K., "Possession by the Holy Spirit in Kimbangu", *International Review of Mission*, Vol. 25/29 (1973), pp. 21-27.

Baeta, C.G., *Prophetism in Ghana: A Study of "Spiritual" Churches*, London: SCM, 1962.

Barrett, C.K., *The Holy Spirit and the Gospel Tradition*, London: SPCK, 1947.

Barrett, D.B., *African Initiatives in Religion*, Nairobi: East Africa Publishing House, 1971.

Barrett, D.B., *Schism and Renewal in Africa: An Analysis of Six Thousand Contemporary Religious Movements*, London: Oxford University Press, 1968.

Barrington-Ward, S., "The Centre Cannot Hold: Spirit Possession as Redefinition", in E. Fashole-Luke et al. (eds.), *Christianity in Africa*, London: Rex Collings, 1978.

Beattie, J.H.M., "Spirit Mediumship in Bunyoro", in J. Beattie and J. Middleton (eds.), *Spirit Mediumships and Society in Africa*, London: Routledge and Kegan Paul, 1969.

Beattie, J.H.M., *Other Cultures*, New York: Free Press of Glencoe, 1964.

Bone, D., "Islam in Malawi", *Journal of Religion in Africa*, Vol. 13 (1982), pp. 126-149.

Bourdillon, M.F.C., *The Shona Peoples: An Ethnography of the Contemporary Shona, with Special Reference to their Religion*, Gweru: Mambo, 1976.

Bourguignon, E., "Introduction: A Framework for the Comparative Study of Altered States of Consciousness", in E. Bourguignon (ed.), *Religion, Altered States of Consciousness, and Social Change*, Columbus: Ohio State University Press, 1973.

Bowen, T.J., *Missionary Labours and Adventures in Central Africa*, New York: Charleston, 1857, 2nd ed., London: Frank Cass, 1968.

Brelsford, W.V., *The Tribes of Northern Rhodesia*, Lusaka: Northern Rhodesia Government Press, 1956.

Bryant, A.T., "The Zulu Cult of the Dead", *Man*, Vol. 95 (1917).

Chilivumbo, A.B., "Vimbuza or Mashawe: A Mystic Therapy", *African Music Society Journal* (1981), pp. 1-7.

Codrington, R., "The Central Angoniland District of the Protectorate", *Geographical Journal*, Vol. 10/15 (May 1898), pp. 11-19.

Colvin, T.S., *Free to Serve: Songs from Africa*, Glasgow: Iona Community, n.d., [1978].

Dammann, E., "A Tentative Philological Typology of some African High Deities", *Journal of Religion in Africa*, Vol. 2 (1969), pp. 81-95.

Daneel, M.L., *Old and New in Southern Shona Independent Churches*, 3 Vols., Vol. 1, *Background and Rise of the Major Movements*, The Hague: Mouton, 1971.

Daneel, M.L., *The God of the Matopo Hills: An Essay on the Mwari Cult in Rhodesia*, The Hague: Mouton, 1970.

Debenham, Frank, *Nyasaland: The Land of the Lake*, London: HMSO, 1955.

Dickson, K.A. and P. Ellingworth (eds.), *Biblical Revelation and African Beliefs*, London: Lutterworth, 1969.

Dillon-Malone, C.M., *The Korsten Basketmakers: A Study of the Masowe Apostles, an Indigenous African Religious Movement*, New York: Fordham University Press, 1976.

Duff, H.L., *Nyasaland under the Foreign Office*, London: George Bell, 1903.

Dunn, J.G.D., *Baptism in the Holy Spirit: a Re-examination of the New Testament Teaching on the Gift of the Spirit in Relation to Pentecostalism Today*, London: SCM, 1970.

Dunn, J.G.D., *Jesus and the Spirit*, London: SCM, 1975.

Edwards, F.S., "Amafufunyane Spirit Possession: A Report on some Recent Developments", *Religion in South Africa*, Vol. 5/2 (July 1984).

Eiselen, M.W. and J. Schapera, "Religious Beliefs and Practices", in I. Schapera (ed.), *The Bantu Speaking Tribes of South Africa*, London: Routledge and Kegan Paul, 1957.

Eliade, M., *A History of Religious Ideas*, London: Collins, 1979.

Elmslie, W.A., *Among the Wild Ngoni: Being Some Chapters in the History of the Livingstonia Mission in British Central Africa*, Edinburgh and London: Oliphant, Anderson and Ferrier, 1899.

Evans-Pritchard, E.E., *Nuer Religion*, Oxford: Clarendon Press, 1956.

Evans-Pritchard, E.E., *The Nuer: a Description of Livelihood and Political Institutions of Nilotic People*, Oxford: Clarendon, 1940.

Field, M.J., "Spirit Possession in Ghana", in J. Beattie and J. Middleton (eds.), *Spirit Mediumship and Society in Africa*, London: Routledge and Kegan Paul, 1969.

Firth, R., "Problems and Assumptions in Anthropological Study of Religion", *Journal of the Royal Anthropological Institute*, Vol. 89/2, 1963.

Fortes, M., "Some Reflections on Ancestors Worship in Africa", in M. Fortes and G. Dieterlen (eds.), *African Systems of Thought*, London: Oxford University Press, 1965.

Fraser, Agnes, *Donald Fraser of Livingstonia*, London: Hodder and Stoughton, 1934.

Fraser, Donald, *African Idylls: Portraits and Impressions of Life on a Central African Mission Station*, London: Seeley, 1923.

Fraser, Donald, *Livingstonia: The Story of Our Mission*, Edinburgh: Foreign Mission Committee of the United Free Church of Scotland, 1915.

Fraser, D., *Winning a Primitive People*, London: Seeley, 1914.

Gamitto, A.C.P., *King Kazembe*, Lisbon: Junta de Investigaçoes do Ultramar, 1960.

Gee, D., *The Initial Evidence of the Baptism of the Holy Spirit*, Surrey: Kenley, 1959.

Hanna, A.J., *The Story of the Rhodesias and Nyasaland*, London: Faber and Faber, 1965.

Hastings, A., *A History of African Christianity 1950-1975*, London: CUP, 1979.

Hastings, A., *African Christianity: an Essay in Interpretation*, London: Geoffrey Chapman, 1976.

Hay, M., *Charles Inwood: His Ministry and his Secret*, London: Marshall, Morgan, Scott, 1929.

Hetherwick, A., *Church Service Annual*, Edinburgh: T. and T. Clark, 1924.

Hetherwick, A., *The Gospel and the African*, Edinburgh: T. and T. Clark, 1932.

Hodgson, A.G.O., "Notes on the Achewa and Angoni of the Dowa District of the Nyasaland Protectorate", *Journal of the Royal Anthropological Institute of Great Britain and Ireland*, Vol. 63 (1933), pp. 123-164.

Hodgson, J., *The God of the Xhosa: A Study of the Origins and Development of the Traditional Concepts of the Supreme Being*, Cape Town: Oxford University Press, 1982.

Hollenweger, W.J., *The Pentecostals*, London: SCM, 1972.

Horton, R., "African Conversion", *Africa*, Vol. 4/2 (1971), pp. 85-108.

Idowu, E.B., *Olodumare: God in Yoruba Belief*, London: Longman, 1962.

Inwood, C., *An African Pentecost*, Edinburgh and London: Longman, 1962.

Irving, E., "The Dealing Virtue of Baptism", Homily 11, Homilies in Baptism, *Collected Writings*, Vol. 2, 1829.

Israel, M., *The Spirit of Counsel: Spiritual Perspectives in the Counselling Process*, London: Hodder and Stoughton, 1983.

Jack, J.W., *Day Break in Livingstonia: the Story of Livingstonia Mission*, Edinburgh and London: Oliphant, Anderson and Ferrier, 1901.

Johnson, W.P., *My African Reminiscences, 1876-1895*, London: UMCA, 1926.

Johnson, W.P., *Nyasa, the Great Water*, London: Humphrey and Milford, 1922.

Johnston, H.H., *British Central Africa*, London: Methuen, 1897.

Jules-Rosette, B., "Songs and Spirit: the Use of the Songs in the Management of Ritual Context", *Africa*, Vol. 45/23 (1975), pp. 150-165.

Kalilombe, P.A., "The African Local Churches and World-wide Roman Catholic Communion", in E. Fashole-Luke et al. (eds.), *Christianity in Independent Africa*, London: Collings, 1978;

Kalilombe, P.A., *Theology at the Grassroots: Theological Essays from Malawi*, Gweru: Mambo, 1998.

Kalu, O., "Gods in Retreat: Models of Religious Change in Africa", *Journal of Humanities* (Lagos), Vol. 1/1 (1977).

Krige, E.J., *The Social System of the Zulus*, London: Longman, 1936.

Lang, A., *The Making of Religion*, London: Longman 1898, 2nd ed. 1900.

Lee, S.G., "Spirit Possession among the Zulu", in J. Beattie and J. Middleton (eds.), *Spirit Mediumship and Society in Africa*, London: Routledge and Kegan Paul, 1969.

Lewis, I.M., "A Structural Approach to Witchcraft and Spirit Possession", in Mary Douglas (ed.), *Witchcraft: Confessions and Accusations*, London: Tavistock, 1970.

Lewis, I.M., *Ecstatic Religion*, London: Penguin, 1971.

Lienhardt, G., *Divinity and Experience: the Religion of the Dinka*, Oxford: Clarendon, 1961.

Linden, I. and J., "Chilembwe and the New Jerusalem", *Journal of African History*, Vol. 12/4.

Linden, I., *Catholics, Peasants and Chewa Resistance in Nyasaland 1889-1939*, London: Longman, 1974.

Livingstone, D. and C., *Narrative of an Expedition to the Zambezi and its Tributaries*, London: Ward, Lock and Co., 1927.

Livingstone, W.P., *Laws of Livingstonia*, London: Hodder and Stoughton, 1921.

Lloyd, A., *Quaker Social History 1669-1738*, London: Longman, 1950.

Ludwig, A.M., "Altered States of Consciousness", in R. Prince (ed.), *Trance and Possession States*, Montreal: R.M. Bucke Memorial Society, 1968.

Mabundo, P., *An African David and Jonathan*, London: Westminster Press, 1926.

MacDonald, D., *Africana: the Heart of Heathen Africa*, 2 vols., London: 1882, [reprint] Dawsons of Pall Mall, 1969.

Mackenzie, D.R., *The Spirit-Ridden Konde*, London: Seeley Service, 1925.

Malingo, E., *The World Between: Christian Healing and the Struggle for Spiritual Survival*, Maryknoll: Orbis, 1984.

Martin, M-L., *Kimbangu: an African Prophet and His Church*, Oxford: Basil Blackwell, 1975.

Marwick, M.G., *History and Tradition in East Central Africa*, London: Longman, 1963.

Mather, A., "Talking Points: the Charismatic Movement", *Themelios: an International Journal of Theological Studies*, Vol. 9/3 (April 1984), pp. 11-22.

Mbiti, J.S., "Spirit Possession among the Lugbara", in J. Beattie and J. Middleton (eds.), *Spirit Mediumship and Society in Africa*, London: Routledge and Kegan Paul, 1969.

MacAlpine, A.G., "Tonga Religious Beliefs and Customs", *African Affairs*, Vol. 5/19 (1906), pp. 187-190, 257-268, 377-380; Vol. 6/24 (1906-1907), pp. 375-384.

McCracken, K.J., *Politics and Christianity in Malawi 1887-1940: the Impact of Livingstonia Mission in the Northern Province*, London: Cambridge University Press, 1977. 2nd edition: Blantyre: CLAIM-Kachere, 2000.

McDonnell, K., *Charismatic Renewal and the Churches*, New York: Seabury Press, 1976.

McMinn, R.D., "Some Tumbuka Dances", *Aurora: a Journal of Missionary News and Christian Work*, Vol. 4/24 (1 December 1900), pp. 2-13.

Moltmann, J., *The Church in the Power of the Spirit*, London: SCM, 1977.

Mufuka, K.N., *Mission and Politics in Malawi*, Kingston, Ontario: Limestone Press, 1977.

Muga, E., *African Response to Western Christian Religion*, Nairobi: East African Literature Bureau, 1975.

Mühlen, H., *A Charismatic Theology: Initiation in the Spirit*, London: Burns and Oats, 1978.

Mulago, V., "Vital Participation", in K.A. Dickson and P. Ellingworth (eds.), *Biblical Revelation and African Beliefs*, London: Lutterworth, 1969.

Mumba, Levi, "The Religion of My Fathers", *International Review of Missions*, Vol. 19 (1930)..

Oliver, R. and A. Atmore, *Africa Since 1800*, London: Cambridge University Press, 1972.

Opoku, K., "When the Spirit of Truth Comes", in S.J. Samartha (ed.), *Faith in the Midst of Faiths: Reflections on Dialogue in Community*, Geneva: World Council of Churches, 1977.

Pachai, B., *Malawi: the Story of the Nation*, London: Longman, 1972.

Pambe, I.M., "The Symbolism of Spirit Possession", in *Service Pastoral Orientation*, Vol. 5.

Parratt, J.K., "Mwasi and the Origin of the Blackman's Church", *Journal of Religion in Africa*, Vol. 9/3 (1978), pp. 193-206.

Parrinder, G., *African Traditional Religion*, London: Sheldon, 1954.

Parrinder, G., *Mysticism in the World's Religions*, London: Sheldon, 1976.

Parrinder, G., *Religion in Africa*, London: Pall Mall, 1969.

Parrinder, G., *Religion in an African City*, London: Pall Mall, 1953.

Payne, E.A., "The Anabaptists", in G.R. Elton (ed.), *The New Cambridge Modern History, Vol. 2: The Reformation*, Cambridge: Cambridge University Press, 1958.

P'Bitek, Okot, *Religion of the Central Luo*, Nairobi: East Africa Literature Bureau, 1971.

Pike, A.H., "A Pre-colonial History of Malawi", *Nyasaland Journal*, Vol. 8/1, 1965, pp. 11-27.

Pobee, J.S., *Toward an African Theology*, Nashville: Abingdon, 1979.

Poole, E.H.L., *The Native Tribes of the East Province of Northern Rhodesia*, Livingstone: Northern Rhodesia Government Press, 1938.

Prince, R. (ed.), *Trance and Possession States*, Montreal: R.M. Bucke Memorial Society, 1968.

Rangeley, W.H.J., "Nyau in Nkhotakota District", *Nyasaland Journal*, Vol. 32 (1949), pp. 19-24.

Ranger, T.O. and J. Weller, *Themes in the Christian History of Central Africa*, London: Heinemann, 1967.

Ranger, T.O., "The Role of Ndebele and Shona Religious Authorities in Rebellions of 1896 and 1897", in E. Stokes and R. Brown (eds.), *The Zambesian Past: Studies in Central African History*, Manchester: Manchester University Press, 1966.

Ranger, T.O., *Revolt in Southern Rhodesia 1896-1897: A Study of African Resistance*, London: Heinemann, 1967.

Rau, W.E., "Chewa Religion and the Ngoni Conquest", in Matthew Schoffeleers (ed.), *Guardians of the Land: Essays on Central African Territorial Cults*, Gweru: Mambo, 1979.

Ray, B.C., "Recent Studies of African Religions", *History of Religions*, Vol. 12 (1972-1973).

Read, M., *The Ngoni of Nyasaland*, London: Oxford University Press, 1956.

Rennie, J.K., *The Ngoni States and European Intrusion in the Zambesian Past*.

Roome, W.J., *A Great Emancipation*, London: World Dominion Press, 1926.

Ross, I., *Margaret Fell: Mother of Quakerism*, London: Longman Green and Co., 1932.

Schneider, H.W., "Religion: the Western Tradition", in C. Moraze (ed.), *History of Mankind: the Nineteenth Century 1775-1905*, London: Allen and Unwin, 1976.

Schoffeleers, Matthew, "The Chisumpi and Mbona Cults in Malawi: A Comparative History", in Matthew Schoffeleers (ed.), *Guardians of the Land: Essays on Central African Territorial Cults*, Gweru: Mambo, 1979.

Schoffeleers, Matthew, "The Interaction of the M'bona Cult and Christianity 1859-1963", in T.O. Ranger and J. Weller (eds.), *Themes in the Christian History of Central Africa*, London: Heinemann, 1975.

Schweitzer, E., "What is the Holy Spirit?", in H. King and J. Mottmann (eds.), *Conflicts about the Holy Spirit*, New York: Seabury Press, 1979.

Scott, D.C., *A Cyclopedic Dictionary of the Mang'anja Language*, Edinburgh: Foreign Missions Committee, 1892.

Shepperson, G. and T. Price, *Independent African*, Edinburgh: E U P, 1958.

Shepperson, G., "The Politics of African Church Separatist Movements 1892-1916", *Africa*, Vol. 24 (1954), pp. 240-248.

Singleton, M., "Spirit and Spiritual Direction: the Pastoral Counselling of the Possessed", in E. Fashole-Luke et al. (eds.), *Christianity in Africa*, London: Cargate Press, 1927.

Soko, Boston, *Nchimi Chikanga: The Battle against Witchcraft in Malawi*, Blantyre: CLAIM-Kachere, 2002.

Southall, A., "Spirit Possession among the Alur", in J. Beattie and J. Middleton (eds.), *Spirit Mediumship and Society in Africa*, London: Routledge and Kegan Paul, 1969.

Stokes, E. and Brown, R., *The Zambesian Past*, Manchester: Manchester University Press, 1966.

Sundkler, B.G.M., *Bantu Prophets in South Africa*, London: 1948, 2nd ed., O U P, 1962.

Swantz, M.L., *Ritual and Symbol in Transitional Zaramo Society with Special Reference to Women*, Uppsala: Gleerup, 1970.

Tanner, R.E.S., "The Theory and Practices of Sukuma Spirit Mediumship", in J. Beattie and J. Middleton (eds.), *Spirit Mediumship and Society in Africa*, London: Routledge and Kegan Paul, 1969.

Taylor, J.V., *The Primal Vision: the Christian Presence amid African Religion*, London: SCM, 1963.

Tempels, P., *Bantu Philosophy*, Paris: Presence Africaine, 1959.

Tew, M., *Peoples of the Lake Nyasa*, London: Oxford University Press, 1950.

Thomas, C., "The Holy Spirit and African Independent Churches: A Case study of the Apostolic Divine Church of Akropong Akwapim, Ghana", *Sierra Leone Bulletin of Religion*, Vol. 2 (November 1984), pp. 19-24.

Thompson, T.J., *Christianity in Northern Malawi: Donald Fraser's Missionary Methods and Ngoni Culture*, Leiden: E.J. Brill, 1995.

Thorndike, L., *A History of Magic and Experimental Science during the First Thirteen Centuries of our Era*, 2 vols., London: MacMillan, 1923.

Tindall, P.E., *History of Central Africa*, London: Longman, 1968.

Turner, H.W., *African Independent Church: the Life and Faith of the Church of the Lord (Aladura)*, Oxford: Clarendon Press, 1967.

Turner, H.W., *Religious Innovations in Africa: Collected Essays on New Movements*, Boston: Hall, 1979.

Turner, V.W., *Revelation and Divination in Ndembu Ritual*, New York: Cornell University Press, 1975.

Turner, V.W., *The Drums of Affliction: a Study of Religious Process among the Ndembu of Zambia*, Oxford: Clarendon Press, 1968.

Turner, V.W., *The Ritual Process: Structure and Anti-structure*, London: Routledge, 1969.

Vail, L., "Religion, Language and Tribal Myth", in Matthew Schoffeleers (ed.), *Guardians of the Land: Essays on Central African Territorial Cults*, Gweru: Mambo, 1979.

Verger, P., "Trance and Convention in Nago-Yoruba Spirit Mediumship", in J. Beattie and J. Middleton (eds.), *Spirit Mediumship and Society in Africa*, London: Routledge & Kegan Paul, 1969.

Vipont, E., *The Story of Quakerism 1652-1952*, London: Bannisdale Press, 1954.

Walker, E.A., *A History of South Africa*, London: Longman, 1940.

Walker, S.S., *Ceremonial Spirit Possession in Africa and Afro-America: Forms, Meanings and Functional Significance for Individuals and Social Groups*, Leiden: E.J. Brill, 1972.

Wallace, A.F.C., *Culture and Personality*, New York: Random House, 1961.

Walls, A.F., "Religion and the Press in the Enclave in the Nigerian Civil War", in E.W. Fashole-Luke et al. (eds.), *Christianity in Independent Africa*, London: Rex Collings, 1978.

Walls, A.F., "The Anabaptists of Africa: the Challenge of African Independent Churches", *Occasional Bulletin of Missionary Research*, Vol. 3/2 (1979), pp. 48-51.

Walls, A.F., "The Gospel as the Prisoner and Liberator of Culture", *Faith and Thought*, Vol. 10/8 (1981), pp. 1-2.

Ware, F.C., *History of Mankind: Cultural and Scientific Development: the Twentieth Century*, London: George Allen and Unwin 1966.

Webb, C. and J.B. Wright (eds.), *A Zulu King Speaks: Statements Made by Cetshwayo Kampande on the History and Customs of his People*, Pietermaritzburg: University of Natal Press, 1978.

Welbourn, F.B., "Spirit Initiation in Ankole and a Christian Spirit Movement in Kenya", in J. Beattie and J. Middleton (eds.), *Spirit Mediumship and Society in Africa*, London: Routledge and Kegan Paul, 1969.

Werbner, R.P., *Regional Cults*, London: Academic Press, 1977.

Westermann, D., *The African Today and Tomorrow*, London: Oxford University Press, 1957.

Whisson, G.M. and M. West, *Religion and Social Change in Southern Africa*, Cape Town: David Phillip, 1975.

Williams, R., *Christian Spirituality: a Theological History of the New Testament to Luther and St John of the Cross*, Atlanta: John Knox Press, 1979.

Willoughby, W.C., *The Soul of the Bantu*, London: SCM, 1928.

Wills, A.J., *The History of Central Africa*, London: Oxford University Press, 1965.

Wilson, M., *Rituals of Kinship among the Nyakyusa*, London: Oxford University Press, 1965.

Wright, L.M., *The Literary Life of the Early Friends*, New York: Columbia University Press, 1932.

Young, T.C., "How far can African Ceremonial be Incorporated in Christian System", *Africa*, Vol. 8/2 (April 1935), pp. 210-217.

Young, T.C., *Contemporary Ancestors*, London: Lutterworth Press, 1934.

Young, T.C., *Notes on the History of Tumbuka-Nkhamanga Peoples: Northern Province of Nyasaland*, London: Lutterworth Press, 1931.

Zaretsky, I., *Bibliography on Spirit Possession and Spirit Mediumship*, Evanston: Northwestern University Press, 1967.

Zuesse, E.M., *Ritual Cosmos*, Athens, Ohio: Ohio University Press, 1979.

Index

www.ingramcontent.com/pod-product-compliance
Lightning Source LLC
Chambersburg PA
CBHW021905020426
42334CB00013B/484